D1083547

Focus on Value:
A Corporate and Investor
Guide to Wealth Creation

James L. Grant

James A. Abate

John Wiley & Sons, Inc.

New York ▪ Chichester ▪ Weinheim ▪ Brisbane ▪ Singapore ▪ Toronto

HG 4028
.V3
G688
2001

JLG
To Robert S. Hamada
friend, mentor, and financial pioneer

D 48559249

JAA
To my family and colleagues

This book is printed on acid-free paper. ∞

Copyright © 2001 by James L. Grant, James A. Abate. All rights reserved.

Published by John Wiley & Sons, Inc.
Published simultaneously in Canada.

No part of this publication may be reproduced, stored in a retrieval system or transmitted in any form or by any means, electronic, mechanical, photocopying, recording, scanning, or otherwise, except as permitted under Sections 107 or 108 of the 1976 United States Copyright Act, without either the prior written permission of the Publisher, or authorization through payment of the appropriate per-copy fee to the Copyright Clearance Center, 222 Rosewood Drive, Danvers, MA 01923, (978) 750-8400, fax (978) 750-4744. Requests to the Publisher for permission should be addressed to the Permissions Department, John Wiley & Sons, Inc., 605 Third Avenue, New York, NY 10158-0012, (212) 850-6011, fax (212) 850-6008, E-Mail: PERMREQ@WILEY.COM.

This publication is designed to provide accurate and authoritative information in regard to the subject matter covered. It is sold with the understanding that the publisher is not engaged in rendering professional services. If professional advice or other expert assistance is required, the services of a competent professional person should be sought.

Library of Congress Cataloging in Publication Data:

ISBN 0-471-21658-5

Printed in the United States of America.

10 9 8 7 6 5 4 3 2 1

Table of Contents

FEB 2 4 2003

About the Authors

James L. Grant is President of JLG Research, a company specializing in economic profit research, and a member of the economics and finance faculty at Baruch College of the City University of New York. Dr. Grant also serves as a Special Adviser to Global Asset Management in New York. Dr. Grant holds a Ph.D. in Business from the University of Chicago's Graduate School of Business and has been a featured speaker at industry conferences on value-based metrics. He has published several articles in investment journals, including the *Journal of Portfolio Management* and the *Journal of Investing*. Dr. Grant is the author of *Foundations of Economic Value Added*, co-author (with Frank J. Fabozzi) of *Equity Portfolio Management*, and coeditor of *Value-Based Metrics: Foundations and Practice*.

James A. Abate is Investment Director, North America, for Global Asset Management in New York. Mr. Abate previously served as Managing Director and Portfolio Manager with Credit Suisse Asset Management and as a Manager in Price Waterhouse's Valuation/Corporate Finance Group. Mr. Abate has written several articles regarding the application of an economic profit framework in financial journals such as *Mergers & Acquisitions* and *Pension Observer* and was a contributing author to *Applied Equity Valuation*. In addition, Mr. Abate has been a frequent speaker to professional societies on valuation and security analysis topics. Mr. Abate holds a B.S. in Accounting from Fairleigh Dickinson University and an M.B.A. in Finance from St. John's University. He is a Chartered Financial Analyst and a Certified Public Accountant.

Preface

Focus on Value weaves together the key issues and provides new insights into the concept of economic profit or economic value-added. Our intention is not to provide yet another back test of data to validate the economic profit linkage to market value, since we believe that the existing evidence supporting this direct relationship is overwhelming. Rather, our goal is to offer practical market-driven advice to corporate executives and sophisticated investors on how best to utilize an economic profit based framework for operational benchmarking and valuation.

Economic profit gained widespread attention from corporate America in the 1980s and early 1990s. Somewhat surprisingly, wide-scale application of a fundamental research framework based on economic profit is really just beginning to make inroads in investment management. Contrary to the recent momentum in its adoption by some investors, it appears that there is growing concern from corporate executives as to whether or not the equity markets recognize the importance of managing to maximize shareholder wealth within an economic profit framework versus a simpler earnings focus. Also, executives in cyclical industries have heightened their questioning of its applicability in an environment dictated by macro forces of supply and demand.

No matter what the forum — be it a financial news interview or a dedicated analysts day held at a company's headquarters — executives are bombarded with questions from investors regarding earnings, usually those of the upcoming quarter. Unfortunately, this concerted focus on income statement results is typical of both traditional growth and value investors alike. Given this environment, imagine how shocking it would be if a chief financial officer turned his or her focus completely away from earnings per share guidance, and instead prioritized managing the company's business and financial risk, capital utilization and investment, and meeting business goals that deliver improving economic profit. And, incidentally, earnings per share will follow as a consequence if management is unwavering in pursuit of such a strategic plan. This may sound like common sense and perhaps is exactly what is going on behind the scenes. The practical need for a redirected focus on value can be validated under almost any market condition. But the reality is that no one dares to break away from the naive long-standing reliance on accounting earnings.

Many corporations have undertaken huge programs at significant expense to teach division-level employees the importance of efficient capital resource allocation, management, and reallocation in an effort to create shareholder wealth. Having introduced the necessary accountability internally for financial management with incentive compensation, it is not surprising that executives championing such programs have found the reception frustrating when articulating the benefits of an economic profit focus and its link to stock price. As investment professionals, we have the benefit of meeting with hundreds of senior executives yearly where we get a chance to discuss misperceptions of value and corporate focus. Reflecting on many of these discussions prompted us to write this book and hopefully address those issues leading to the frustrations.

In its basic form, an economic profit framework captures many different research insights and provides impetus for further company analysis including operating and capital condition, risk profile, and market expectations of future performance. These major elements are important in determining "true value" and uncovering investment opportunities. In contrast, traditional accounting-based measures such as price-to-earnings, earnings growth rate, and reported book value have been shown to be relatively unimportant in this regard. Superior investment performance can be achieved by identifying good companies (improving operating condition, steady or decreasing risk, and economic profit growth) that are also good stocks (low market expectations).

One unfortunate disservice hindering greater acceptance of economic profit based analysis comes directly from consultants and others who help implement such programs at their corporate clients. What we mean is that the amount of time and effort spent bickering over the necessity and magnitude of various accounting adjustments to enhance the connection between economic profit and market valuation dominate many efforts without material benefit. We do recognize the necessity to translate accounting information into usable financial information, as we believe accounting statements have become less reliable over time. That being said, as far as the capital markets are concerned, the incremental benefit of fine-tuning a LIFO reserve add-back, for example, is generally minimal in terms of importance. Rather, having consistently applied data for peer benchmarking and drilling down on company specific issues concerning the cost of capital or future growth rate of economic profit embedded within today's stock price are areas of higher significance deserving much closer attention.

Economic profit based analysis can be a powerful tool in the hands of executives heading firms and competing for investment dollars, as well as investors trying to spot opportunities away from the general investment crowd. However, its power of bringing insights to the surface is relevant only if the key issues are identified. We hope that this book shines new light on the building block concepts of economic profit and provides an unbiased view in applying this approach with a singular goal — to help focus on value through a practical and market-driven framework.

Before proceeding to the economic profit matter at hand, we acknowledge the following individuals for their insightful comments and helpful assistance — Frank Fabozzi of Frank J. Fabozzi Associates and Mickey Nguyen of Global Asset Management (USA). We also thank Al Ehrbar of Stern Stewart and Co. for providing independent economic profit data that we use in real world application of key economic profit valuation concepts.

James L. Grant
James A. Abate

Chapter 1

Reenergizing Economic Profit

Over the past two decades, the utilization of economic profit (EP) measurement has gained a large following by corporations, consultants, and portfolio managers. The 1980s and early 1990s, with its emphasis on identifying "undiscovered value," focused principally on revitalizing underperforming or mismanaged businesses. The mechanism to drive higher economic profit was accomplished mostly by eliminating inefficiencies within corporations, changing capital structures by introducing leverage, or other variables thought — whether correctly or incorrectly — by managers to raise the "spread" that firms could deliver between their invested capital returns and the cost of capital.[1] The tremendous restructuring activity that we have witnessed over the past two decades is a testament to this renewed *focus on* shareholder value.

However, as part of the daily task of portfolio management in meeting with companies who have embraced some type of economic profit measure, we hear increasing frustration that the marketplace is rewarding only short-term improvement in earnings. Even acquisitions have been more closely scrutinized for goodwill and dilution issues rather than strategic purpose and value creation. This narrow market focus is causing some corporations and Wall Street analysts to re-think — or worse yet, abandon — their focus on economic profit measurement. Simply put, why have some of the great companies of the 1980s and early 1990s with transparent economic profit management guidelines — such as AT&T, Coca-Cola, and Disney — been stock market underperformers in the second half of the 1990s?[2]

Another frustration with economic profit measurement is coming from companies that operate in commodity price and interest rate sensitive sectors of the economy. For examples, in the basic materials (commodity price) and financial sectors (interest rate sensitive) of the economy, corporate managers express frustration that their economic profit achievements can be dissipated by macro-economic happenings having little to do with their company-specific effort to improve economic profit. Obviously, the loudest cry about the limitations of economic

---

[1] Restructuring a stale business in need of change should obviously improve the economic profit outlook and enhance shareholder value. However, simply changing a company's mix of debt and equity securities on the corporate balance sheet may only give investors an "illusion" of economic profit and value creation. We seek to explain the real sources of wealth creation.

[2] During the six years spanning December 1994 to December 2000, the cumulative total returns on AT&T, Coca-Cola, and Disney shares were −12.1%, 152.5%, and 96.5%, respectively. Over the same time span, the S&P 500 earned a total return of 219%.

profit measurement is coming from companies with EP-based incentive compensation plans — as volatility in economic profit and stock price leads to unexplained and possibly negative changes in incentive compensation.[3]

While we sympathize with the arguments, we believe that the success to applying economic profit principles in corporate planning and investment analysis has shifted. So many times we have heard a disproportionate amount of time being spent by corporate managers and investors/analysts on a numbing set of EP-based accounting adjustments — such as the impact of LIFO/FIFO inventory and deferred tax accounting adjustments — to calculate economic profit. In our view, this is time better spent on the real economic and financial factors that drive economic profit change and stock market success. Taken together, these "big picture" EP factors include:

- generating favorable returns on existing assets
- examining risk (to value) in a cost of capital context
- investing positively for economic profit growth
- understanding the magnitude of external influence (industry, sector and macroeconomic factors) on corporate performance
- reconciling market versus internal ("warranted"[4]) expectations of economic profit growth

In large part, corporate managers have paid considerable attention over the last few decades to revitalizing their cash flow and improving the return on existing capital assets — via restructurings, corporate downsizing, and the like. Coupled with the decline in interest rates and, arguably, a decline in the risk of equities as a whole, this has led to significant improvement in stock market performance as Wall Street has reacted favorably to the rising spread between a firm's return on invested capital and the cost of capital. However, unless forward thinking managers pay particular attention to all five of the key economic profit influences — including, assessing the financial risk impact of cost of capital change, investing positively for EP growth, understanding internal as well as external economic profit influences, and just as importantly, reconciling market versus company expectations of economic profit growth — then it is unlikely that we will see a repeat of the spectacular stock market performance that distinguishes the truly "great companies" from the rest of the pack.

Along this line, this book is targeted to those who are interested in knowing how the major economic profit influences (cited above) can lead to substantial

---

[3] Since volatility says nothing about stock price direction, it's interesting that we don't hear any EP measurement limitations from corporate managers when independent macroeconomic forces — such as a decline in interest rates — drive stock prices up.

[4] The "warranted" value of a company refers to the discounted value of its cash flow and economic profit based on firm-specific internal assets and company fundamentals. Due to differing growth perceptions between managers and investors, this value may or may not be consistent with the capital market's assessment of enterprise value and stock price.

shareholder value improvement. In our effort to re-direct and, yes, reinvigorate the economic profit movement, we assume that our targeted audience — ranging from corporate executives to "sell side" analysts and "buy side" portfolio managers — are primarily interested in a "big picture" perspective on the EP factors that can lead to substantial wealth creation — rather than the myriad accounting adjustments that can be made to estimate a firm's economic profit in practice.[5]

THE EVOLUTION OF ECONOMIC PROFIT

The evolution of economic profit theory is a fascinating study, with robust historical roots that we only introduce in this book. In a nutshell, economic profit is simply the classical economist's notion of "residual income" from days gone by. For instance, consider the oft-cited reference to economic profit made in 1890 by famous British economist, Alfred Marshall, regarding the real meaning of a business owner's "profit:"[6]

> "What remains of his profits after deducting interest on his capital at the current rate may be called his earnings of undertaking or management."

Based on Marshall's statement, it is evident that the economists' interpretation of profit — namely, residual income or economic profit — is radically different from today's accounting view of earnings as measured by "net income."

The key distinction between accounting profit and economic profit lies in the classical economists' assertion that a company is not truly profitable unless its revenues have not only covered production and operating expenses, but also when the firm's profits are sufficient enough to provide its owners with a normal return on invested capital. In a fundamental sense, this residual view of income is what today's economic profit movement is really all about.[7]

While economic profit is rooted in classical economic theory, three pioneering 20th Century American economists — Irving Fisher during the 1930s,[8] and Nobel Laureates Franco Modigliani and Merton Miller in the late 1950s to early 1960s[9] — expanded upon the fuller meaning of economic profit in a corpo-

---

[5] Having said that, we do of course cover the major accounting adjustments that enhance the accurate measurement of economic profit. See Chapter 7.

[6] Alfred Marshall, *Principles of Economics*, Vol. 1 (New York: MacMillan & Co., 1890) p. 142.

[7] We emphasize later that "profits" need also be sufficient enough to justify the market expectations implied by the firm's current stock price.

[8] Irving Fisher's pioneering work on the NPV theory of the firm is described in *The Theory of Investment* (New York: Augustus M. Kelley Publishers, 1965, Reprinted from the original 1930 edition).

[9] See Franco Modigliani and Merton H. Miller, "The Cost of Capital, Corporation Finance, and the Theory of Investment," *American Economic Review* (June 1958), and "Dividend Policy, Growth and the Valuation of Shares," *Journal of Business* (October 1961).

rate valuation context. In particular, Irving Fisher established a fundamental link between a company's net present value (NPV) and its discounted stream of expected cash flows. Modigliani and Miller then showed that corporate investment decisions — as manifest in positive NPV decisions — are the primary determinant of a firm's enterprise value and its stock price — as opposed to the firm's capital structure mix of debt and equity securities. We in turn acknowledge these pioneering economists for providing a foundation for the economic profit insight that we offer in this book.

REFLECTION

In this chapter, we introduce five economic profit factors that are central to the process of wealth creation. These strategic EP considerations for managers and investors include (1) generating favorable returns on existing assets, (2) examining risk (to value) in a cost of capital framework, (3) investing positively for economic profit growth, (4) understanding the magnitude of external influence, and (5) reconciling market versus internal expectations of economic profit growth.

We emphasize that a keen understanding of wealth creation involves much more than knowledge of the myriad set of accounting adjustments that are necessary to measure economic profit. Indeed, it is possible for a manager or investor to be the "best of the best" value-based accountants, and yet still have very little understanding of how economic profit is fundamentally linked to wealth creation. In our view, an understanding of what the economic profit movement is really all about involves a comprehensive knowledge of not only the traditional EP-based accounting adjustments but also a detailed understanding of the strategic forces that drive economic profit change and wealth creation.

We also provided an overview of the evolution of economic profit theory. On balance, the theory of economic profit rests on two principle assertions: (1) a company is not truly profitable unless it earns a return on invested capital that exceeds the opportunity cost of capital, and (2) that wealth is created when managers undertake positive NPV investment opportunities for the shareholders. We will of course expand on the EP tenets of wealth creation as we proceed in this book. In the next few chapters, we'll look at prominent value-based players and metrics that have shaped the economic profit movement, and we'll provide a basic link between a company's economic profit and its enterprise value.

Chapter 2

The Tribes of Economic Profit

E conomic profit players have made great strides in demonstrating the supe-riority of value-based metrics over traditional accounting measures of corporate success, including net income and return on equity. However, economic profit advocates — particularly, value-based consultants — have all too often missed the "big picture" perspective on economic profit and wealth cre-ation by getting tangled up in a "my metric is better than your metric" mentality, or, worse yet, a litigious set of claims that effectively say that "your metric is really our metric." This unfortunate and negative side of the economic profit movement is aptly captured by Randy Myers in a CEO magazine article titled "Metric Wars."[1]

In this chapter, we focus on the value-based contributions of consulting firms, corporations, and investment firms. We like to call this diverse set of groups — with seemingly different corporate cultures and motivations — the "tribes of economic profit." We emphasize value-based players that have advanced the development and application of economic profit measures in prac-tice. Yet we recognize up front that these are the same value-based constituencies — especially, value-based consulting firms — that constitute the warring eco-nomic profit tribes that are all too quick to espouse a "my economic profit metric way of evaluating companies and/or investment opportunities is really better than yours" philosophy.

We attribute in a hopefully positive manner the development and applica-tion of value-based decision tools to several tribes of economic profit including corporations, value-based consulting firms, investment banking firms, and money management companies. We believe that what is most important in the advance-ment of economic profit thinking is not so much the particular value-based metric used in practice, but rather the recognition by corporate managers, consultants, and investors alike that economic profit — regardless of whose measure or analy-sis is being employed — is inextricably linked to wealth creation.

EP TRIBES AND METRICS

Like the theory of economic profit, the application of economic profit principles in practice is not new. We trace the development and application of basic and

---

[1] Randy Myers, *CEO*, "Metric Wars," (October 1996).

sophisticated economic profit metrics to value-based groups that — in our words — constitute the tribes of economic profit:[2]

- Corporations
- Value-based consultants
- Sell-side equity analysts
- Buy-side portfolio managers

Along the way, we refer to three distinct value-based groups: (1) The Corporate Tribe of Economic Profit, (2) The Consultant Tribe of Economic Profit, and (3) the Investor Tribe of Economic Profit.

The Corporate Tribe of Economic Profit

Economic profit concepts have been used for many years in the corporate sector to measure success and to align manager interests with those of shareholders. In 1922, General Motors developed a basic EP metric and a bonus plan for its managers that provided for a 10% bonus pool based on profits in excess of a 7% return on capital.[3] During the 1950s and 1960s, General Electric, among others, utilized the concept of *residual income* — earnings less a capital charge — to assess profit center performance.[4] In 1983 Coca-Cola's chairman, Roberto Goizueta, emphasized economic profit decision-making and measurement with the goal of creating tremendous shareholder value.[5]

The wealth creation (or NPV) numbers tell the story for Coke's shareholders under Roberto Goizueta's watch. Over the ten years spanning 1983 to 1992 — when Coca-Cola changed its strategic financial mission from sales growth to shareholder value maximization — this beverage firm added some $47 billion to its economic book capital.[6] Moreover, many of today's corporations with an economic profit focus include some of the world's largest and best-known companies. Exhibit 1 shows a diversified list of U.S. companies that employ economic profit measurement tools to enhance shareholder value.

---

[2] A discussion of EP players and metrics can also be found in Frank J. Fabozzi and James L. Grant, "Value-Based Metrics: Motivation and Practice," Chapter 1 in Frank J. Fabozzi and James L. Grant (Eds.), *Value-Based Metrics: Foundations and Practice* (New Hope PA: Frank J. Fabozzi Associates, 2000).

[3] For in-depth discussion on the role of EP measurement in incentive compensation programs, see Stephen F. O'Byrne, "Does Value-Based Management Discourage Investment in Intangibles?" Chapter 5 in *Value-Based Metrics: Foundations and Practice*.

[4] For an interesting application of EP measurement using General Electric data, see James M. McTaggart, Peter Kontes, and Michael C. Mankins, *The Value Imperative: Managing for Superior Shareholder Returns* (New York: The Free Press, 1994).

[5] Also, in 1984, The Walt Disney Company gave Michael Eisner an annual bonus equal to 2% of net income in excess of a 9% return on equity. This incentive compensation example is noted by Stephen O'Byrne in "Does Value-Based Measurement Discourage Investment in Intangibles?"

[6] Stern Stewart reports that Coca-Cola's Market Value Added (MVA, or estimated NPV) was $51.06 billion at year-end 1992, and $4.015 billion at year-end 1982.

Exhibit 1: Representative Companies using Economic Profit Measurement

American Express	Boise Cascade
Coca-Cola	Diageo
Equifax	Entergy
FMC	Georgia Pacific
Guidant	Home Depot
Lilly (Eli)	Lucent Technology
MCI Communications	Olin
Peoplesoft	Nestle
Sprint	Unilever

Exhibit 2: Economic Profit Approach cited by Large U.S. Corporations

EP Approach	% Companies
Economic Value Added	47
Risk adjusted Return on Capital Employed	27
Economic Profit	9
Shareholder Value Added	7
Other*	10

* Includes: Earned Value Added, Economic Value Created, Economic Profit Realized, Value Created, among other economic profit descriptors.

Source: James A. Abate, white paper, January 2001: Sample includes 192 firms based on publicly available information.

In a recent survey of major U.S. companies (primarily S&P 500 companies), one of the authors[7] found that 192 firms stated in publicly available documents that they use some form of economic profit measurement in profit center planning and their incentive compensation programs. Exhibit 2 shows a percentage breakdown of these large cap companies by EP-related measure that they employ in practice. The most frequently cited economic profit metrics by companies in the survey include, Economic Value Added (EVA[8]), Risk-adjusted Return on Capital Employed (or Risk-adjusted Return on Invested Capital), "Economic Profit," and Shareholder Value Added.

The economic profit survey is interesting in several respects. With 192 firms, it suggests that there are many large US companies that utilize economic profit measurement in their profit center planning and incentive compensation programs. This is especially important since EP measurement programs are designed to enhance shareholder value. On the other hand, Exhibit 2 reveals that there is a diversity of opinion as to what economic profit measurement is really

---

[7] James A. Abate, white paper, January 2001.

[8] EVA® is a registered trademark of Stern Stewart & Co. While many firms use Stern Stewart's commercial EVA metric, the author did not examine whether EP reporting companies use EVA® or *generic* economic value added (EVA).

all about — with 47% of sample companies using a formal EP metric like Economic Value Added (EVA), and 27% of the value-based companies using a simple risk-adjusted return on invested capital metric.

Also, at 10%, the category labeled "Other," in Exhibit 2 seems to include several "home grown" metrics that firms utilize to measure economic profit. Given this disparity, we seek to point companies in a direction that focuses on the "real key" to economic profit and wealth improvement. This includes an EP focus on not only existing corporate assets (as manifest in the restructuring and downsizing movement), but also the economic profit improvement from anticipated future growth assets not currently in place.

The Consultant Tribe of Economic Profit

While corporations were gearing up for EP measurement, several value-based consulting firms were founded during the 1970s and early 1980s with the expressed goal of linking economic profit to shareholder value. These EP consulting pioneers include Marakon Associates — founded in 1978 by James McTaggart and Peter Contes[9] — and The Alcar Consulting Group — founded in 1979 and directed by long-time shareholder value proponent Alfred Rappaport of Northwestern University.[10] Also, in 1974, University of Chicago trained Joel Stern published his insightful article in the *Financial Analysts Journal* titled "Earnings Per Share Don't Count."[11] This EP-focused article — with its emphasis on the importance of discounted cash flow as opposed to accounting profit — provided a motivation for the creation in 1982 of the financial advisory firm of Stern Stewart & Co.

One of the more notable events among EP consultants is the release in 1982 of Stern Stewart's commercial economic profit metric, called EVA® — for Economic Value Added.[12] Also, the HOLT Value Associates — founded several years ago by Robert Hendricks — developed an economic profit-based metric called CFROI — for Cash Flow Return on Investment.[13] This value-based metric was designed for portfolio managers seeking a percentage based economic profit

---

[9] For a description of Marakon's innovative approach to economic profit measurement, see McTaggart, Kontes, and Mankins, *The Value Imperative: Managing for Superior Shareholder Returns.*

[10] In 1993, the The Alcar Consulting Group became part of LEK/Alcar Consulting Group — with a primary emphasis on shareholder value advisory. For Rappaport's insightful views on creating shareholder value added, see Alfred Rappaport, *Creating Shareholder Value: A Guide for Managers and Investors* (Free Press, 1997, revised from the original 1986 edition), and "New Thinking on How to Link Executive Pay with Performance," *Harvard Business Review* (March/April, 1999).

[11] Joel M. Stern, "Earnings Per Share Don't Count," *Financial Analyst Journal* (July-August 1974).

[12] As noted before, EVA® is a registered trademark of Stern Stewart & Co. For a rigorous discussion of their economic profit model, along with many applications in a corporate finance setting, see G. Bennett Stewart III, *The Quest for Value* (New York: Harper Collins, 1991) and Al Ehrbar, *EVA: The Real Key to Creating Wealth* (New York: John Wiley and Sons, 1998).

[13] For a complete discussion of the CFROI approach to measuring economic profit, see Bartley J. Madden, *CFROI Valuation: A Total Systems Approach to Valuing the Firm* (Woburn, MA: Butterworth-Heinemann, 1999).

figure (much like an IRR) to compare companies as opposed to a dollar EP measure. Moreover, HOLT's CFROI provides insight on the nature of competition and defendable business franchises via the notion of competitive "fade" — whereby a company's invested capital returns converge over time to a long-run average return on capital of about 6% per year when stated in real terms.[14]

In today's sophisticated world of economic profit measurement there exists a variety of value-based measures and acronyms. These metrics include (1) Stern Stewart's MVA and EVA — for Market Value Added and Economic Value Added, (2) HOLT's CFROI — for Cash Flow Return on Investment, (3) Boston Consulting Group's CVA — for Cash Value Added, (4) LEK/Alcar Consulting Group's SVA and TSR — for Shareholder Value Added and Total Stock Return, and (5) the Economic Margin (EM) approach of the Applied Finance Group of Chicago. Exhibit 3 lists some of the prominent EP advisory firms and their metrics. The list of value-based consulting firms includes early EP riser, Marakon Associates — with economic profit efforts that date back to the 1970s — to EP newcomer, Shareholder Value Advisors, directed by Stephen O'Byrne.[15]

While several economic profit metrics exist in practice, it should be noted that in theory they must *all* give the same warranted (or intrinsic) value of the firm and its outstanding shares. In practice, however, the economic profit metrics promoted by today's financial advisory firms can be differentiated along several lines. These include (1) the number of accounting adjustments that are made to determine a firm's "cash" operating profit and its economic book (or invested) capital, (2) whether the economic profit metric provides an answer that is stated in dollars (like EVA) or percentage terms (CFROI), and (3) whether the economic profit analysis is conducted using nominal or inflation-adjusted estimates of operating profit and book capital.

Exhibit 3: Shareholder Value Advisory Firms

Company	Metric(s) or Focus
Applied Finance Group	EM
Boston Consulting Group	CVA
HOLT Value Associates	CFROI*
LEK/Alcar Group	SVA, TSR
Stern Stewart & Co.	MVA, EVA
Marakon Associates	SV improvement**
Shareholder Value Advisors	EP improvement

* Also promoted by Boston Consulting Group
** SV = Shareholder value

[14] There is, however, considerable disagreement among EP players about the competitive decay rate in a firm's economic profit over time.
[15] While Shareholder Value Advisors, Inc. was founded in the late 1990s, we note that its managing director, Stephen O'Byrne, is hardly a newcomer to the economic profit movement. His writings on "EP improvement" have raised the awareness of corporate managers and investors alike on the importance of managing for shareholder value added.

In our view, the advent of sophisticated EP metrics and measurement systems by consultants is a step in the right direction — as corporate managers and investors can gain insight on the economic profit factors that drive enterprise value and stock price. Sometimes, however, the real economic profit message from consultants can be muted by their inter-company squabbling in the midst of a "cacophony" of EP acronyms that seem more focused on accounting adjustments rather than advancing the economic profit movement more generally.[16]

The Investor Tribe of Economic Profit

Although economic profit measures have been successfully applied in the corporate world — both with and without EP consultants — the large-scale application of these metrics in securities analysis and equity portfolio management in particular is a relatively recent occurrence. We trace Wall Street's interest in the application of economic profit measurement to several pioneering developments on both the "sell side" and "buy side" of the Street.

On Wall Street's "sell side," we include CS First Boston's 1996 "Economic Value Added Conference,"[17] and — providing academic impetus in that same year — the economic profit article published by one of the authors in the *Journal of Portfolio Management*.[18] In turn, these 1996 developments were followed by two significant EP events including (1) the 1997 Goldman Sach's client conference, "EVA and Return on Capital: Roads to Shareholder Wealth" — where Steven Einhorn "rolled out" this investment bank's EP company research platform[19] — and (3) the 1999 Information Management Network's Inaugural Conference on Value-Based Metrics — with economic profit applications in the fields of banking, corporate finance, and investment management.

On Wall Street's "buy side," several investment players have embraced the economic profit approach to equity portfolio management. Buy-side institutions like Global Asset Management, Oppenheimer Capital, and RS Investment Management have successfully integrated EP measurement in their stock selection and portfolio construction processes. Indeed, with its emphasis on economic profit as opposed to GAAP earnings, Wall Street's movement toward economic profit measurement at the century-turn has led to a whole new school of investment research called the "economic profit approach to equity securities analysis."[20]

---

[16] As mentioned in the introduction, Randy Myers in "Metrics Wars" voiced this negative side of value-based consultants.

[17] For economic profit research at CS First Boston, see Al Jackson, Michael J. Mauboussin, and Charles R. Wolf, "EVA Primer," *Equity-Research Americas* (CS First Boston: February 20, 1996).

[18] See James L. Grant, "Foundations of EVA for Investment Managers," *Journal of Portfolio Management* (Fall 1996).

[19] For a description of Goldman Sach's economic profit approach to company analysis, see Steven G. Einhorn, Gabrielle Napolitano, and Abby Joseph Cohen, "EVA: A Primer," *U.S. Research* (Goldman Sachs, September 10, 1997).

[20] A foundation for the economic profit approach to equity securities analysis *and* portfolio management is described in James A. Abate, "*American Focus* Equity Investment Strategy Profile," Global Asset Management (USA) (January 2001) and James L. Grant, *Foundations of Economic Value Added* (New Hope, PA: Frank J. Fabozzi Associates, 1997).

Moreover, we believe that recent interest in economic profit measurement among corporate managers and investors is based on a convergence of value-based thinking in the corporate and institutional world of portfolio management. As equity analysts — and buy-side investors — we find this corporate-investor synergy especially exciting and also consistent with Wall Street's long-standing penchant for embracing financial theories that seek to distinguish between companies that create wealth and firms that, unfortunately, destroy it.

Equally important, the economic profit approach to stock selection is transparent. Other things the same — such as macroeconomic and geo-political happenings — we can say at this early juncture that stocks of companies with *positive* economic profit momentum — both now *and* in the anticipated future — are potential buy candidates for investors. However, the stocks of companies having negative economic profit characteristics are trading opportunities at best, and sell or short-sell candidates most of the time. We will of course expand upon the real meaning of the economic profit approach to equity securities analysis and portfolio management as we proceed in this book.

SUMMARY

We explained in this chapter the evolutionary — and yes, revolutionary — events that shape today's economic profit movement. In this context, we discussed the value-based metrics that are advocated by corporations, value-based consulting firms, and investment management companies to enhance shareholder (investor) value. Given the jointly peaceful coexistence and sometime warring actions of these constituencies — especially among value-based consulting firms — we referred to today's economic profit players as the "tribes of economic profit."

We emphasized at the outset of the chapter that what is most important for senior corporate managers and investors to realize is that it's not so much the economic profit metric per se that matters most, but rather a value-based mindset that leads managers and investors to become educated about the inextricable link between economic profit and wealth creation. Upon taking this critical first step, senior managers and investors will then search for the fundamental factors that lead to substantial economic profit — and therefore substantial shareholder value — improvement.

We believe that a heightened *focus on value* leads to the same set of economic profit factors — generating favorable returns on existing capital, understanding risk in a cost of capital context, investing positively for economic profit growth, and reconciling market versus company expectations of economic profit growth — that we introduced in Chapter 1. Before getting into a rigorous explanation of these central economic profit factors, let's first make sure that we understand the basic link between economic profit and wealth creation. We provide a basic economic profit valuation foundation in the next chapter with a more advanced treatment of economic profit valuation issues later on.

Chapter 3
Basic Economic Profit Link to Valuation

Before looking at the connection between economic profit and enterprise value — as well as the drivers of economic profit — we provide an overview of how it differs from traditional accounting earnings and its general appeal to corporate managers and investors. As noted in Chapter 1, economic profit is the classical economists notion of *residual* income. In this context, a company is deemed "profitable" when its revenues not only cover the usual production/operating expenses of running a business, but also when the firm's profit is sufficient enough to provide a fair return on the owner's invested capital — including a required return to debt *and* equity suppliers of financial capital. With this introduction, we'll begin with the basic ingredients of the economic profit calculation.

BASIC ECONOMIC PROFIT

While there are many accounting adjustments that can be made to estimate a firm's economic profit in practice — far too many, quite frankly[1] — Exhibit 1 shows the basic ingredients in the economic profit calculation. In this context, economic profit — or in popular jargon, economic value added (EVA) — can be defined in simple terms as the difference between a firm's net operating profit after tax (NOPAT) and a dollar charge for the capital employed in the business. The invested capital charge is measured by the firm's economic book capital times its weighted average cost (expressed as a percentage) of debt and equity capital, *wacc* — a cost of capital term that should be familiar to any corporate manager or investor who has had a basic course in finance.[2]

With this economic profit definition, we see that a company's residual income is positive when its cash revenue is more than sufficient to cover production/operating expenses and *unlevered* taxes,[3] as well as providing a required return

---

[1] Indeed, Stern Stewart and Goldman Sachs U.S. Research (among others) have discovered some 160 accounting adjustments that can be made to estimate a firm's cash operating profit and its economic book capital. Just as important, we will show that there are several "cost of capital" issues that complicate the correct estimation of economic profit.

[2] We cover the estimation of *wacc* in Chapter 8.

[3] A *levered* firm is simply a company that has some form of interest-bearing debt outstanding including leases, while in principle an *unlevered* firm has no interest bearing securities whatsoever. Thus, the term "unlevered taxes" refers to the taxes that a company would owe if it were in fact an unlevered firm. Without getting into accounting detail here, we note that unlevered taxes should be used in the NOPAT measure of operating profit because a firm's dollar cost of capital already reflects the annual interest tax subsidy from its debt (and debt equivalent such as operating leases) financings.

on invested capital. On the other hand, economic profit is negative when a company's revenue and profit fall short of covering its normal operating expenses and taxes and — just as importantly — the owners' opportunity cost of invested capital.

The basic economic profit formula shown in Exhibit 1 can be used to highlight the distinction between accounting profit and economic profit — and, from our perspective, why economic profit principles should be of keen interest to corporate managers and investors. Specifically, we know that accounting profit is positive when revenue covers production/operating expenses, interest expense, and corporate taxes. But interest expense is a dollar payment to the providers of only one source of the firm's capital — namely, debt holders as opposed to equity holders. Therefore, accounting profit does not provide investors with a *direct* indication as to whether a firm is profitable in the economist's view of a residual amount of income that is left after owners have been compensated for what Alfred Marshall viewed as a normal "interest" return on invested capital.[4]

Consequently, the accounting profession's measure of profit — namely GAAP earnings — does not provide investors with a direct measure of whether a firm is creating wealth or destroying it. That is not to say that accounting earnings are irrelevant since many of its components — including revenue, cost of goods sold (COGS), and selling, general, and administrative expenses (SG&A) — are included in the economic profit calculation. Aside from many accounting adjustments that are necessary to get at the firm's operating cash, it should be apparent that the distinction between the two profit measures lies in the classical economists' notion that equity capital has an opportunity cost, and in no way is a "free" source of financial capital.

Exhibit 1: Basic Economic Profit

EP = NOPAT − $ Capital Charge
Where:
Revenue
Less:
Production/Operating Expenses*
Less:
Unlevered Taxes
Equals:
NOPAT
$Capital Charge = $Capital × *wacc*

* Production and operating expenses include cost of goods sold, selling, general, and administrative expenses, and a charge for economic wear and tear — namely, depreciation that results in an erosion of value or useful life. In practice, we note that there are many EP-based accounting adjustments that can be made to assess a firm's net operating profit after tax (NOPAT) and, consequently, its economic book capital. On the positive side though, EP measurement links a firm's income statement and balance sheet in a way that is *directly* related to shareholder value.

---

[4] Alfred Marshall, *Principles of Economics*, Vol. 1 (New York: MacMillan & Co., 1890), p. 142.

In the next section we reflect on some concepts that are central to the appeal of economic profit. Specifically, we emphasize that wealth creators have positive (discounted) economic profit. Wealth wasters have negative economic profit, even though they may have positive accounting profit. This is a meaningful analytical distinction for corporate managers who are interested in using economic profit measures to create shareholder wealth and for investors who seek to discover mispriced securities in the capital market.

BASIC ECONOMIC PROFIT LINK TO VALUATION

In an attempt to show the basic relationship between wealth creation and economic profit (EP), we can establish a synergy between value-based concepts used by corporate managers and investors. On the corporate side, we know that if managers are acting in the best interest of shareholders then they will make capital budgeting decisions according to the market value rule.[5] Simply put, this means that corporate managers should only invest in real assets (physical and human) if they add value to the economic capital employed. In more familiar terms, corporate managers should only invest in capital assets having a *positive* net present value (NPV).

In turn, the firm's aggregate net present value — or total value added to invested capital — is the collective sum of the NPV that is generated on each of its capital investment projects. But what does this have to do with economic profit? As we explain in a later chapter, the firm's NPV is equal to the present value of its anticipated economic profit stream generated by existing assets and anticipated future assets (growth assets) not currently in place. Without getting into formalities here,[6] we express the basic NPV-EP relationship as:

NPV = Present Value of Expected EP

From this expression, we can say that wealth creators have positive NPV because the present value of expected economic profit is positive. On the other hand, wealth destroyers have negative NPV because their (capitalized) economic profit stream is on average negative. Exhibit 2 shows the basic NPV-EP link for wealth creators, wealth neutral companies — firms that are neither adding wealth nor destroying it — and wealth wasters.[7]

---

[5] For a theoretical discussion of the "market value" rule of corporate finance, see Chapter 2 in Eugene F. Fama and Merton H. Miller, *The Theory of Finance* (Holt, Rinehart, and Winston: 1972). For an explanation of the classic NPV rule in an economic profit (EP) context, see Frank J. Fabozzi and James L. Grant, "Value-Based Metrics in Financial Theory," Chapter 2 in *Value-Based Metrics: Foundations and Practice*.

[6] We cover the economic profit approach to enterprise valuation in Chapter 6.

[7] We assume in this exhibit that the capital market is efficient in the sense that investor-assessed NPV "fully reflects" a firm's economic profit outlook. If the capital market is not price efficient, then a company's stock may be undervalued or overvalued — a powerful stock selection theme that we expand upon in a later discussion of the economic profit approach to equity securities analysis.

Exhibit 2: Financial Characteristics of
Wealth Creators and Wealth Destroyers

Wealth Creator:	NPV > 0, EP > 0, RROC > 0*
Wealth Neutrality:	NPV = 0, EP = 0, RROC = 0
Wealth Waster:	NPV < 0, EP < 0, RROC < 0

* RROC = ROIC − *wacc*

Exhibit 2 also shows that if a company's after-tax return on invested capital, ROIC = NOPAT/Capital, is higher than its weighted average cost of capital, *wacc*, then the firm will (on average) have positive economic profit — and therefore, positive NPV.[8] If ROIC falls short of the *wacc*, then the firm will have negative economic profit, even though its after-tax return on capital is more than sufficient to cover the after-tax debt cost. In this latter instance, the firm's residual return on capital, RROC, is negative. In economic profit jargon, the firm is a wealth destroyer (having negative NPV) because it has a negative residual return on capital — and, in equivalent economic profit terms, a negative economic profit spread.

A Look at Wealth Creators

In an attempt to provide some real world insight on these economic profit relationships, Exhibit 3 shows the estimated NPV for the "top 10" U.S. wealth creators that were listed in the Stern Stewart Performance 1000 Universe at year end 1998.[9] In turn, Exhibit 4 shows the after tax return on invested capital, ROIC, versus the cost of capital, *wacc*, for these powerful wealth creators. As we noted before, wealth creators have positive NPV because their economic profit is positive and their invested capital returns exceed the cost of capital — thereby producing a positive EP spread.

Exhibit 3 shows that wealth creators add tremendous value to the physical (and human) capital in their employ. At year-end 1997, GE, Coca-Cola, and Microsoft's estimated NPV were $195.83 billion, $158.25 billion, and $143.74 billion, respectively. This is especially astonishing for Coca-Cola and Microsoft since their invested capital at that time was only $10.96 billion and $8.68 billion. On balance, the combined NPV for all 10 U.S. wealth creators was $1,117 billion. The average dollar amount of value added to invested capital employed at these firms was $111.71 billion. Moreover, the NPV of the 10 firms ranged from $195.83 billion for General Electric down to $81.31 billion for Bristol-Myers Squibb.

---

[8] Some equivalent financial characteristics of wealth creators include (1) positive economic profit, (2) a positive residual or surplus return on invested capital, ROIC less *wacc* > 0, and (3) a profitability index ratio that exceeds unity, ROIC/*wacc* > 1.

[9] While in principle, a firm's NPV is the present value of its anticipated future economic profit, we can measure the market's assessment of this value as the difference between its observable enterprise value and total capital employed in the business.

Exhibit 3: Net Present Value of Top 10 U.S. Wealth Creators in 1997

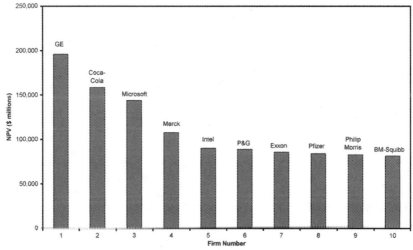

Data source: 1998 Performance 1000 Universe

Also, Exhibit 4 reveals that wealth creators have positive economic profit. In this context, 9 out of the top 10 U.S. wealth creators at year-end 1997 had a positive spread between their after-tax return on invested capital and the cost of capital. At that time, the return on capital employed figures for Coca-Cola, Microsoft, and Intel were 36.33%, 52.94%, and 42.71%, while their respective cost of capital figures (using a simple Capital Asset Pricing Model framework)[10] were noticeably lower — at 12.13%, 14.2%, and 15.14%, respectively. At about 8%, the positive economic profit spreads on wealth creators within the pharmaceutical industry — including, Merck, Pfizer, and Bristol-Myers Squibb — were attractive too. On balance, the average return on invested capital for the top 10 U.S. wealth creators at year-end 1997 was 26.24%%, while the average capital cost was 12.90% — producing an average economic profit spread of 13.34%.

Investor Link to Economic Profit

Since Wall Street analysts typically speak in terms of price-to-earnings and price-to-book value ratios when evaluating stocks, we can make a simple economic profit transition to a ratio format to introduce the benefit of using economic profit concepts in equities securities analysis. In this context, we know that the enterprise value of the firm (V) is simply the market value of its outstanding debt (D) and equity securities (E). That is,

$$V = D + E$$

---

[10] We cover CAPM and alternative cost of capital measurement approaches in Chapter 8.

Exhibit 4: Return on Invested Capital versus Cost of Capital: Top 10 U.S. Wealth Creators in 1998 Performance Universe

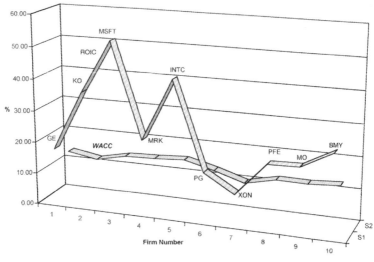

However the basic balance sheet relationship — expressed in market value terms — doesn't really tell the investor anything about how the firm derives its corporate value, V, in the first instance.

Here's where the basic NPV-EP link can provide some practical insight on corporate value and equity securities valuation in particular. First, we can express the intrinsic worth of the firm as being equal to its book capital (C) plus the net present value (NPV) that has been added to the invested capital (C). This is shown as:

$$V = C + \text{NPV}$$

Dividing the firm's enterprise value by its book capital, we obtain a powerful NPV-EP relationship for the firm's enterprise value-to-capital ratio. Accordingly, we have:

$$V/C = 1 + \text{NPV}/C$$
$$= 1 + [\text{PV of Expected EP}]/C$$

In this ratio, we see that a firm's enterprise value-to-capital ratio is higher than one — in a well-functioning or efficient capital market — if the firm has positive net present value. The source of the firm's positive NPV is in turn due to positive (discounted) economic profit.

On the other hand, the firm's enterprise value/capital ratio falls below unity when the capitalized economic profit stream is less than zero. In essence, the invested capital is more valuable outside its current economic profit stream usage. Building on our earlier NPV-EP relationship (see Exhibit 2), the basic corporate- and investor-linked measures of economic profit for wealth creators and wealth wasters are shown in Exhibit 5.

Relative Valuation of Wealth Creators

Based on the previous sample of wealth creators, we can shed some insight on the relationship between the EP-to-Capital and the NPV-to-Capital ratios. In this context, Exhibit 6 shows a scatter plot of these ratios for the 10 largest wealth creators (ranked by unadjusted NPV) in the Performance Universe at year-end 1998.[11]

The cross-sectional scatter (Exhibit 6) shows that there is a strongly positive relationship between the EP-to-Capital ratio and the NPV-to-Capital ratio. With respect to the individual data points, it's interesting to see that Microsoft has a higher NPV-to-Capital ratio than Coca-Cola — at 16.57 and 14.44, respectively. This seems to be a reflection of the fact that Microsoft's EP-to-Capital ratio, at 0.32, is higher than the size-adjusted EP for Coca-Cola, at 0.24.

***

Exhibit 5: Corporate and Investor Economic Profit Links

	Valuation	Profitability
Wealth Creator:	V/C > 1*	EP/C > 0, RROC > 0**
Wealth Neutrality:	V/C = 1	EP/C = 0, RROC = 0
Wealth Waster:	V/C < 1	EP/C < 0, RROC < 0

* V/C = Value/Total Capital ratio
* RROC = ROIC − *wacc* (assumes average values)

Exhibit 6: EP/Capital versus NPV/Capital: Top 10 U.S. Wealth Creators in 1998 Performance Universe

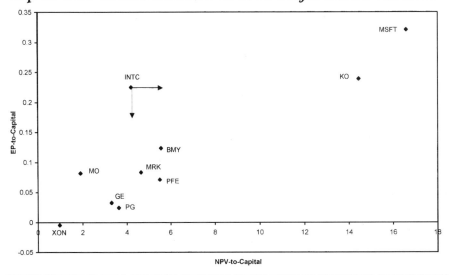

---

[11] In this illustration, we again use Stern Stewart's EVA® metric to estimate economic profit (EP).

If one posits a positive (albeit a linear one, for now[12]) relationship between EP and NPV ratios, then Exhibit 6 suggests that Intel was an attractive investment opportunity at year-end 1997. There's two ways of seeing this in the exhibit: At 0.23, Intel's EP/Capital ratio was similar to that observed for Coca-Cola. Yet at 4.2, its NPV-to-Capital was considerably lower than the NPV-to-Capital ratio for Coke, at 14.44. In practical terms, this means that if Intel's EP returns were to hold steady (or surprise positively), then its stock was due for a substantial revaluation. This favorable price revision is captured by the horizontal arrow shown in Exhibit 6.

Also, with an NPV-to-Capital ratio at about the same level (around 4) as that observed for Procter & Gamble and Merck, one sees that Intel's relative economic profit is noticeably better. At that valuation, it appears that investors were anticipating a sizable deterioration in Intel's forward economic profit-to-capital ratio. This potential EP compression is reflected in the downward pointing arrow shown in Exhibit 6.[13] Yet with "undiscovered" economic profit stability, the chip-maker turned out to be an attractive "buy" opportunity among the top 10 wealth creators at year-end 1997.[14] Moreover, the Intel illustration is consistent with a "buy side" view of wealth creation. That is, it suggests that a contrarian position based on an economic profit framework can lead to substantial discovery of value for astute investors.

Economic Profit Anomaly for Wealth Creators

Another look at Exhibit 6 reveals an interesting economic profit anomaly for Exxon Corporation. The exhibit shows that at year-end 1997, the energy company has positive NPV in the presence of its currently negative economic profit. Not surprisingly, there are several possible economic profit explanations for this financial occurrence.

On the one hand, if the capital market is "price efficient," then investors at that time must have been optimistic about the *future* ability of this oil producer to generate economic profit. On the other hand, the stock may have been overvalued in light of the firm's negative economic profit. About all we will say at this point is that a wealth creator cannot have persistent negative economic profit. At some point there must be a fundamental economic profit-growth "catalyst" that turns the negative economic profit situation around. Otherwise, the firm loses its premium valua-

---

[12] In Chapter 11, we emphasize that in theory the EP-to-Capital and NPV-to-Capital relationship is *non-linear*. This can be attributed to the NPV impact of changes in the economic profit growth rate and the cost of invested capital.

[13] There are at least two reasons why the capital market may have anticipated a sharp contraction in Intel's economic profit: (1) the chip-maker may have been at the peak of its competitive cycle, and (2) the firm's cyclicality in markets may have led to a higher cost of capital (at that time) than that which is reflected in the conventional "CAPM approach" to estimating the cost of (equity) capital. We capture firm-specific volatility in economic profit in our cost of capital model explained in Chapter 8.

[14] It is interesting to see that Intel's total return over the 1998 and 1999 period was 135.1%, while the S&P 500 had a cumulative total return of 55.6%.

tion. In Exxon's case, the sharp upward movement in oil prices during year 2000 and Exxon's resulting economic profitability eventually led to such a turnaround.

A WORD ON VALUE AND GROWTH STOCKS

Since "value stocks" — in Wall Street speak — have low price-to-book value and low price-to-earnings ratios, we can also use economic profit principles to gain some insight on enterprise valuation and stock valuation in particular. Specifically, if the capital market is reasonably efficient, then not all firms with low price relatives are "real value" opportunities — an important stock selection theme that we build upon at a later point in this book.

Specifically, the equities of companies having a combination of low price relatives and a poor economic profit outlook are a "value trap." In this context, the price-to-book capital ratio *and* the price-to-earnings ratio[15] for such troubled companies are low because they should be (low)! On balance, it is likely that these firms are "plagued" by a troublesome combination of high credit risk, adverse economic profit, and, therefore, negative NPV.[16] Barring turnaround, either internally or externally sparked, these equities offer low long-term capital appreciation.

We would also argue that high price-to-book value stocks (and high price-to-earnings stocks) operating in growth sectors like healthcare and technology are in many instances a reflection of their abundant and sustainable economic profit opportunities. This is an important recognition for investors in the former "high flying" internet and biotechnology stocks that were incorrectly perceived to be in a "world of their own."[17] Indeed, discovering those stocks having *real value* opportunities (via economic profit improvement) among the conventional universes of value and growth stocks is one of the key insights offered by the economic profit approach to securities valuation.

Moreover, with a sharpened focus by corporate managers and investors on the financial characteristics of wealth creators and wealth destroyers, the economic profit approach is the essence of a company research transformation that is reshaping the world of corporate finance and investment management. Indeed, the economic profit revolution transcends the mere labeling of companies as either "growth stocks" or "value stocks."

---

[15] Like the price/book capital ratio, we can (and will) show that a low (high) price/earnings ratio may be a sign of the firm's limited (abundant) growth opportunities. In principle, the price-to-earnings ratio for a firm with no future growth is a meager, $1/wacc$ — where $wacc$ is the firm's discount rate or cost of capital. Hence, in the economic profit approach, a so-called "value stock" does not necessarily mean a real value opportunity for investors.

[16] One of the authors emphasizes that wealth-destroying firms are plagued by an abundance of adverse managerial noise having negative NPV consequences for the shareholders. See Grant, *Foundations of Economic Value Added*.

[17] Unfortunately, many of these firms held no entrenched competitive advantage and therefore fell victim to commoditization quite rapidly. Ironically, the framework for looking at internet related companies is presently (years 2000-2001) similar to the "value-oriented" approach to evaluating negative NPV companies.

Chapter 4

Economic Profit View of Indexing and Equity Styles

One of the most misunderstood investment issues concerns the relevance (or lack thereof) of indexing and equity management "styles."[1] On the one hand, the breakdown of common stock portfolios into "style boxes" such as value, "blend," and growth along various capitalization dimensions adds structure to a complex world of stock selection, portfolio construction, and risk control. On the other hand, corporate pension plan sponsors and other investors are becoming increasingly aware of several equity style limitations — especially, investment style inadequacies that can be explained by sector-based and macro-economic profit considerations.

Equity style limitations can be explained on both empirical and theoretical grounds. On the empirical side, Jacobs and Levy[2] show that abnormal returns to value, growth, and small cap stock portfolios are inconsistent over time. That is, value portfolios do not always outperform growth-oriented portfolios and vice versa. Also, empirical evidence by Jensen, Johnson, and Mercer[3] suggests that equity style performance is endogenous to macroeconomic and monetary forces. In a similar manner, equity style performance can be traced to sector and industry factors. Moreover, from a theoretical perspective, the mere labeling of common stock portfolios as value, growth, or small capitalization says little if anything about the real economic profit characteristics — or wealth creating and wealth destroying potential — of companies in the investment portfolio.[4]

Our goal in this chapter and the next one is to explain the real meaning of indexing and equity management styles in an economic profit context. To achieve this objective, we begin with a review of Modern Portfolio Theory (MPT) and the Capital Asset Pricing Model (CAPM).[5] The capital market theory foundation provides a conceptual basis for understanding the accompanying discussions on (1) indexing (a pop-

---

[1] We treat "indexing" in this chapter as a special type of equity style — namely, a "blend" of conventional value and growth stocks.

[2] See Bruce Jacobs and Kenneth Levy, "Investment Management: An Architecture for the Equity Market," Chapter 1 in Frank J. Fabozzi (ed.), *Active Equity Portfolio Management* (New Hope, PA: Frank J. Fabozzi Associates, 1998).

[3] See Gerald R. Jensen, Robert R. Johnson, and Jeffrey M. Mercer, "The Inconsistency of Small-Firm and Value Stock Premiums," *Journal of Portfolio Management* (Winter 1998).

[4] One only needs to look at the many "growth funds" that held copious amounts of wealth-wasting technology stocks during year 2000.

ular blend type of equity style) and (2) how equity styles evolved from empirical challenges to the single (beta) factor CAPM. It also provides a framework for understanding why the practice of indexing (to the S&P 500, for example) and equity management styles more generally are inconsistent with the tenets of Modern Portfolio Theory — especially, when examined through an economic profit lens.

After providing a review of Modern Portfolio Theory, we propose a central tenet of the economic profit view of indexing and equity styles (of which the latter is explained more fully in the next chapter). Specifically, we contend that economic profit analysis is the "bottom up" means by which investors can hope to build "efficient portfolios" that maximize expected returns while maintaining risk at a desired level. After all, maximizing expected return while minimizing risk exposure is the essence of Modern Portfolio Theory. Following the MPT-EP link, we use economic profit principles to "debunk" indexing as well as the accounting factors used to classify common stock portfolios according to equity style — namely, the price-to-book value and price-to-earnings ratios.

Taken together, the MPT-EP focus on indexing and equity styles sheds light on the danger of having a naive view on what stock selection and portfolio management is really all about. We conclude with a "thinking out of the box" approach to the question of equity style management. We argue that a proper perspective on equity style management is one that sees styles as conditional on micro- and macro-economic profit influences. Conversely, we argue that a misguided style interpretation is one that views economic profit fundamentals as a mere byproduct of conventional indexing and value-growth styles of equity management.

MODERN PORTFOLIO THEORY

In 1952, Harry Markowitz provided the foundation for what is known today as Modern Portfolio Theory.[6] In a nutshell, he argued that investors have an incentive to diversify their portfolios to achieve the best possible expected returns with the least amount of investment risk. In more formal terms, Markowitz argued that investors — whether large players like corporate pension plans or small investors — should hold portfolios that are "mean-variance efficient." Exhibit 1 illustrates the benefits of portfolio diversification in a world consisting of two securities or two asset classes.[7]

Exhibit 1 shows the feasible set of portfolios that can be constructed from two asset classes. The feasible set is represented by the curve connecting point L (for, say, low-risk securities) with point H (for high-risk securities) in the

---

[5] In this chapter and the next one, we get at the heart of indexing and equity style dilemmas using Modern Portfolio Theory and economic profit (EP) principles. For additional insight on capital market theory, economic profit, and empirical challenges that have, ironically, led to a proliferation of equity styles, see Frank J. Fabozzi and James L. Grant, *Equity Portfolio Management* (New Hope, PA: Frank J. Fabozzi Associates, 1999).

[6] Harry M. Markowitz, "Portfolio Selection," *Journal of Finance* (March 1952).

[7] We show a real world efficient frontier in the next section with U.S. and international equities.

exhibit. Notice as the investor allocates investment funds to the higher volatility asset H that portfolio risk goes down while expected portfolio performance goes up. For example, portfolio 2 — with a 75%/25% mix of asset class L and H — has a noticeably lower level of volatility (typically measured by standard deviation of portfolio return) and a higher level of anticipated return when compared to portfolio 1 having a 100% allocation to asset class L.

Another look at Exhibit 1 reveals the set of portfolios that describe the efficient frontier. In this context, portfolios 2 through 5 provide investors with the highest level of expected return for a given level of investment risk. In this context, no rational investor would have an incentive to hold just asset class L when efficiently diversified combinations of assets L and H are available. Moreover, it should be evident that rational-minded investors would not hold any portfolio within the feasible set — such as portfolio 6 — when diversified combinations of assets L and H offer either higher expected return for a given risk level — see, portfolio 4 — or lower expected risk for the same expected portfolio return — see, portfolio 2.

With more stocks or asset classes, it should be no surprise that investors have added opportunities to enhance portfolio return while reducing investment risk. The efficient frontier again looks similar to that depicted in Exhibit 1, while its exact shape depends on expected returns, risk estimates, and correlation among asset class returns. A noteworthy extension of the multi-asset framework is the concept of the market portfolio. Specifically, in the Markowitz portfolio world, we know that investors have an incentive to hold mean-variance efficient portfolios — namely, those portfolios lying on the positively sloping portion of the feasible set of portfolios.

Exhibit 1: Feasible and Efficient Set of Portfolios for Asset L and Asset H

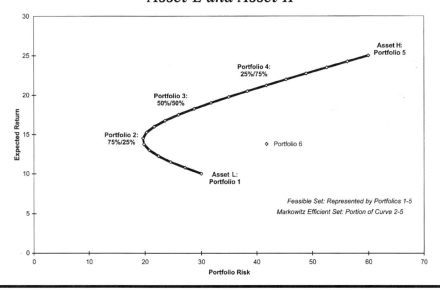

Exhibit 2: Benefit of Global Investing: 1970-1997 Period

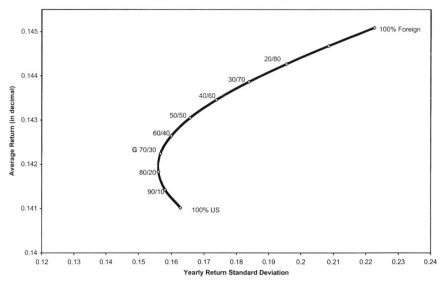

In theory, the market portfolio is simply the capitalization weighted average of all the presumed efficient holdings of investors. Therefore, in Modern Portfolio Theory, the market portfolio is also efficient and must lie on the *positively* sloping portion of the feasible set of investment choices. Viewed in practical terms, Modern Portfolio Theory provides investors with an expected return and diversification incentive for the management of portfolios on a globally diversified basis as well as the creation of world index funds.[8]

Empirical Look at Global Efficient Frontier

With this portfolio background, let's look at efficient diversification using recent empirical data. Exhibit 2 illustrates the real world implications of portfolio diversification with U.S. and international stock market returns. Specifically, the exhibit shows the portfolio return and risk management benefits of constructing a two-asset class frontier consisting of U.S. and international equities estimated over the 1970 to 1997 period. The Standard and Poor's 500 (S&P 500) index is used to represent U.S. stocks, while the Morgan Stanley Capital International "EAFE" index denotes the returns to international equities.[9]

---

[8] While MPT provides a basis for the creation of world index funds, what we see in practice is hardly a reflection of the theory. As we explain shortly, indexing to (say) the S&P 500 is really a local form of indexing which represents an active tilt away from the globally diversified market portfolio. Perhaps most troubling, indexing — whether locally or globally — presumes that capital market valuations "fully reflect" the economic profit potential of all companies in the index.

[9] Morgan Stanley Capital International EAFE represents the returns to a diversified mix of 21 developed stock markets — namely, Europe (15) plus Pacific (6).

Exhibit 2 shows that as an investor moves away from a 100% U.S. equity position, average portfolio return rises while investment risk — as measured by portfolio return standard deviation — goes down. For instance, the 80/20 mix of U.S. and international stocks has an average portfolio return of 14.18% with portfolio volatility of 15.6%. In contrast, the 100% U.S. equity allocation has a 28-year average return of 14.10% with a portfolio risk of 16.27%. With the potential for higher expected return and lower portfolio risk, the two-asset global frontier illustrates the benefit of Markowitz portfolio diversification. This portfolio return enhancement and risk management benefit is available on any set of asset classes as long as (1) the more volatile asset class — such as EAFE equities (with higher currency and political risk attributes for U.S. investors) — provides higher expected return, and (2) the correlation among asset (class) returns is less than unity.[10]

Another look at Exhibit 2 reveals the set of two-asset class portfolios that are mean-variance efficient — in the Markowitz sense of providing the highest expected reward for a given amount of global investment risk. These efficient portfolio combinations range from the 70/30 mix (noted as G70/30 in the exhibit) on up to the 100% asset allocation in international equities. Most importantly, the exhibit shows that no rational investor would hold just U.S. equities when the globally diversified 60/40 mix of U.S. and EAFE stocks has higher average return — at 14.26% over the sample period — for the same amount of equity portfolio risk. Again, these global-based findings illustrate the expected return enhancement and risk management benefits of the Markowitz portfolio model.[11]

Misguided Indexing

While portfolio theory was developed several decades ago, we find that all too many misguided applications of the theory arise in practice.[12] First, the "market portfolio" envisioned by Harry Markowitz (and others[13]) consists of a capitalization weighted average of the returns on all risky assets, including U.S. equities, international equities, U.S. and international bonds, U.S. and international real

---

[10] In recent years, the average return on the more volatile international asset class — namely, EAFE — has been lower than that earned on U.S. equities. This has produced a "backward bending" frontier that is inconsistent with global diversification tenets. For a fuller explanation, see Fabozzi and Grant, *Equity Portfolio Management.*

[11] Having reiterated that, we note that the average return spread between the domestic and international opportunity over the 28-year reporting period — at 40 basis points in Exhibit 2 — is surprisingly small and does not include transaction cost differentials.

[12] As we will shortly see, investor confusion over indexing and equity styles can be eliminated when explained in an economic profit context.

[13] Several individuals are credited with the development of Modern Portfolio Theory. These pioneers include (in alphabetical order) Fischer Black, Eugene Fama, John Lintner, Jan Mossin, Paul Samuelson, William Sharpe, and James Tobin. We'll also show how the introduction of a risk-free asset changes the portfolio opportunity set and, in turn, leads to the familiar CAPM. While several authors were involved in the development of CAPM, William Sharpe is most often cited in practical discussion and application of the single (beta) factor model.

estate, and other global-based assets classes.[14] Even if we were to allow a representative market portfolio to be comprised of all equities, it would need to consist — according to recent developed world equity capitalization estimates by Morgan Stanley Capital International — of about 50% U.S. equities (measured by the S&P 500) and the balance of portfolio funds in the stocks of Europe, Australia, and the Far East (EAFE).

Second, the popular "top down" global allocation approach used by many of today's investors to capture relative economic conditions is based on large capitalization stocks in each respective regional market. The global orientation of many of these money management firms leads sometimes to inherent biases that contradict the local economic condition insights. This global allocation approach may also miss the expected return and risk management benefits of mid-to-small capitalization stocks — to the extent that we use style labels in this book — within U.S. and developed foreign markets. Nor does it say anything about the performance benefits of stock selection in emerging markets of Asia, Latin America, Eastern Europe, and Africa.

MPT AND ECONOMIC PROFIT

At this point, the reader is probably wondering what our theoretical and empirical discussion of Modern Portfolio Theory has to do with economic profit analysis. The answer to this question is simple. In our view, economic profit measurement is the "bottom-up" foundation on which Modern Portfolio Theory rests. Specifically, if the capital market is price efficient, then current security prices should "fully reflect"[15] the firm's underlying ability to generate economic profit on both existing and anticipated future assets not currently in place. In turn, if the capital market is efficient at the company stock level, then investors have a "top down" incentive to diversify their portfolios in order to achieve the highest expected reward for the least amount of company-specific risk.

Hence, the incentive for investors to hold well-diversified portfolios in the first place rests on the more fundamental notion that company stock valuations reflect the underlying economic profit potential of companies in the global marketplace. If correct, then economic profit analysis at the company level is the "bottom-up" means by which the capital market not only becomes efficient, but also the means by which investors can hope to achieve the "top-down" portfolio

---

[14] While we'll cover the question of equity styles, notice that Modern Portfolio Theory says nothing about the risk-adjusted performance benefits of equity styles *per se*. Capital market theory focuses on discovering the set of portfolios that offer the highest expected reward for any given level of risk. This performance goal transcends the popular value and growth equity styles — and, is entirely consistent with economic profit principles that we espouse in this book.

[15] The words "fully reflect" are aptly captured in Fama's now classic explanation of an efficient capital market. See Eugene F. Fama, "Efficient Capital Markets: A Review of Theory and Empirical Work," *Journal of Finance* (May 1970).

management benefits espoused by Markowitz portfolio diversification — namely, maximum expected return for any given level of expected portfolio risk.

Practical Considerations

In this *combined* MPT and economic profit framework, we argue that indexing (to the S&P 500, for example) and equity styles more generally are misguided investment strategies because they limit expected return and/or increase risk. That is, an index fund or a particular equity style doesn't guarantee that all companies in the portfolio sell at prices that "fully reflect" their underlying economic profit potential. Unfortunately, indexing and equity styles more generally presume that the capital market is largely price efficient with respect to the relevant indexes at hand.

Also, to the extent that capital market inefficiencies exist (as they surely do in the real world), the need for an economic profit approach to stock selection and portfolio construction is further enhanced for any active investor (corporate plan sponsor and like-minded investor) who seriously wants to maximize expected portfolio return while limiting risk exposure. In terms of investment strategy, the "long only" portion of an economic profit approach to portfolio construction would maintain index weights on those stocks (in industries, sectors, and even countries) that are price efficient, while tilting both toward and away from those companies having attractive and unattractive economic profit valuations, respectively.

If short selling is permitted, the active component of the economic profit strategy could be implemented by a "long-short" approach to equity portfolio management. In such a market-neutral strategy, the portfolio manager would utilize economic profit analysis to add positive "alpha" to the risk-free rate of interest. Stock index futures could be added to an economic profit strategy to the extent that plan sponsors and other institutional investors want to amplify the alpha with market exposure. Hence, the economic profit approach to stock selection and portfolio construction is not only consistent with the expected return and risk management tenets of Modern Portfolio Theory, but it also provides corporate plan sponsors and other sophisticated investors with the means to discover the "best of the best" companies in a world where capital market inefficiencies most certainly exist.

CAPITAL ASSET PRICING MODEL

The Capital Asset Pricing Model (CAPM) is of course another tenet of modern investment theory that is relevant to our economic profit discussion of indexing and equity styles. In the following sections, we'll provide (1) a review of the single (beta) factor CAPM, (2) a discussion of empirical challenges to CAPM, and (3) a discussion of studies that point to limitations of a strict "value versus growth" style of managing a common stock portfolio. This introductory focus on CAPM and equity styles will provide a helpful background for our examination in the next chapter of the real meaning of equity styles — and style fundamentals such as the price-to-book value and price-to-earnings ratio — in an economic profit context.

Exhibit 3: Efficient Portfolios With and Without Risk Free Asset

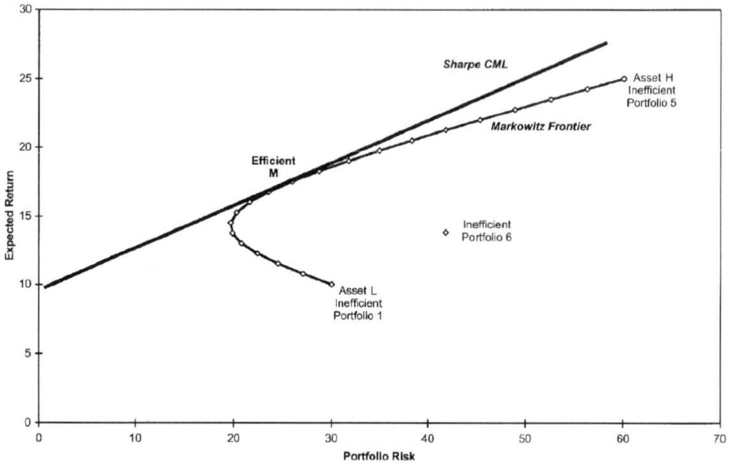

CAPM Theory

In the mid-1960s, William Sharpe *et al* revolutionized the world of portfolio management by introducing a "risk-free" asset into the portfolio opportunity set. Although many debates have ensued about the existence of such an asset — an asset with positive return and zero return volatility — the investment management implications of the Sharpe *et al* model are abundantly clear: rational investors should strive to hold a two-asset portfolio consisting of a risk-free Treasury security in combination with the capitalization-weighted world market portfolio, *M*. As indicated before, the market portfolio consists of all risky assets (any asset having a positive return standard deviation) including the capitalization-weighted combination of returns to all sorts of assets including domestic and international equities, bonds, real estate, art, coins, and even "human capital."

Exhibit 3 shows how the introduction of a risk-free asset into the portfolio set leads to additional opportunities for investors to enhance portfolio returns and to reduce investment risk. That is, the introduction of a risk-free asset into the portfolio opportunity set leads to a "Capital Market Line" that dominates the Markowitz portfolio frontier in expected return and risk space at every point on the CML except for the tangency point, *M*. In principle, this means that two-asset class combinations of the risk-free asset and risky market portfolio dominate all portfolio choices on the now inefficient — from a portfolio efficiency perspective[16] — investment opportunity set described by Harry Markowitz.

---

[16] As Eugene Fama points out in *The Theory of Finance*, an efficient portfolio provides an investor with the best possible expected return for a given level of risk. Investors have an incentive to diversity their portfolios in this way if the capital market is price efficient. Strictly speaking, the presumption of capital market efficiency is a pre-condition for the creation of a Markowitz efficient portfolio.

Expected Security Return

Up to this point, we have been speaking in terms of portfolio choices as opposed to expected return and risk relationships for individual securities. As MPT theory would have it, there exists a linear relationship between expected security return and "systematic" risk for each and every security (or portfolio) within the market portfolio, M. The familiar CAPM describes this asset-pricing relationship as follows:

$$r_e = r_f + MRP \times \beta_{e,m}$$

In this expression, r_e is the expected return on a security or portfolio, r_f is the "risk-free" rate of interest, and MRP and $\beta_{e,m}$ measure the expected market risk premium (expected market return less the risk-free rate) and the level of systematic (beta) risk, respectively. In CAPM, there is only one systematic risk factor that is "priced" into equilibrium expected security returns — namely, the beta measure that captures a security's sensitivity or relative risk in the market portfolio, M.

According to CAPM, high beta stocks (or portfolios) should produce high-expected returns, while low beta stocks should have comparatively low expected returns. Indeed, if the CAPM is the correct specification of capital market equilibrium, then the predicted expected return-beta risk relationship should — on the average — be seen in the performance of real-world portfolios. However, this is where financial theory and reality depart, as CAPM falters due to several empirical inconsistencies that have been discovered since the inception of this model. Unfortunately, the CAPM void has *not* been filled but simply replaced — as we will shortly see — with equity "styles" that say little if anything about the economic profit and risk potential of companies in the marketplace.

CAPM Anomalies

Since the inception of CAPM, there have been numerous empirical challenges to the notion that beta is the only risk factor that investors need to know when setting equilibrium expected security returns. Early CAPM studies by Rolf Banz and Marc Reinganum[17] to more recent studies by Eugene Fama and Kenneth French, Richard Roll, and Rex Sinquefield[18] have all documented the inability of the sin-

---

[17] For early CAPM studies, see (1) Rolf Banz, "The Relationship Between Return and Market Value of Common Stocks," *Journal of Financial Economics* (March 1981), and (2) Marc Reinganum, "Misspecification of Capital Asset Pricing: Empirical Anomalies Based on Earnings Yield and Market Values," *Journal of Financial Economics* (March 1981).

[18] For recent studies that challenge the single-(beta) factor CAPM, see (1) Eugene Fama and Kenneth French, "The Cross-Section of Expected Stock Returns," *Journal of Finance* (June 1992), (2) Richard Roll, "Style Return Differentials: Illusions, Risk Premiums, or Investment Opportunities," Chapter 5 in Daniel Coggin, Frank Fabozzi, and Robert Arnott (eds.), *The Handbook of Equity Style Management* (New Hope, PA: Frank J. Fabozzi Associates, 1997), and (3) Rex Sinquefield, "Where are the Gains from International Diversification?" *Financial Analysts Journal* (January/February 1996).

gle-factor CAPM to adequately explain the average return and risk relationship observed in real world capital markets — both in the U.S. and in international capital markets.

In a now classic study, Fama and French find that two easily measured variables including equity size and book-to-price ratio adequately describe the cross section of expected security returns over the 1963 to 1990 period.[19] As a direct assault on CAPM, they argue that the traditionally celebrated relationship between average returns and beta risk is "weak" and perhaps "nonexistent." Also, Richard Roll — using stock returns over the 1985 to 1994 period — shows that a low risk (measured by CAPM beta) equity portfolio strategy produces abnormally high returns, regardless of whether one focuses on the common stocks of small or large capitalization companies.

Studies by David Leinweber, Robert Arnott, and Christopher Luck[20] as well as Rex Sinquefield find that a relatively low risk "value strategy" produces abnormally high average returns relative to a high-risk "growth strategy" in international capital markets. Thus, empirical challenges to CAPM are not just confined to the U.S. stock market, but also appear endemic to global equity markets. Moreover, as we mentioned at the outset of this chapter, Jensen, Johnson, and Mercer find that equity style performance is endogenous to macroeconomic and monetary forces.[21] Their empirical findings are in turn consistent with our primary investment view — explained in detail in the next chapter — that equity styles are secondary to economic profit fundamentals.

Specifically, the classification of a stock as either value or growth says little about why a company is so classified. For example, consider the approach used to construct the S&P/BARRA Growth and S&P/BARRA Value indexes. In these well known indexes, stocks of companies that have a relatively low price-to-book value ratio are classified as value stocks — up to 50% of the S&P 500 market cap — while stocks with high price-to-book value ratio are considered growth stocks — with nothing in between the value/growth classifications. Unfortunately, in this naive style-based portfolio construction process,[22] there is no focus whatsoever on the more fundamental question of why a company's stock has a low (or high) price-to-book ratio, and the economic profit meaning of this low (or high) price relative in the portfolio construction process.

---

[19] The Fama-French finding that small cap stocks with low price-to-book value ratios have positive abnormal returns (when examined in a CAPM context) should not be taken to mean that small cap value stocks are a "free lunch" approach to investing. Indeed, Fama and French point out that the seemingly positive abnormal returns on these stocks may be due to credit and default risk considerations.

[20] See David Leinweber, Robert Arnott, and Christopher Luck, "The Many Sides of Equity Style: Quantitative Management of Core, Value, and Growth Portfolios," Chapter 11 in *The Handbook of Equity Style Management*.

[21] Jensen, Johnson, and Mercer, "The Inconsistency of Small-Firm and Value Stock Premiums."

[22] In 2001, JDS Uniphase, widely recognized as a momentum growth stock, was included in the BARRA Value Index due to a high amount of intangible book value emanating from a recent purchase acquisition. Thus, when the stock price fell, the low price to book ratio resulted in its "value" classification.

Exhibit 4: Large-Cap Growth Stocks Outperform Large-Cap Value in Some Periods and Underperform in Other

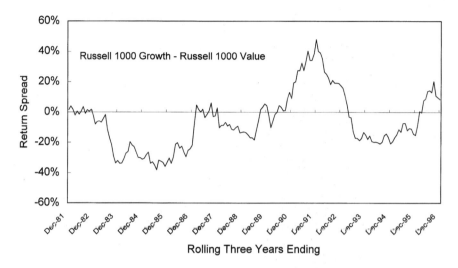

Rolling Three Years Ending

Source: Bruce I. Jacobs and Kenneth N. Levy, "Investment Management: An Architecture for the Equity Market," Chapter 1 in Frank J. Fabozzi (ed.), *Active Equity Portfolio Management* (New Hope, PA: Frank J. Fabozzi Associates, 1998).

Style-Based Performance Inconsistencies

Having recognized the theoretical inconsistency of a strict value (or growth) strategy,[23] it is also important to emphasize that value does not always outperform growth — even though several studies suggest that "value wins" over the long term. Along this line, Bruce Jacobs and Kenneth Levy[24] report (see Exhibit 4) the relative performance of large cap growth stocks, measured by the difference in cumulative return performance on the Russell 1000 Growth index less the Russell 1000 Value index over the December 1981 to December 1996 period. In contrast with other studies, their empirical findings show that there are extended periods when the return to value investing — such as the early to mid-1980s — was more attractive than growth stock investing, while a growth style of equity management was more attractive during the late 1980s and early 1990s, and again during the mid 1990s.[25]

---

[23] In the next chapter, we'll examine the inconsistency of equity style fundamentals — including the price-to-book value and price-to-earnings ratio — from an economic profit perspective.

[24] See Bruce Jacobs and Kenneth Levy, "Investment Management: An Architecture for the Equity Market," Chapter 1 in *Active Equity Portfolio Management*.

[25] Also, growth stock investing was back in favor during the late 1990s — and then preempted by value stock investing in year 2000.

Exhibit 5: Range of Equity Management Styles

	Value	Blend	Growth
Maxi-Cap	Max V	Max B	Max G
Large-Cap	Lge V	Lge B	Lge G
Mid-Cap	Mid V	Mid B	Mid G
Small-Cap	Sm V	Sm B	Sm G
Micro-Cap	Mic V	Mic B	Mic G

We now see that a compartmentalized equity style approach — as manifest in the range of equity management styles shown in Exhibit 5 — where investors naively follow a value or growth strategy is both inconsistent with financial theory and empirical evidence. As explained later in an economic profit context, we believe that investment managers should be given the flexibility to search for the best opportunities within the overall universe of equity securities — including, of course, the conventional value and growth styles. Such a synthesized economic profit approach to stock selection and portfolio construction is neither growth nor value, nor can it be conveniently brushed off as a "market-oriented" style of equity portfolio management.[26] It is "true value" and consistency in the purest sense.

EQUITY STYLE CONUNDRUM

Based on the above evidence, we believe that a disciplined economic profit approach to investment management is the correct approach. Clearly, the creation by pension plan consultants of normalized portfolios or similarly designed value and growth style benchmarks make little sense if the fundamentals for portfolio construction and risk control have little to do with the underlying economic profit considerations that drive security prices. Economic profit fundamentals should come first — as we explain more fully in the next chapter — while indexing and equity styles *per se* are secondary.

Because of this priority, we advocate a "core-satellite" approach for overall pension or investment plans. In this approach, the low value-added core is made up of the S&P 500 index or structured portfolios to gain the desired level of market risk. This is then surrounded by alpha-seeking satellite portfolios that are not constrained by style or size but rather analyzed for consistency of company-specific alpha generation over many periods.

---

[26] Note that indexing (a blend, or market-oriented style) a portfolio to a beta of 1 says nothing about economic profit fundamentals — albeit, whether they are positive for wealth creators or negative for wealth destroyers — of companies in the overall portfolio. This economic profit criticism will be launched in the next chapter against equity styles more generally.

Chapter 5

Debunking Equity Style Fundamentals

O ne of the benefits of looking at a company — and therefore its stock — in an economic profit context is that it provides the investor (or manager) with meaningful information about why an equity style fundamental such as the value-to-capital ratio (or in more popular terms, the price-to-book value ratio) for a company's stock is low or high. In the economic profit approach, investment fundamentals come first while equity styles *per se* are secondary. This economic profit view of "value investing" is radically different from the conventional view because it transcends the standard value and growth equity styles. Specifically, real value investing means discovering companies selling at prices that are not fully reflective of their attractive economic profit fundamentals.

In this chapter, we look at two equity style determinants in an economic profit context — namely, the price-to-book value ratio and the price-to-earnings ratio. These are two of the more important variables used in practice to define the conventional growth and value styles of investing. Value stocks in a strict style view are thought to be attractive simply because their price relatives are low, while growth stocks are thought to be attractive because high price relatives conveys positive information about future revenue and earnings growth. We in turn argue that many so-called "value stocks" have low price-to-book ratio, for example, because they should have — their economic profit outlook is unattractive. In a similar manner, we argue that "growth stocks" can at times be undervalued or overvalued when their price relative measures are examined in an economic profit context.

DEBUNKING THE PRICE-TO-BOOK RATIO

The fundamental inconsistency of a naive value or growth style of investing becomes transparent when examined in an economic profit context. We'll examine this equity style limitation in terms of "value stocks."[1] In principle, the low price-to-book ratio for value stocks may — and in many instances will — be a reflection of the firm's currently assessed negative net present value. The negative NPV is in turn a present value reflection of the firm's negative assessed economic profit. Moreover, as we noted before, economic profit is negative when the after-tax return on invested capital falls short of the cost of capital.

---

[1] We examine the growth style of investing from an economic profit lens in the next section.

35

We can express these economic profit ideas in more formal terms.[2] Specifically, the enterprise (or warranted) value of any company — small, medium or large — can always be expressed as total invested capital, C, plus aggregate net present value, NPV, according to:

$$V = C + \text{NPV}$$

Upon dividing this expression by invested capital, we obtain a simple — yet powerful — characterization of a company's value-to-capital (or in popular jargon, the price-to-book ratio) ratio in terms of its NPV-to-Capital ratio:

$$V/C = 1 + \text{NPV}/C$$

Moreover, since NPV is equal to the present value of expected economic profit, the relationship between a firm's value-to-capital ratio and its economic profit is transparent:

$$V/C = 1 + [\text{PV of Expected EP}]/C$$

Taken together, we see that the value-to-capital ratio for a company is higher than unity when it has positive NPV. The positive NPV is attributed to the firm's discounted positive economic profit. In contrast, the value-to-capital ratio for a company is less than one when the firm has discounted negative economic profit. This adverse economic profit happening occurs when the return on invested capital falls short of the weighted average cost of capital *and* is expected to remain there over time.[3]

Danger of Naive Value Investing

Exhibit 1 provides a powerful depiction of why the popular value style of investing is not only inconsistent with capital market theory, but also dangerous to an investor's financial health! The exhibit shows why not all value is "real value," and therefore why many value stocks in the conventional view may be a "value trap." In this context, the exhibit reports the NPV-to-Capital ratio versus the Economic Profit (EP)-to-Capital ratio for the bottom 50 companies in the Stern Stewart Performance 1000 Universe for 1998.[4]

Notice that the stocks of all 50 of these companies could be considered "value stocks." This is because their price-to-book value ratio is not only low, but also because it is less than unity. At the same time, there are 46 companies shown

---

[2] The enterprise valuation discussion that follows parallels a similar discussion that we had in Chapter 3 concerning the value-to-capital ratio. We believe it worth repeating here given our goal of debunking equity styles in an economic profit context.

[3] We cover the strategic role of the cost of capital in enterprise and stock valuation in Chapter 8.

[4] As shown in Chapter 3, we can just as easily explain our NPV and economic profit findings in the context of the EP-to-Capital versus the NPV-to-Capital ratio.

in Exhibit 1 having *jointly* negative economic profit in the presence of their currently negative NPV. Consequently, these so-called value stocks have low positive to negative NPV because they should have! There are of course several reasons why the companies shown in Exhibit 1 have a negative economic profit outlook. These include (1) limited to poor future growth opportunities, (2) a relatively high cost of capital due to excess economic profit volatility, and, as Jensen, Johnson, and Mercer[5] point out, (3) an unfavorable economic profit outlook that is largely driven by adverse monetary and macroeconomic forces.

There are also some interesting extreme cases shown in Exhibit 1. At year-end 1997, Apple Computer and Digital Equipment Corporation had sharply negative NPV-to-Capital ratios, each at about −0.37, in the presence of their negative EP-to-Capital ratios. Based on these findings, it appears that blindly betting on a value portfolio constructed with a simple price-to-book sort — the S&P/ BARRA approach, for example — is tantamount to investing in a portfolio of currently wealth destroying firms. Equally naive, the investor may be betting on companies having economic profit outcomes that are mostly driven by monetary and macroeconomic forces. The source of their negative economic profit (and therefore, negative NPV) is due to their current *inability* to earn a sustainable after-tax capital return that exceeds the cost of capital.

Exhibit 1: NPV-to-Capital versus EP-to-Capital Ratio: 50 Largest Wealth Destroyers in 1998 Performance Universe

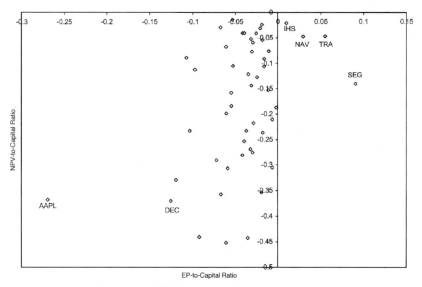

Data Source: 1998 Stern Stewart Performance Universe

---

[5] See Gerald Jensen, Robert Johnson, and Jeffrey Mercer, "The Inconsistency of Small-Firm and Value Stock Premiums," *Journal of Portfolio Management* (Winter 1998).

Another look at Exhibit 1 reveals the potential benefit of "bottom up" company analysis over blindly choosing a value style of investing.[6] Specifically, economic profit tools can be used to discover the real value stocks within the universe of so-called value stocks. In this context, one sees that there are four companies in the sample of 50 companies having jointly positive economic profit in the presence of their currently negative assessed NPV. With pricing inefficiencies, firms like Integrated Health Services (IHS), Navistar International (NAV), Seagate Technologies (SEG), and Terra Industries (TRA) were good candidates to investigate further among a set of value stocks having low price relative and negative NPV. Indeed, these four companies had the beneficial combination of low price-to-book value ratio with currently positive economic profit.[7] Clearly, analyzing the persistency of future economic profit is the focus for these companies rather than "timing" a turnaround as would be necessary for the other group of so-called value stocks reported in Exhibit 1.

Economic Profit within Growth Investing

The benefit of looking at economic profit fundamentals is not unique to just value stocks. That is, fundamental economic profit research may also prove helpful in identifying superior stocks within a universe of growth stocks. In this regard, Exhibit 2 shows the NPV-to-Capital ratio versus the EP-to-Capital ratio for the 50 largest wealth creators in the 1998 Performance Universe.[8] Notice that powerful wealth creators such as Coca Cola (KO), Microsoft (MSFT), and Cisco Systems (CSCO) stand out with their strongly positive economic profit in the presence of their NPV that was some 10 to 17 times the invested capital employed in these wealth creating firms.

Dell Computer, however, went to the head of the growth stock class with a relatively small amount of capital being used to generate a powerful economic profit — hence, a powerful wealth creator with strongly positive net present value. Indeed, Dell's NPV at year-end 1997 was an astounding 47 times the relatively *small* amount of capital employed. Moreover, economic profit for Dell was positive at 1.77 times the computer maker's invested capital. These findings suggest that an economic profit approach to stock selection with a dual focus on companies that can generate a powerful economic profit on a small amount of invested capital is a winning "opportunistic" growth strategy for the future.

Based on the empirical findings shown in Exhibit 2, we see that growth companies have high NPV-to-Capital ratios because they should have![9] The

---

[6] The display of negative NPV and EP (economic profit) companies in the exhibit shows just how important it is to employ company analysis in the stock selection process.

[7] There are of course other economic profit issues that need to be addressed before outright investing in companies with currently positive economic profit and low NPV-to-Capital ratios — such as an investigation of future economic profit opportunities and invested capital growth rates as we explain in Chapter 10.

[8] Exhibit 2 provides a basis for expanding on our discussion in Chapter 3 of the importance of looking at growth stocks in an economic profit context.

[9] Of course, the real key for investors is to ascertain whether the future growth potential is "fully reflected" in the current stock price, and whether the stability of economic profit will remain constant.

attractive future growth potential is largely reflected in stock price. In effect, real growth-oriented companies generate powerful economic profit because their after-tax return on invested capital *far* exceeds the weighted average cost of debt (to the extent that growth firms have any debt) and equity capital. Moreover, as we discuss later, the key is to determine the persistence of the high returns on invested capital and stability of the company's risk profile. We believe that an economic profit framework is best suited for this type of company analysis.

DEBUNKING THE PRICE-TO-EARNINGS RATIO

We can also use economic profit thinking to "debunk" another popular equity style fundamental — namely the price-to-earnings ratio. In particular, we noted in the above formulation that the firm derives its enterprise value from the NPV addition to capital employed within the business. In a helpful and equivalent manner, we can split the firm's enterprise value into two components: namely, the NOPAT contribution to market value generated by the firm's existing assets *plus* the economic profit contribution to enterprise value generated by expected future assets not currently in place — that is, future growth opportunities.

Exhibit 2: NPV-to-Capital versus EP-to-Capital Ratio:
50 Largest Wealth Creators in 1998 Performance Universe

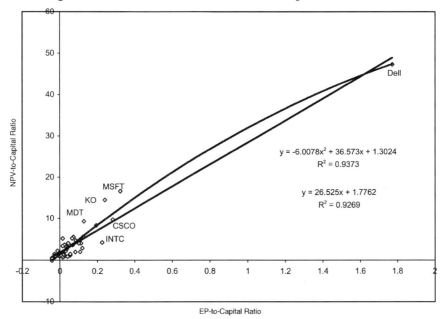

Data Source: 1998 Stern Stewart Performance Universe

In this context, we can express the enterprise (or warranted) value of the firms as:[10]

$$V = \text{NOPAT}/wacc + G_f$$

In this expression, V is the firm's enterprise value, $\text{NOPAT}/wacc$ is the present value contribution to enterprise value from existing assets, and G_f is the present value of firm's anticipated growth opportunities. Without getting into large detail here,[11] it should be of little surprise to managers and investors that the firm's future growth value, G_f, is positive if on the average future investment opportunities earn a capital return that exceeds the assessed future cost of capital.

Dividing the firm's enterprise value by its net operating profit after tax, NOPAT, we obtain the enterprise value-to-earnings ratio:

$$V/E = 1/wacc + G_f/\text{NOPAT}$$

With this development, we see that the firm's "price-to-earnings" ratio is equal to the "P/E" ratio for a firm having no expected growth opportunities — namely, 1/$wacc$ — plus the relative contribution to enterprise value generated by expected future assets not currently in place, G_f/NOPAT.

Decomposition of Price-to-Earnings Ratio for Wealth Creators

Exhibit 3 shows a decomposition of enterprise value-to-earnings ratio for the 10 largest U.S. wealth creators in the 1998 Performance Universe. Consistent with economic profit growth principles, the exhibit reveals that the enterprise value-to-earnings ratio for growth companies is largely comprised of future growth opportunities — that is, G_f/NOPAT makes up most of the observed value-to-operating earnings ratio for wealth creating firms. For examples, at year-end 1997, the enterprise value-to-NOPAT ratios for General Electric, Coca-Cola, Microsoft, and Merck were 27.45, 43.09, 40.11, and 25.37, respectively.

In turn, the growth multiples (of NOPAT) for these large U.S. wealth creators were 20.19, 34.85, 33.07, and 18.48, respectively. Expressed in percentage terms, the NPV (and future EP "improvement") contribution of expected future assets to the value/earnings ratio for GE and Merck was about 73%, while the relative future growth contribution to enterprise value for Coca-Cola and Microsoft was up to 81% to 82%. Conversely, the anticipated NOPAT perpetuity from existing assets made up only 19% to 18% of the observed enterprise value-to-earnings ratio for powerful wealth creators such as Coca-Cola and Microsoft.

---

[10] For a robust explanation of how a firm derives its enterprise value from existing and future assets not currently in place, see the "Investment Opportunities Approach to Valuation" (Chapter 2) in Eugene F. Fama and Merton H. Miller, *The Theory of Finance* (Holt, Rinehart and Winston, Inc., 1972).

[11] We'll cover the development and application of economic profit models in Chapter 6.

Exhibit 3: Enterprise Value/NOPAT Ratio: Growth and Operating Asset Components for Top 10 Companies in 1998 Performance Universe *

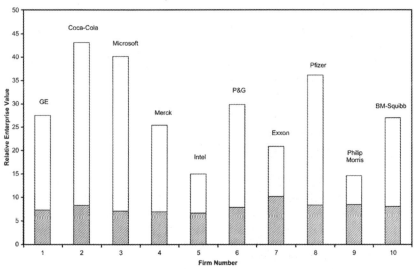

* Operating asset component ($1/wacc$) represented by shaded portion of each bar.

At 48% and 58%, the highest contribution among the U.S. wealth creators from existing assets to enterprise value is observed for Exxon and Philip Morris. With $1/wacc$ multiples of 10.09 and 8.38, operating earnings from existing assets — again, measured by NOPAT — comprise a relatively high proportion of the enterprise value-to-earnings ratios of 20.81 and 14.54, respectively. On the average though, the contribution of existing assets to the enterprise value-to-earnings ratio, $V/NOPAT$, for the 10 largest U.S. wealth creators at year-end 1997 was about 32%. This implies that the economic profit contribution from future growth opportunities, at 68%, mostly drives the enterprise value-to-earnings ratio for wealth creating firms.[12]

Economic Profit-Driven Sectors

Another economic profit strike against a naive view of equity styles is that the styles themselves are endogenous to sector and macroeconomic forces.[13] For examples, common stocks within the financial sector and utility sector are highly

---

[12] While we emphasize the firm's future growth opportunities in this section, we should equally emphasize the importance of a company's economic profit risk profile in determining the enterprise value-to-earnings ratio. We cover economic profit risk issues in a cost of capital context in Chapter 8.

[13] Jensen, Johnson, and Mercer provide compelling evidence on why small cap *and* value styles are driven by macroeconomic and monetary forces. See Jensen, Johnson, and Mercer, "The Inconsistency of Small-Firm and Value Stock Premiums."

correlated due to their heightened sensitivity to interest rate changes. Also, the stocks of companies within the energy and basic material sectors of the economy are positively correlated due to their high positive association with commodity prices — another macroeconomic factor. On the other hand, the stocks of companies within the health care and technology sectors have a relatively low correlation with the market, therefore allowing for a more bottom-up approach to equity securities analysis.

With a naive focus on equity styles, it is possible that an investor might select what appears to be a "winning style" — such as the value style of investing — but show low to poor stock market performance due to adverse sector and/or macro happenings associated with, say, interest rate uncertainty and commodity price fluctuations. These are just two of many pervasive macroeconomic and sector-based factors. Moreover, a misguided style focus can also arise within a growth strategy if there is no attention being paid to the micro (or company specific) and/or macro economic profit considerations that are driving the sector.

As we discuss in later chapters, the economic profit approach to investing should commence with an understanding of how external influences — such as interest rates and commodity price developments — impact the company-level economic profit outlook. In sectors that are largely driven by unique circumstances at the company-specific level, clearly, an understanding of external influences is less important. Whatever the case, stocks of *all* companies should be evaluated from a fundamental economic profit perspective to ensure that wealth creators are selected for the portfolio.

Thinking "Out of the Box"

By now, it should be clear that we advocate a "thinking out of the (style) box" approach to evaluating companies and their investment opportunities. For what is the meaning of labels such as value and growth stocks when the simple categorization by equity style has little if anything to do with the economic profit potential of companies within the portfolio?

Also, does it really make sense to index or benchmark a portfolio to an equity style when some of the component companies have currently negative economic profit, as can be the case of all too many value stocks? In a similar vein, does it make sense to benchmark to a growth style while ignoring overly optimistic valuations that may be placed on the future economic profit generation of some companies within the growth sector? We think not.

More to the point, does it make sense to blindly assume that all stocks in a conventional value or growth index are efficiently priced if it is widely recognized that metrics used for style determination (price to book, price to earnings) have significant shortcomings? Given that pricing inefficiencies do arise within real world capital markets, we recommend an economic profit approach to looking at stocks within *and* across conventional value, blend, and growth universes. By employing such a discipline, a good investment manager should be able to perform well independently of the current investment style in vogue. With an emphasis on economic profit fundamentals — especially the key economic profit drivers that we introduced in Chapter 1 — an investor or corporate manager can hopefully see whether or not a company is trading for its full warranted value.

REFLECTIONS ON INDEXING AND EQUITY STYLES

The central message in our economic profit treatment of equity styles (explained thus far) for corporate managers — especially plan sponsors — and investors is that economic profit analysis is the *bottom-up* means by which investors can hope to build portfolios that have the best risk-adjusted returns. As we noted in the previous chapter, if the capital market is price efficient, then current security prices should "fully reflect" the economic profit potential of companies in the marketplace.

Given that capital market inefficiencies do exist, this provides a value-added incentive for active-minded investors to employ an economic profit approach to equity analysis during the price adjustment period to full equilibrium. Thus, whether or not the capital market is highly efficient or less efficient, an investor can see that economic profit valuation lies at the heart of stock selection, portfolio construction, and risk control.

Our view that modern portfolio theory and economic profit principles are inextricably joined challenges the conventional notions of equity management styles. In our overall discussion of investment style, we argue that indexing and equity styles *per se* are misguided investment strategies (to the extent that they are investment "strategies") because there is no explicit evaluation of whether companies in the respective portfolios or tracking indexes have negative or positive economic profit characteristics.

Moreover, as we explained before, many so-called "value stocks" have low price-to-book value and low price-to-earnings ratios because of limited to poor future growth opportunities and/or a high degree of economic profit volatility (cyclicality). In contrast, a bottom up economic profit strategy looks across the universe of value and growth stocks to discover real value in the marketplace. Indeed, we contend that the economic profit approach to stock selection and portfolio construction is entirely consistent with the return enhancement and risk management goals of modern portfolio theory.

Chapter 6

Economic Profit Approach to Enterprise Valuation

One of the major criticisms voiced against economic profit measurement (like earnings per share) is that the profit measures themselves are too short-term focused and, therefore, inconsistent with shareholder value maximization. While it is true that misguided short-term applications of economic profit measurement have occurred in practice — and that value-based consultants with a "cacophony" of metrics may have led corporate managers astray — the broader assertion that economic profit measurement is inconsistent with shareholder wealth maximization is incorrect.

Economic profit measurement is the quintessential way of looking at corporate profitability because it fully recognizes that invested capital has a capital *charge* associated with it. We know that shareholders invest in companies with the expectation of earning a normal return on their invested capital. Indeed, the shareholder's required return for bearing business and financial risk is an *explicit* opportunity cost, and one that must duly be recognized by corporate managers and investors when assessing the firm's short- and long-term viability. Economic profit measurement recognizes this normal return requirement on a periodic basis by deducting a capital charge from the firm's net operating profit after tax (NOPAT). Unlike accounting measures, economic profit places a value on the timing and consistency of the capital charge.

We also know that from a corporate valuation perspective, the firm's net creation of wealth — as measured by its net present value (NPV) — is equal to the discounted value of its economic profit stream.[1] Equivalently, it can be shown that the firm's average economic profit is the *annualized* equivalent of its NPV. Thus, economic profit is central to the measurement of shareholder value added. In contrast with traditional accounting profit measures — like EBITD, net income, ROE, and even NOPAT — economic profit (specifically, the capitalized value thereof) provides a *direct* means of assessing the wealth impact of capital budgeting decisions made by the firm's corporate managers.

Our goal in this chapter is to provide a foundation on the economic profit approach to enterprise valuation. We begin by looking at the similarities and differences between the free cash flow (FCF) and economic profit (EP) approaches

---

[1] For a theoretical discussion on the link between NPV and economic profit, see James L. Grant, *Foundations of Economic Value Added* (New Hope, PA: Frank J. Fabozzi Associates, 1997).

to enterprise valuation. We then demonstrate that the economic profit approach provides the same estimate of enterprise value and warranted stock price as that obtained using the conventional free cash flow model. With a joint emphasis on discounted cash flow, the FCF-EP linkage is important for corporate managers and investors who are unfamiliar with economic profit valuation tools, and for managers and analysts who *incorrectly* perceive that economic profit measurement is a shortsighted measurement and valuation tool.

Following our examination of enterprise valuation models, we look at the sensitivity of enterprise value and warranted stock price to varying assumptions about the economic profit growth period — as manifest in a company's competitive advantage — and the cost of capital. Based on the valuation concepts presented in this chapter, corporate managers and investors can see how seemingly small changes in key economic profit parameters — such as the economic profit growth period and the cost of capital — can impact enterprise value and warranted equity price in a meaningful way.

ENTERPRISE VALUATION MODELS

Myriad approaches available to value a company and its stock can confuse corporate managers and investors. Along this line, we are asked whether it is better to value a company based on a discounted streams of dividends, free cash flows, or economic profit. While several valuation approaches exist in practice, the overriding valuation principle to keep in mind is that the value of the firm is, after all, the value of the firm! That is, at any given moment in time, the firm's market value reflects a discounted set of cash flows generated by its existing and anticipated future assets not currently in place. Regardless of how one packages these cash flows — as dividends, free cash flow, or even economic profit — the firm's enterprise value and its warranted stock price must be consistent across all approaches to corporate valuation.[2]

Given that there are several equivalent ways to value a company, we believe that it makes sense for corporate managers and investors to focus their valuation efforts on a measure of profitability — specifically, economic profit — that is directly related to wealth creation via positive net present value. While dividends are in theory the ultimate source of investor value, it is often difficult to see how a dividend stream relates on a periodic basis to the real investment decisions made by corporate managers in large ongoing companies with multiple divisions and subsidiaries. Moreover, dividend valuation lacks practical relevance for companies that retain most all of their earnings for (hopefully) positive future growth.

Free cash flow utilization is a step in the right direction because it looks at net operating profit after tax (NOPAT) less the required working capital and net

---

[2] This pricing equivalence among enterprise valuation models is an outgrowth of the equal (risk-adjusted) rate of return principle explained in Eugene F. Fama and Merton H. Miller, *The Theory of Finance* (Holt, Rinehart and Winston, Inc., 1972).

capital additions to support a growing revenue (and earnings) stream. However, economic profit provides a more transparent look at wealth creation because it makes a periodic assessment of whether the firm's invested capital return exceeds the weighted average cost of capital and the EP measure includes the impact from changes to invested capital; i.e., net investment. Also, the sign of the economic profit is a key determinant of whether the firm's net present value is positive — a reflection of wealth creating investment decisions — or negative — as in corporate investment decisions that waste shareholder value. Again though, we emphasize that all enterprise valuation models must in principal yield the same intrinsic worth of the firm and its outstanding shares of common stock.

FREE CASH FLOW MODEL

We'll begin our discussion of enterprise valuation models with an application of the traditional free cash flow model.[3] In this approach, the enterprise value of the firm is expressed as the present value of the anticipated free cash flow stream generated by the firm's existing and expected future assets not currently in place. In formal terms the FCF model can be expressed as:

$$V = \sum \frac{\text{FCF}(t)}{(1 + wacc)^t}$$

In this expression, V is the firm's estimated enterprise value, $\text{FCF}(t)$ is the assessed free cash flow at year t, and $wacc$ is the familiar weighted average cost of debt and equity capital.[4] Unless otherwise noted, t runs from 1 to infinity.

In turn, the firm's assessed free cash flow at year t, $\text{FCF}(t)$, is equal to the anticipated net operating profit after tax, NOPAT, less annual net investment, NI, to support the firm's growth. Gross annual investment expenditures include (1) working capital additions to support a growing revenue base, (2) capital expenditures to maintain economic productivity of the firm's existing assets, and (3) any new capital investment by the firm's managers at period t. In turn, net investment is equal to gross investment less (in principle) economic depreciation.[5]

---

[3] For an interesting early application of the free cash flow model, see Alfred Rappaport, "Strategic Analysis for More Profitable Acquisitions," *Harvard Business Review* (July/August 1979). Recent insight on how to apply the traditional free cash flow model can be found in (1) Thomas Copeland, Timothy Koller, and Jack Murrin, *Valuation: Measuring and Managing the Value of Companies, Second Edition* (New York: John Wiley & Sons, 1994), and (2) Frank J. Fabozzi and James L. Grant (eds.), *Value Based Metrics: Foundations and Practice* (New Hope, PA: Frank J. Fabozzi Associates, 2000).

[4] Anyone who has had a basic course in finance is familiar with the cost of capital. We explore some pricing implications of *wacc* fluctuations later in this chapter. We also devote a chapter to the estimation and measurement of this key economic profit factor.

[5] For insight as to how to properly measure economic depreciation, see Stephen F. O'Byrne, "Does Value-Based Management Discourage Investment in Intangibles?" Chapter 5 in *Value-Based Metrics: Foundations and Practice*. We'll cover the economic profit problem of using GAAP-pronounced straight line versus economic depreciation in Chapter 7.

We can now express the firm's enterprise value, V, as the capitalized value of its expected NOPAT less annual net investment at time period t according to:

$$V = \sum \frac{\text{NOPAT}(t) - \text{NI}(t)}{(1 + wacc)^t}$$

As noted above, we take net investment (NI) to mean gross capital expenditures at period t less maintenance expenditures (measured by economic depreciation) on the firm's existing assets.[6] Net annual investment also includes the change in working capital to support a growing revenue base.

Forecasting Free Cash Flow

While several approaches can be used to forecast a company's free cash flow, we'll use the traditional revenue forecasting approach described by Alfred Rappaport.[7] In this context, the free cash flow estimate for any given year is based on forecasted *sales* net of both operating and investment expenditures. Operating and investment expenditures are expressed as a fraction of the growing revenue stream. In more formal terms, the sales forecasting equation that is used to produce a free cash flow estimate for any given year t is given by:

$$
\begin{aligned}
\text{FCF}(t) &= \text{NOPAT}(t) - \text{NI}(t) \\
&= \text{EBIT}(t)(1 - t_u) - \text{NI}(t) \\
&= S(t - 1)(1 + g_s)p(1 - t_u) - (w + f)[(S(t) - S(t - 1)]
\end{aligned}
$$

Note that in the second free cash flow expression, $\text{FCF}(t)$ is expressed as tax adjusted EBIT (earnings before interest and taxes) less net investment, $\text{NI}(t)$, at period t. We use the unlevered tax rate in this expression, t_u, because the weighted average cost of capital, $wacc$, presumably includes the interest tax shield (if any) received on the firm's outstanding debt.

Also, in the third free cash flow expression, the letter S is used to denote sales, g_s is the forecasted sales or revenue growth rate, p is the pre-tax operating (net of depreciation) margin, and the letters w and f, respectively, are working capital and net investment proportions that are applied to the forecasted change in sales, $S(t) - S(t - 1)$. These investment percentages account for the fact that a growing company will not only invest in more capital, but it will also need additional working capital (added inventory, etc.) to support the growing revenue base.

---

[6] In this chapter, we explain the free cash flow model in the context of the firm's NOPAT and net investment. We could obtain the same free cash flow results by focusing on the firm's gross operating profit after tax (GOPAT) less its gross investment each year. For further discussion of this issue, see Fabozzi and Grant, *Value-Based Metrics: Foundations and Practice*.

[7] See Rappaport, "Strategic Analysis for More Profitable Acquisitions." Also, applications of the revenue forecasting model using free cash flow and economic profit approaches can be found in Fabozzi and Grant, *Value-Based Metrics: Foundations and Practice*.

To see how this works, we'll make the following assumptions to obtain an estimate of free cash flow at year 1:

- Base Revenue = 100
- Revenue growth rate = 25%
- Pre-tax operating margin (EBIT/Sales) = 20%
- Net capital investment = 20% of increased sales
- Working capital additions = 5% of increased sales
- Unlevered tax rate = 35%[8]

Based on these assumptions, the free cash flow estimate at year 1 is given by:

$$
\begin{aligned}
FCF(1) &= NOPAT(1) - NI(1) \\
&= \$125 \times 0.2 \times 0.65 - [0.2 + 0.05][\$125 - \$100] \\
&= \$16.25 - \$6.25 = \$10
\end{aligned}
$$

Notice that in the free cash flow model, the focus is on the firm's net operating profit after tax less the net investment to maintain existing assets and to support a growing revenue stream. Free cash flow makes sense from a valuation perspective because the firm cannot expect to produce the NOPAT estimate of $16.25 without a supporting net investment expenditure of $10 at year 1.

Exhibit 1 shows a 10-year stream of free cash flow estimates that were produced by the revenue-forecasting model. We'll use the assessed NOPAT, net annual investment, and resulting free cash flow figures in the next section to estimate the enterprise value of the firm and its outstanding equity shares.

Exhibit 1: Forecasting Free Cash Flow: NOPAT Approach

Period	1	2	3	4	5	6	7	8	9	10
Sales	125.00	156.25	195.31	244.14	305.18	381.47	476.84	596.05	745.06	931.32
Op. Exp.	100.00	125.00	156.25	195.31	244.14	305.18	381.47	476.84	596.05	745.06
EBIT	25.00	31.25	39.06	48.83	61.04	76.29	95.37	119.21	149.01	186.26
Taxes	8.75	10.94	13.67	17.09	21.36	26.70	33.38	41.72	52.15	65.19
NOPAT	16.25	20.31	25.39	31.74	39.67	49.59	61.99	77.49	96.86	121.07
NCapInv.	5.00	6.25	7.81	9.77	12.21	15.26	19.07	23.84	29.80	37.25
Work Cap	1.25	1.56	1.95	2.44	3.05	3.81	4.77	5.96	7.45	9.31
Net Inv.	6.25	7.81	9.77	12.21	15.26	19.07	23.84	29.80	37.25	46.57
FCF	10.00	12.50	15.63	19.53	24.41	30.52	38.15	47.68	59.60	74.51

[8] As mentioned before, it is standard practice to use an un-levered tax rate when estimating NOPAT because any tax benefit associated with corporate debt financing (including operating leases) should already be reflected in the firm's weighted average cost of capital, *wacc*.

Exhibit 2: Free Cash Flow Valuation: Horizon Years

Cost of Capital = 9%

Year	NOPAT	Net Invest	FCF	Pres.Val. 9%	Cum. PV
1	16.25	6.25	10.00	9.17	9.17
2	20.31	7.81	12.50	10.52	19.70
3	25.39	9.77	15.62	12.06	31.76
4	31.74	12.21	19.53	13.84	45.59
5	39.67	15.26	24.41	15.86	61.46
6	49.59	19.07	30.52	18.20	79.66
7	61.99	23.84	38.15	20.87	100.52
8	77.49	29.80	47.69	23.93	124.46
9	96.86	37.25	59.61	27.45	151.90
10	121.07	46.57	74.50	31.47	183.37
11 Plus	121.07				

FREE CASH FLOW VALUATION

When valuing a company using the free cash flow model, one typically sees the value of the firm split up into two components — namely, the valuation of free cash flow estimates over the "horizon" years and the intrinsic worth of free cash flow generated during the "residual" years. In this breakout, the horizon years capture that portion of the firm's life where the analyst feels comfortable projecting cash flows on a periodic basic. In our illustration, we'll use the 10 years of free cash flow estimates produced by the revenue-forecasting equation to assess the horizon value of the firm. We'll then look at how the firm derives a large portion of its enterprise value and warranted stock price from free cash flow generated during the post-horizon or residual years. Indeed, our decomposition of enterprise value in Chapter 5 for the 10 largest U.S. wealth creators is consistent with the view that the majority of value is embedded outside the horizon years.

FCF Valuation: Horizon Years

Exhibit 2 shows how to "roll up" the 10 years of free cash flow estimates for the horizon years. The exhibit reports NOPAT, net investment, free cash flow, the present value of free cash flow for any given year, and the *cumulative* present value of the free cash flow estimates over the horizon period. Based on a "cost of capital" (discount rate) of 9%, we see that the $10 free cash flow estimate for year 1 has a current market value of $9.17.

Upon calculating the present value of the 10 free cash flow estimates and then cumulating these values, we see that the firm's warranted horizon value is $183.37. With long-term debt at, say, $30, and 20 shares of common stock outstanding, the warranted horizon value of each share of stock would be $7.67.

Horizon-Year Stock Price
    = [Horizon-Year Enterprise Value – LT Debt]/Equity Shares
    = [$183.37 – $30]/20 = $7.67

However, stopping here in the enterprise valuation process presumes that the firm is unable to generate positive free cash flow beyond the horizon period. Such an unfortunate state of affairs might exist for the shareholders if a company has no future growth opportunities because its existing capital assets at that time (year-end 10) were obsolete.

FCF Valuation: Residual Years

While several assumptions can be made about free cash flow generation (real inflation adjusted) during the post-horizon years,[9] we'll make the simplifying assumption that revenue growth ceases at year 10 and that *net* annual investment is zero thereafter. This latter assumption is tantamount to saying that net investment beyond year 10 equals zero because gross annual investment is equal to the maintenance expenditure required to maintain a perpetual cash flow (measured by NOPAT) on the firm's existing assets in place at the end of the horizon period.

Exhibit 3 shows how to estimate the enterprise value of the firm for both the horizon and residual years. Based on our simplifying assumption, the residual value at year-end 10 is $1345.22. This residual value estimate was calculated using a 9% discount rate.

$$RV(10) = FCF(11)/(wacc - g)$$
$$= NOPAT(11)/wacc$$
$$= \$121.07/0.09 = \$1345.22$$

Exhibit 3: Free Cash Flow Valuation: Horizon and Residual Years

Cost of Capital = 9%

Horizon Value		183.37
Residual Value	1345.22	568.24*
Corporate Value		751.61
LT Debt		30.00
Equity		721.61
Share OS		20.00
Price		36.08

* RV(0) = [121.07/0.09]PV(9%,10)

---

[9] Such possibilities include constant and variable growth in free cash flow beyond year 10 (at a growth rate *less* than *wacc*) to some form of competitive "decay" in the firm's estimated free cash flow during post-horizon or residual years.

Upon discounting RV(10) back 10 years, we obtain the intrinsic worth, at $568.24, of the free cash flow generated in the post-horizon or residual years. As summarized in Exhibit 3, we see that the enterprise or corporate value of the firm is $751.61. This value consists of the $183.37 in horizon value *plus* $568.24 of current residual value. With long-term debt at $30, and 20 shares of common stock outstanding, the warranted equity price is *now* $36.08.

Before proceeding, it is important to note that the current residual value, at $568.24, makes up some 76% of the firm's warranted enterprise value. This large residual value impact is a common finding when using discounted cash flow approaches to estimate enterprise value and stock price. As stated previously, in the real world, the residual value impact is especially pronounced for growth-oriented companies[10] since most of their enterprise value comes from distant — and usually difficult to predict — cash flows that are a reflection of future investment opportunities.

ECONOMIC PROFIT MODEL

The economic profit model differs from the free cash flow model in that it provides a *direct* assessment of value added to the firm's invested capital.[11] The wealth added to the firm's invested capital is called its net present value. In principle, the firm's net present value is equal to the present value of the anticipated economic profit stream generated by both existing and anticipated future assets. In more formal terms, we can express the general NPV and economic profit relationship as:

$$V = C + NPV$$

where

$$NPV = \text{Present Value of Economic Profit}$$
$$= \sum \frac{EP(t)}{(1 + wacc)^t}$$

In the net present value expression, EP is the estimated economic profit at time period t, and *wacc* is the weighted average cost of debt and equity capital. Other things the same,[12] we see that the firm's managers create wealth by making

---

[10] We use the term "growth-oriented companies" to mean those firms that can earn *discounted* positive economic profit (and therefore, positive NPV) on future investment opportunities. They do so with an after-tax return on future investments that exceeds *wacc*.

[11] As noted before, this does *not* mean that the economic profit approach to enterprise valuation gives a better answer than that available from other valuation models, including DDMs and free cash flow approaches.

[12] When evaluating companies and their stocks, managers and investors must be keenly aware of possible economic profit influences due to industry, sector, and market effects. We cover these *non*-company-specific economic profit effects in Chapter 9.

discounted positive economic profit — and therefore positive NPV — decisions. They destroy wealth when economic profit is on the average negative.

As we said before, the firm's estimated economic profit is positive when its expected after-tax return on invested capital exceeds the cost of capital. Economic profit — and its discounted NPV equivalent — is negative when corporate managers invest in assets (both tangible and intangible) having an after-tax capital return that on balance falls short of the *wacc*.

EP Link with Free Cash Flow

There are two things to keep in mind when exploring the relationship between the traditional free cash flow model and the economic profit model. The first is obvious — namely, both models must produce the same internal or warranted value of the firm and its outstanding shares of stock. In this sense, the two models are equivalent. Having said that, we believe that the economic profit approach to valuation provides corporate managers and investors with a transparent look at how the firm derives its overall net present value. Simply put, has the firm created value up and above the cash invested in the operating assets, either tangible or intangible?

The second item to keep in mind between the two valuation models pertains to the capital charge on invested assets. Specifically, in the free cash flow model, the present value of the capital charge on the firm's annual net investment is *implicitly* recognized in the same year that the capital expenditure is incurred. In contrast, in the economic profit approach to enterprise valuation an *explicit* charge on the beginning of year invested capital is assessed each year.

To see how this works, suppose — as in our free cash flow application at year 1 — the firm spends $6.25 in capital improvement during a particular year. In the free cash flow model, the entire annual investment would be subtracted from NOPAT in the year incurred. As mentioned above, this is equivalent to recognizing the present value of the yearly capital charge that would be assessed in the economic profit model. Assuming that the capital charge can be expressed as perpetuity, we have:

$$\text{Net Investment}(1) = \$6.25$$
$$= wacc \times \text{NI}(1)/wacc = \$6.25$$

Notice that the free cash flow model subtracts the entire investment of $6.25 from NOPAT in the year incurred. In the economic profit approach, the periodic capital charge of $0.563 (assuming a 9% cost of capital) would be deducted from each year's NOPAT beginning in the first year following the capital expenditure. Of course, annual investment expenditures (initially, at $6.25) are added to the *beginning* of year capital base in the economic profit model.

Forecasting Economic Profit

With these basic FCF-EP relationships, let's now see how economic profit can be estimated using the revenue forecasting approach that we introduced before. In this context, Exhibit 4 shows how to estimate the firm's economic profit over the horizon years. With NOPAT at \$16.25 for year 1, an initial (net[13]) capital investment of \$90, and a cost of capital at 9%, we see that the firm's assessed economic profit for year 1 is \$8.15:

$$EP(1) = NOPAT(1) - wacc \times C(0)$$
$$= \$16.25 - 0.09 \times 90.00 = \$8.15$$

Likewise, at \$11.65, economic profit for year 2 is just NOPAT less the assessed capital charge on net invested capital at the end of year 1.

$$EP(2) = NOPAT(2) - wacc \times C(1)$$
$$= \$20.31 - 0.09 \times \$96.25 = \$11.65$$

At \$96.25, the capital investment at the start of year 2 is a reflection of the initial capital, $C(0)$ of \$90.00, plus the net annual investment of \$6.25 that occurred during year 1.

In a similar manner, Exhibit 4 shows how to estimate economic profit for the rest of the horizon years, covering years 3 to 10. Notice that the estimated economic profit for year 11, at \$94.27, is equal to the assessed NOPAT for year 10, at \$121.07, less the capital charge on beginning of year 11 (or end of year 10) capital at \$26.80. This economic profit figure results because of our previous simplifying assumption of no future growth beyond the horizon period.

Exhibit 4: Forecasting Economic Profit: Horizon Years
Cost of Capital = 9%

Year	Yearly Net Inv.	Total Net Capital	NOPAT	Capital Charge	Economic Profit
0		90.00			
1	6.25	96.25	16.25	8.1000	8.1500
2	7.81	104.06	20.31	8.6625	11.6475
3	9.77	113.83	25.39	9.3654	16.0246
4	12.21	126.04	31.74	10.2447	21.4953
5	15.26	141.30	39.67	11.3436	28.3264
6	19.07	160.37	49.59	12.7170	36.8730
7	23.84	184.21	61.99	14.4333	47.5567
8	29.80	214.01	77.49	16.5789	60.9111
9	37.25	251.26	96.86	19.2609	77.5991
10	46.57	297.83	121.07	22.6134	98.4566
11 Plus			121.07	26.8047	94.2653

---

[13] Since we are using NOPAT on the income statement side, we must also use *net* (of accumulated depreciation) operating assets on the balance sheet side. As noted earlier, we could use gross operating profit after tax (GOPAT) on the income side and gross operating assets on the balance sheet to obtain the same operating cash flow and enterprise valuation results.

Exhibit 5: Valuation of Economic Profit: Horizon and Residual Years

Cost of Capital = 9%

Year	Economic Profit	Pres.Val. 9%	Cum. PV
1	8.15	7.48	7.48
2	11.65	9.81	17.28
3	16.02	12.37	29.65
4	21.50	15.23	44.88
5	28.33	18.41	63.30
6	36.87	21.98	85.28
7	47.56	26.02	111.30
8	60.91	30.57	141.87
9	77.60	35.73	177.60
10	98.46	41.59	219.19
11 Plus	94.27		

Residual Value	1047.44	442.45
NPV		661.64
Capital		90.00
Corp.Val		751.64
LT Debt		30.00
Equity		721.64
Share OS		20.00
Price		36.08

VALUATION OF ECONOMIC PROFIT

Exhibit 5 shows how to "roll up" the economic profit estimates into the NPV generated during the horizon years *plus* the NPV generated during the residual period. The sum of these two NPV figures is the net creation of wealth that has been added to the firm's invested capital. Holding market forces constant, this is a reflection of the wealth that has been created (or destroyed) by the firm's capital investment decisions.

Exhibit 5 shows that the cumulative present value of the estimated economic profit stream during the horizon period is $219.19. This figure can also be interpreted as the NPV generated from economic profit during the horizon years. In turn, with economic profit perpetuity of $94.27 commencing in year 11, we see in Exhibit 5 that the firm's residual economic profit value (or NPV) at year 10 is $1,047.44. With our simplifying assumptions, this NPV at year 10 is calculated according to:

$$NPV(10) = \text{Residual Value of Future EP at Year 10}$$
$$= EP(11)/(wacc - g)$$
$$= EP(10)/wacc$$
$$= \$94.27/0.09 = \$1,047.44$$

Upon discounting the residual economic profit value back to the current period, we obtain the NPV of the economic profit stream generated during the post-horizon years, at $442.45. Also, upon adding up the NPV of economic profit generated during horizon and residual years, we obtain the firm's overall net creation of wealth as follows:

$$NPV(0) = \text{NPV(Horizon Years)} + \text{NPV(Residual Years)}$$
$$= \$219.19 + \$442.45 = \$661.64$$

With an initial capital base of $90.00, the firm's estimated enterprise value is $751.64. Moreover, with long-term debt at $30.00 and 20 shares of common stock outstanding, the firms warranted stock price is:

$$\text{Warranted Stock Price} = [V - \text{LT Debt}]/\text{shares}$$
$$= [\$751.64 - 30]/20 = \$36.08.$$

Not surprisingly, both the enterprise value and the warranted equity price are the same figures that we obtained using the conventional free cash flow approach to corporate valuation. However, as emphasized before, the economic profit approach to enterprise valuation provides corporate managers and investors with a *direct* assessment of the wealth that is being added (via discounted economic profit) to the firm's invested capital.

COMPETITIVE FADE PERIOD

In our illustration of the economic profit approach to enterprise valuation, we made the simplifying and questionable assumption that the firm could generate EP perpetuity of $94.27 during the residual period. In a more realistic setting, one might argue that at some point competitive market forces would drive the firm's (marginal) economic profit to zero. While several sophisticated approaches exist to modeling a company's competitive "fade period,"[14] we'll provide some basic insight on fade by varying the number of years (T) that a company can earn positive economic profit on investment during the residual years.

For convenience,[15] we'll use the numbers from our previous illustration and *now* assume that the economic profit earned during the horizon years is attrib-

---

[14] For example, Stewart provides an insightful discussion on fade in the context of the generalized T period economic profit model. See G. Bennett Stewart III, *The Quest for Value* (New York: Harper Collins, 1991). We'll provide an overview of this competitive fade model in an upcoming section.

[15] We realize that in our previous illustration, *no* future growth was assumed. While we utilize the same numbers in the growth illustration that follows, our goal here is to shed some basic insight on economic profit growth effects (and periods) without having the reader get bogged down in detailed formulas that model the firm's investment opportunities.

uted entirely to existing assets, while any economic profit generated in the residual period is due to future growth opportunities. We'll also make the simplifying assumption that the estimated economic profit for year 11, at $94.27, can be used as a proxy for the average economic profit generated during the residual years. Based on these simplifications, the competitive fade approach suggests that a large portion of the firm's NPV and enterprise value can be determined by estimating the number of periods that it can generate positive economic profit on investment during the residual years.

Competitive Fade: A Simple Example

With no restriction on the number of years that the firm can earn an economic profit of $94.27 in the residual period, we found that the firm's estimated NPV at year 10 was $1,047.44 [$94.27/0.09]. This residual value has a current NPV of $442.45. Notice that in the *absence* of additional economic profit opportunities during the residual years that the NPV of $442.45 is the maximum value of the firm's estimated economic profit stream from the post horizon years. This, in turn, sets upper limit values on both the firm's aggregate NPV and its warranted enterprise value. Drawing values from before, we have $661.64 and $751.64, respectively.

In general, the notion of competitive fade presumes that a firm's opportunity to earn positive economic profit is limited by technological obsolescence and/or competition in the productive market for goods and services. If correct, corporate managers and investors must make an assessment of the number of periods that a company can *realistically* generate positive economic profit for the future. By implication, we can say that investors will not "pay" for negative economic profit earned on future investment opportunities.

With these considerations, Exhibit 6 shows how the NPV of the firm's future growth opportunities varies as the number of positive economic profit years goes from 5 years to 50 years. At $442.45, the exhibit shows the upper limit value of the economic profit stream generated during the residual (assumed future growth) period. Notice how the residual value of the firm changes as "*T*" varies from 5 to 50 years of positive economic profit. Based on present value dynamics, we see that the residual value function asymptotically approaches the line that represents the present value of the economic profit perpetuity.

Exhibit 6 shows that with five years of positive economic profit in the post horizon years, the NPV of future growth opportunities is only $154.89. When expressed in terms of the firm's enterprise value and its warranted stock price, we obtain $464.08 and $21.70. In contrast, with 15 and 30 years of positive economic profit during the residual period, the NPV values for future growth opportunities are $320.98 and $409.10. The exhibit also suggests that with "*T*" of 15 and 30 years, the firm's enterprise values are $630.17 and $718.29, respectively. Also, the corresponding stock price estimates are $30.01 and $34.41.

Exhibit 6: NPV Impact of "T" Periods of Positive Economic Profit

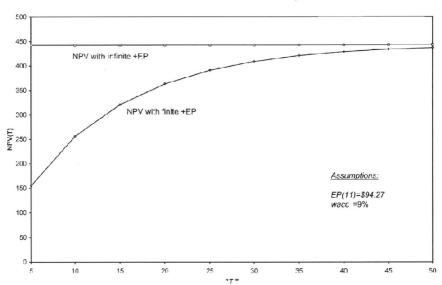

With *unlimited* positive economic profit in the residual years, we see that the firm's estimated enterprise value is $751.64 and its warranted stock price is $36.08. These are the values that we initially obtained before. Notice that with just 5 years of positive economic profit in residual years that the estimated stock price is only 60% ($21.70/$36.08) of the price obtained with unlimited positive economic profit. With 15 and 30 years of positive economic profit in post horizon years, the warranted equity prices are 83% and 95%, respectively, of the price obtained with unlimited positive economic profit. Thus, corporate managers and investors must be keenly aware of the number of periods that a company can *realistically* earn economic profit for the future.

Some Trading Implications

Based on our simple competitive fade application, it is worth noting that if the actual number of positive economic profit periods was, say, five years rather than 15 years, then the firm's enterprise value and stock price would be *overvalued* in the capital market. Based on the figures supplied before, the firm's stock price would fall over time from $30.01 to $21.70 — unless of course the firm's managers could preempt the decline by surprising investors positively about the number of periods that the firm could earn positive economic profit on its investment opportunities. Conversely, a company's stock would be *undervalued* if the capital market at large incorrectly perceived that the number of positive economic profit periods was, say, 15 years when in fact the warranted period was longer. In general, the authors believe that one of the key inefficiencies in the equity markets is investors' optimism regarding the persistence and stability of economic profit periods, particularly in technology and consumer discretionary companies.[16]

OVERVIEW OF COST OF CAPITAL SENSITIVITY

As with future growth opportunities, another economic profit factor that is central to enterprise valuation is the cost of capital. While we devote Chapter 8 to cost of capital estimation and measurement, we show here how seemingly small changes in *wacc* can have a large impact on corporate value and warranted stock price. Specifically, Exhibit 7 shows what happens to enterprise value and warranted stock price when the cost of capital rises by 100 basis points (due to rising interest rates, for example) and falls by 100 basis points (due to declining interest rates or business uncertainty).

With a 9% cost of capital, we found that the firm's enterprise value was $751.64. This figure includes (along with the initial $90 capital investment) the NPV of economic profit generated during the horizon and post-horizon years — at $219.19 and $442.45, respectively. At that discount rate, the firm's warranted stock price is $36.08. However, Exhibit 7 also reveals that if the cost of capital were to decline from 9% to 8% — due perhaps to a general decline in interest rates or a decline in the required business risk premium — then the firm's enterprise value and warranted stock price would rise to $895.90 and $43.29, respectively. This change in *wacc* translates into a 19% rise in the firm's enterprise value.

On the other hand, if the firm's cost of capital were to rise by 100 basis points — from 9% to 10% — then Exhibit 7 shows that the firm's enterprise value and warranted stock price would decline to $639.50 and $30.48, respectively. This in turn represents a 15% decline in the firm's warranted enterprise value. As with the present value impact of changes in a company's future growth opportunities, we see that enterprise value and warranted stock price are impacted in a meaningful and *non*-linear way by fluctuations in the firm's cost of capital.

Exhibit 7: Cost of Capital Effect

wacc %	Change in Basis Points	Enterprise Value	Warranted Stock Price
8	−100	895.90	43.29
9	0	751.64	36.08
10	100	639.50	30.48

[16] Moreover, we emphasize in Chapter 11 that if managers truly want to have a great company with a great stock, then they must reconcile differences between internal and market-implied expectations of economic profit growth.

Corporate Implications

The above illustrations on the economic profit importance of the competitive growth period and the cost of capital provides some basic pricing insight on managerial issues that are central to this book. First, it appears that uncertainty about the number of years that a firm can generate positive economic profit on new investments and/or uncertainty about the firm's true cost of capital can have a material impact on both its enterprise value and its stock price. Second, there are changes in both T and $wacc$ that can produce the same impact as with the $30 stock price obtained in our illustrations.

Hence, anything that corporate management can do to either increase the economic profit growth period and/or decrease the weighted average cost of capital will surprise investors positively and have a meaningful impact on enterprise value and stock price. By taking stock (pun intended) of how variations in T and $wacc$ can have a jointly positive influence on enterprise value and wealth creation, we believe that these are two of the critical economic profit factors.

A CLOSER LOOK AT GROWTH OPPORTUNITIES

In the economic profit model, the firm's enterprise value is defined as total invested capital *plus* aggregate net present value. With some simple re-arrangements to the model, we can take a closer look at that part of the firm's enterprise value that is attributed to economic profit generated by existing assets and the economic profit contribution due to future growth opportunities. Taken together, the two economic profit sources determine the firm's aggregate net present value.

In this context, the firm's enterprise value, V, can be split into two components: (1) the present value of the assumed NOPAT perpetuity generated by existing assets, NOPAT/$wacc$, and (2) the net present value of the firm's anticipated future growth opportunities, G_f.[17] That is,

$$V = \text{NOPAT}/wacc + G_f$$

The obvious question at this point is how to estimate the NPV contribution of the firm's anticipated growth opportunities, G_f.

In an attempt to answer this question, we'll look at two general approaches to modeling the firm's future growth opportunities. The two valuation approaches include the constant EP growth model — a variation on the traditional Gordon model — and the generalized T-period growth model described by Stewart.[18] Both of these EP growth models reinforce *and* expand upon our previous explanation of the economic profit approach to enterprise valuation.

---

[17] The growth model presented here is based on the "Investment Opportunities Approach to Valuation" described by Fama and Miller — see *The Theory of Finance*. For a discussion of the classic IOAV model in an economic profit context, see Grant, *Foundations of Economic Value Added*.

[18] For example, see Stewart, *The Quest for Value*.

First, the constant growth economic profit model. In this model, the firm's NPV of future growth opportunities is expressed as a function of the *one-period ahead* economic profit forecast and the firm's long-term capitalization rate. The "cap rate" is equal to the cost of capital *less* the long-term economic profit growth rate — of which these EP factors were shown before as, *wacc–g*. In formal terms, the present value of the firm's future growth opportunities is expressed as:

$$G_f = EP/(wacc - g)$$

In this growth expression, it is understood that (1) the one-step ahead economic profit forecast, EP, is positive because ROIC > *wacc* on future investment, and (2) the cost of capital exceeds the long-term EP growth rate (namely, *wacc* > *g*). Of course, when a company has multiple stages of economic profit growth — such as super growth followed by mature EP growth — the NPV expression for future investment opportunities, G_f, becomes more complex, but the present value principle remains intact.[19]

If we assume that the EP perpetuity of $94.27 from our previous application is growing at a long-term rate of, say, 3%, then the net present value at year 10 of the firm's opportunity to earn positive economic profit during the residual years is

$$G_f(10) = \$94.27/(0.09 - 0.03) = \$1,571.17$$

Discounting this figure back 10 years yields the NPV of the firm's economic profit opportunity from the residual years — that is, G_f equals $663.68. Based on this investment application, we see that the 3% EP growth assumption during the residual period has added $221.23 ($663.68 – $442.45) to the net present value of the firm's future growth opportunities.

Moreover, as we emphasize in Chapter 11, sizeable differences between the market implied EP growth rate and the actual internal growth in economic profit that a company can realistically achieve have both corporate and investment implications. Differences between market implied and internal (or warranted) EP growth rates can lead to trading opportunities for investors on the firm's incorrectly priced shares. From a corporate perspective, we'll see that managers to reconcile stock price with internal valuation of company shares must evaluate differences between market-implied and warranted EP growth projections.

Generalized T-Period Growth Model

One of the obvious limitations of the constant growth EP model is that it presumes that a firm can grow its economic profit forever. As we explained in our

---

[19] Multiple stage growth models are common in the finance and investment literature. A three-stage EP growth model might be characterized by super growth, transitional growth, and then mature growth. As we explain later though, competitive market inconsistencies arise when we speak of a company having the opportunity to forever growth its economic or abnormal profit.

simple application of the competitive fade concept, it is inconsistent with competitive goods and product markets for a company to have an unchecked opportunity to both earn and grow its economic profit forever. Such growth might make sense if we were talking about growing a revenue or cash flow stream at a constant rate, but here we are talking about permanently growing the firm's abnormal profit — indeed, a growing "profit" stream that forever widens the gap between a firm's after-tax operating profit, NOPAT, and the dollar cost of invested capital. All of this being said, such an approach can still be used effectively for benchmarking between firms so long as the calculations remain consistent. While one might disagree with the theory, capital markets may be biased towards the shorter horizon years and so a relative value using "apples-to-apples" comparisons can use a constant growth approach with success.

On the other hand, Bennett Stewart,[20] among others, recognizes a growth limitation and instead proposes an economic profit growth model that recognizes that a firm has a limited set of opportunities — or a limited number of time periods that we can represent by the familiar "T" notation — to generate a set of EP perpetuities on future investment opportunities.[21] In formal terms, the generalized T period approach to modeling the value of future growth opportunities can be expressed as:

$$G_f = (AEP \times T)/wacc(1 + wacc)$$

In this expression, AEP represents average economic profit (which of course must be positive) on future investments, T is the number of growth periods that the firm can generate EP perpetuities — each valued at $1/wacc$ — and $wacc$ is the familiar weighted average cost of capital. Based on the generalized T period model, we can show that the maximum present value of the residual period economic profit stream, at $442.45, from our simple competitive fade illustration is a special case (where $T = 1$) of the generalized T approach to modeling a company's future investment opportunities in the presence of competitive fade.[22]

Market Implied Growth Period

In practice, the generalized T-period growth model can be re-arranged to solve for the market-implied period of positive economic profit on future investment opportunities. The following inputs are required to solve for market implied T that is embedded in a firm's NPV and enterprise value:

---

[20] Stewart develops a T period economic profit growth model in the context of a firm's current operations and a "forward plan." See Stewart, *The Quest for Value.*

[21] In our simple application on competitive fade, we were speaking about the possibility that the period 11 economic profit, at $94.27, would last forever. In the generalized T period model, one speaks of multiple investment opportunities, each with the capacity to generate perpetuity of economic profit. In turn, the individual perpetuities are valued at $1/wacc$.

[22] With $T = 1$, we can show this equivalence by multiplying the numerator in the generalized T period growth model by $(1 + wacc)$.

• Enterprise value (outstanding debt plus equity values[23])
• NOPAT perpetuity (or annualized equivalent of periodic NOPAT on existing assets)
• Average economic profit on new investments (AEP)
• Cost of capital (*wacc*)

Upon solving for the number of periods, T, that the market expects a firm to earn positive economic profit perpetuity on new investments, we obtain:

$$T = \left[V - \frac{\text{NOPAT}}{wacc} \right] \times \frac{wacc(1 + wacc)}{\text{AEP}}$$

Also, upon calculating market implied T, managers and investors can then assess whether this figure is consistent with a company's internal or "warranted" number of periods of positive economic profit perpetuity on future investment opportunities. While the math is more complex here, the notion of comparing market implied and internal T values is consistent with our previous — and yet simplistic — discussion of the competition fade period.

Another Look at the Enterprise Value-to-Earnings Ratio

In Chapter 5, we introduced the enterprise value-to-earnings ratio in the context of popular value and growth styles of investing. Using economic profit concepts, we learned that managers and investors must exercise caution when evaluating companies that have unusually low or excessively high enterprise value-to-earnings ratios.

While some low price-to-earnings ratio stocks may be attractive buy opportunities, many such companies have low price-to-earnings (and low price-to-book value) ratios because of limited economic profit opportunities. Also, while high price-to-earnings ratio stocks can signal attractive future growth opportunities, managers and investors must be wary of the lack of economic profit sustainability and, consequently, pay too much for a company's future growth opportunities. As a notable case in point, high price-to-earnings ratio stocks can incur severe compression in their price-to-earnings ratio as witnessed in the technology sector during year 2000 when growth potential began to weaken.

We can gain some further insight on the enterprise value-to-earnings ratio by utilizing the T period valuation concepts presented above. Upon dividing the firm's enterprise value by the NOPAT stream generated by its existing assets, we (again[24]) obtain:

$$V/E = 1/wacc + G_f/\text{NOPAT}$$

---

[23] In practical application of enterprise valuation models, long-term debt is often measured at book value while equity capitalization — number of shares of stock outstanding *times* stock price — is used for the common stock.

[24] We provided a basic discussion — with real world application — of the enterprise value-to-earnings ratio in Chapter 5.

In this expression, $1/wacc$ is the enterprise value-to-earnings ratio for a company with no expected future growth opportunities, while G_f/NOPAT is the growth component of a firm's enterprise value-to-earnings ratio.

In turn, upon substituting the T-period growth function into the enterprise value-to-earnings ratio produces:

$$V/E = 1/wacc + G_f(\text{AEP}, T, wacc)/\text{NOPAT}$$

From this expression, we see that a company will have a price-to-earnings ratio that exceeds $1/wacc$ when it has the opportunity to invest in future assets having positive average economic profit. These future investment opportunities have positive NPV because the after-tax return on future invested capital exceeds the anticipated weighted average cost capital.

With the 9% cost of capital that we used before, and no opportunity to earn positive economic profit on future investments — that is, T equal zero — the firm's enterprise value would sell for a rather meager 11.11 times its un-levered operating (NOPAT) earnings. On the other hand, the T-period growth model reveals that with a period of positive economic profit on future investments (T greater than zero), the firm's price-to-earnings ratio will exceed the no-growth price relative of $1/wacc$. Of course the source of the firm's positive growth multiple, G_f/NOPAT, is due to its underlying ability to earn an after-tax return on future investments that exceeds the future $wacc$.

RECONCILIATION OF ECONOMIC PROFIT MODELS

While explaining the economic profit approach to enterprise valuation, we introduced two standard formulations for the firm's enterprise value. In this context, we said that the firm's enterprise value is equal to (1) total invested capital plus aggregate NPV and, equivalently, (2) the present value of the NOPAT perpetuity on exist assets plus the NPV of all future growth opportunities — as captured by G_f. We'll now reconcile these equivalent expressions for the firm's warranted enterprise value.

We begin by noting that NOPAT is equal to the capital charge earned on the firm's existing assets plus the economic profit earned on corporate assets already in place. From this, we can see that the firm's enterprise value is equal to invested capital, C, plus the NPV contribution of all future economic profit generated by both existing assets, $\text{EP}/wacc$, and expected future assets, G_f, according to:

$$
\begin{aligned}
V &= \text{NOPAT}/wacc + G_f \\
&= [wacc \times C + \text{EP}]/wacc + G_f \\
&= C + [\text{EP}/wacc + G_f] \\
&= C + \text{NPV}
\end{aligned}
$$

As before, the firm's enterprise value is in fact equal to its invested capital *plus* aggregate NPV. In turn, the firm's aggregate NPV is equal to the present value of all future economic profit.

Based on the preceding developments, we see that economic profit valuation has two primary sources: (1) the assessed value of economic profit generated by the firm's existing assets — represented by EP/*wacc*, and (2) the NPV contribution attributed to economic profit "improvement" from anticipated growth assets not currently in place — as captured by G_f in the enterprise valuation model. Moreover, economic profit — whether earned on existing or future assets — is positive if and only if the firm invests in real assets having an after-tax return on invested capital that on average exceeds the weighted average cost of capital.

SUMMARY

The economic profit approach to enterprise valuation has several attractive features and — like all DCF models — some limitations. On the positive side, the economic profit model provides a *direct* means by which corporate managers and investors can assess the NPV contribution from existing assets as well as future growth opportunities. In this context, the firm's total creation of wealth — as measured by its NPV — is equal to the present value of all future economic profit generated by existing assets and anticipated future assets (growth opportunities) not currently in place. With positive discounted economic profit a company is a wealth creator, while with negative discounted economic profit a company is — unfortunately — a wealth destroyer and, perhaps, should identify an alternative use for the assets as currently operated.

While economic profit valuation is intuitively appealing, managers and investors need to realize that the resulting estimates of enterprise value and warranted stock price are highly sensitive to the model inputs. A seemingly small change in the firm's anticipated future growth period (or growth rate) and/or its cost of capital can have a meaningful impact on the value of the firm and its outstanding shares. With uncertainty about true model inputs, corporate managers must do everything within their control to surprise investors *positively* about key economic profit parameters such as the future growth period and the cost of capital.

In this context, we learned that the firm can significantly increase its warranted value by increasing — relative to market implied economic profit parameters embedded in stock price — the number of positive economic profit periods on future investments, and/or by finding ways to decrease business risk and, consequently, the weighted average cost of capital. Indeed, we saw that a rise in "T" and a concomitant decline in the firm's *wacc* is a "win-win" combination for the firm's shareholders.

Chapter 7

Estimating the Return on Invested Capital

One of the more transparent factors that impact a company's economic profit is the return on invested capital (ROIC). Given the firm's existing assets, one can measure whether current economic profit from observable assets is either favorable or unfavorable. While simplifying perpetuity assumptions are often used to value the economic profit stream from a company's existing assets, it should be recognized that corporate managers can — and should — take decisive actions to improve the anticipated return on a firm's invested capital.

This ROIC emphasis should not be interpreted to mean that the return on existing capital is the most important economic profit factor in measuring a company's net creation of wealth. Indeed, the economic profit stream earned on future growth assets can (and most certainly does) make a sizable contribution to the firm's net present value (NPV). Moreover, some companies spend far too much time on their so-called downsizing, rightsizing, and restructuring efforts to improve currently visible economic profit from existing assets, while spending far too little time on corporate strategies that will enhance the firm's economic profit from future growth opportunities (namely, positive NPV investments). We cover the importance of strategic growth opportunities in Chapter 10.

Managerial steps to improve current economic profit include (1) engaging in a more aggressive marketing campaign to promote the firm's products and services, (2) making a candid assessment of the short and long-term impact of currently reducing the firm's operating expenses, and (3) finding profitable ways to use less capital rather than more.[1] Moreover, managers and investors must recognize that the return on a firm's existing capital stock (and future capital stock for that matter) is never really static because of competitive forces that operate within industries as well as economy-wide influences (interest rate and commodity price developments, for examples) that impact capital returns in a favorable or unfavorable way. In accordance, current economic profit trends can provide insight into future actions and wealth creation in industries with stable characteristics, such as food and retail. In more cyclical industries such as mining and capital goods, a multi-year historical trend analysis can highlight peaks and troughs in economic profit.

In this chapter we show how to measure the return on a company's existing capital. In simple terms, we see that ROIC is just the firm's net operating profit after

---

[1] Economic profit actions that management can take to improve a company's return on invested capital are also recognized in Shawn Tully, "The Real Key to Creating Wealth," *Fortune* (September 20, 1993).

tax (NOPAT) divided by its invested capital. Although simple in concept, there are many accounting adjustments that could be made when assessing the firm's cash-based operating profit and its book capital.[2] In the next section, we'll review some of the more important accounting adjustments that could impact a firm's NOPAT and its invested capital.[3] These NOPAT adjustments include implied interest expense on operating leases, increase (decrease) in LIFO reserve, increase in accumulated good-will amortization, increase in capitalized R&D, and the rise in cumulative special items (like restructuring charges) to the extent included in operating results.

We then provide a numerical illustration on how to estimate NOPAT, invested capital, and the after-tax return on invested capital. We also take a look at an ROIC decision-making tree in the context of a company's NOPAT margin and its net invested capital turnover ratio. Following that, we'll show how economic depreciation can be used to correct for bias in conventional ROIC estimates. We conclude with an explanation of how the concept of negative economic depreciation can be used to obtain improved estimates of invested capital returns in the case of corporate acquisitions.

In the next chapter, we tie these economic profit findings together with the firm's weighted average cost of capital (*wacc*) and the excess return on invested capital (or the "EVA spread").[4] Taken together, we'll see that ROIC and *wacc* — along with a realistic assessment of a company's economic profit growth rate (covered later) — are primary factors in the assessment of any company's ability to create shareholder value.

ACCOUNTING ADJUSTMENTS

Bennett Stewart provides an insightful guide to estimating a firm's net operating profit after tax and its invested capital.[5] In this context, he shows equivalent "bottom-up and top-down" approaches to estimating a company's net operating profit after taxes (NOPAT) along with equivalent "asset and financing" approaches to estimating book capital. Exhibit 1 shows some of the key accounting adjustments in the equivalent NOPAT approaches recommended by Stewart, while Exhibit 2 shows the companion accounting adjustments that must be made when estimating a company's invested capital in practice.

---

[2] We use the terms "invested capital" and "book capital" interchangeably in this chapter. Also, for a detailed treatment of the many accounting issues that arise when estimating NOPAT, invested capital, and economic profit in practice, see G. Bennett Stewart III, *The Quest for Value* (New York: Harper Collins, 1991).

[3] Ehrbar also emphasizes these economic profit accounting adjustments. See Al Ehrbar, *EVA: The Real Key to Creating Wealth* (New York: John Wiley and Sons, 1998).

[4] We feel that the cost of capital is such an important economic profit factor that it deserves a separate chapter in its own right. With knowledge of the return on invested capital and the cost of capital, we can then speak more clearly about the excess return on invested capital — namely, the "EVA spread" which equals ROIC less *wacc*.

[5] See Stewart, *The Quest for Value*.

Exhibit 1: Calculation of NOPAT from Financial Statement Data

A. Bottom-up approach
Begin:
    Operating profit after depreciation and amortization
Add:
    Implied interest expense on operating leases
    Increase in LIFO reserve
    Increase in accumulated goodwill amortization
    Increase in bad-debt reserve
    Increase in capitalized research and development
    *Increase in cumulative write-offs of special items**
Equals:
    Adjusted operating profit before taxes
Subtract:
    Cash operating taxes
Equals:
    NOPAT

B. Top-down approach
Begin:
    Sales
Subtract:
    Cost of goods sold
    Selling, general, and administrative expenses
    Depreciation
Add:
    Implied interest expense on operating leases
    Increase in equity reserve accounts (see above listing)
    Other operating income
Equals:
    Adjusted operating profit before taxes
Subtract:
    Cash operating taxes
Equals:
    NOPAT

* To the extent that write-offs are included in operating results rather than an extraordinary or unusual item.
Note: Exhibit based on information in G. Bennett Stewart III, *The Quest for Value* (New York: Harper Collins, 1991).

In the bottom-up approach to estimating NOPAT, the manager or investor begins with net operating profit before taxes. This is just the familiar earnings before interest and taxes (EBIT) figure on a company's income statement. To this amount, several value-based adjustments are made to move toward a closer approximation of the firm's pre-tax cash operating profit. For examples, the increase in the LIFO reserve account is added back to pre-tax operating profit to adjust for the overstatement of cost of goods sold — due to an overstatement of product costing — in a period of rising prices, while the net increase in research and development expenditure is added back to operating profit to recognize that R&D investment generates a *future* stream of benefits.[6]

Likewise, the change in accumulated goodwill amortization is added back to operating profit to reflect the fact that goodwill is a form of capital investment that needs to earn a cost of capital return just like expenditures on physical capital. In a value-based (economic profit) context, annual corporate restructuring write-offs get added back to operating profit since they are viewed as a form of restructuring "investment."

Exhibit 2: Calculation of Capital Using Accounting Financial Statements

A. *Asset approach*
Begin:
    Net (short term) operating assets
Add:
    Net plant and equipment
    Other assets
    LIFO reserve
    Accumulated goodwill amortization
    Bad-debt reserve
    Capitalized research and development
    Cumulative write-offs of special items
    Present value of operating leases
Equals:
    Capital

B. *Sources of financing approach*
Begin:
    Book value of common equity
Add equity equivalents:
    Preferred stock
    Minority interest
    Deferred income tax
    Equity reserve accounts (see above listing)
Add debt and debt equivalents:
    Interest-bearing short-term debt
    Long-term debt
    Present value of operating leases
Equals:
    Capital

Note: Exhibit based on information in G. Bennett Stewart III, *The Quest for Value* (New York: Harper Collins, 1991).

---

[6] In other words, R&D expenditures should be capitalized and amortized over a useful time period such as five years — rather than incorrectly expensed in the current year as if these expenditures have no future cash flow benefits.

Also, the implied interest expense on operating leases is added to operating profit to recognize that leasing is a form of debt financing such that the implied interest costs should be reflected in the firm's cost of debt financing — rather than showing up in its *un-levered* operating profit. However, in industries where operating leases are common and similar in financial magnitude, certain segments of retail, for example, analysts may use their judgement to determine whether the leasing adjustment will materially enhance the accuracy of the economic profit calculation used for peer benchmarking.

Moreover, from a tax perspective, the increase in deferred taxes should be subtracted from reported taxes to adjust for the overstatement of the firm's actual cash taxes, while tax subsidies from debt financings (including operating leases) should be added back to reported taxes to adjust for the understatement of *un-levered* cash taxes.

Invested Capital

A look at Exhibit 2 shows the companion accounting adjustments that must be made to arrive at invested capital. Based on the assets approach, we begin with net short term operating capital. This reflects moneys tied up in current asset accounts such as accounts receivables and inventories as well as a normal amount of cash needed for operations.[7] Current liabilities such as accounts payable, accrued expenses, and taxes payable are of course netted from the short term operating asset accounts. Notes payable are excluded because they represent a source of debt financing. Also, their interest cost is reflected in the calculation of a company's dollar cost of capital.

Net plant, property, and equipment is then added to capital along with other assets and several equity-based reserve accounts. Some analysts may choose to adjust property, plant, and equipment to a gross basis by adding back accumulated depreciation in an effort to eliminate differing depreciation policies and to approximate replacement cost. Obviously, the accumulated depreciation adjustment would be made in both asset and financing approaches to calculating capital along with an appropriate (annual) depreciation adjustment to NOPAT.

As shown in Exhibit 2, the adjustments to arrive at invested capital include the add back of LIFO reserve, accumulated goodwill amortization, bad debt reserve, capitalized research and development, and cumulative write-off of special items like restructuring and re-engineering costs. Unfortunately, some companies view a write-off of restructuring costs that result in a reduction of capital as an immediate boost to return on invested capital and then profess progress in operations. However, unless there is an outright asset disposal, with proceeds received in the sale or liquidation, then this latter adjustment is critical for objec-

---

[7] Research estimates on a normal range of cash required for operations vary by industry — such as 0.5% to 2% of net sales. Also, one can make a distinction between invested capital and operating capital. Operating capital is viewed as invested capital net of excess cash and marketable securities and goodwill accounts. We generally focus on invested capital in the economic profit illustrations that follow.

tive benchmarking and analysis. Additionally, the present value of operating leases, if any, would also be added to arrive at a company's invested capital.

In the sources of financing approach (see Exhibit 2), the analyst begins with the book value of common equity. To this, one adds several "equity equivalent" accounts including preferred stock, minority interest, deferred income tax reserve, and other equity reserve accounts that were listed in the assets approach to invested capital. Debt and debt equivalents are then added to arrive at a value-based figure for invested capital. These debt-related accounts include interest bearing short-term debt, long-term debt, and the present value of operating leases. Either way — the assets or financing approach — we arrive at adjusted book capital for use in calculation of a firm's economic profit.[8]

RETURN ON INVESTED CAPITAL

Having introduced the "conventional"[9] accounting adjustments to estimate NOPAT and invested capital, we'll now provide a numerical illustration to show how these adjustments get "rolled up" into the after-tax return on book capital (ROIC). Before getting immersed in the economic profit calculations, it is important to realize that (in this chapter) we are estimating the after-tax return on the firm's *existing* assets. Estimates of future capital returns — on both existing and future growth assets — will not only require similar value-based adjustments, but the forecasts themselves will also be sensitive to unforeseen industry and macro economic developments.

In other words, an undue focus on all the accounting adjustments that might be made when estimating existing asset returns may cause the manager or investor to miss key valuation and economic profit effects from future growth assets. Having said that, let's now look at how to estimate NOPAT, invested capital, and the ROIC for a home improvement supply company that we'll call "Do-It-Yourself Company."[10] In this illustration, we'll include several of the accounting adjustments that are listed in Exhibits 1 and 2. Also, we use the "bottom up" approach to estimating NOPAT and the "assets approach" to estimating invested capital.[11]

---

[8] Another refinement to adjusted book capital may be the subtraction of excess marketable securities or the value of equity held in strategic partners. This value should simply be kept separate and added back after the economic profit value determination to calculate business value.

[9] There are several economic profit refinements that can be made to standard accounting adjustments that we cite in the text. At a later point, we'll see how the concepts of positive *and* negative economic depreciation can be used to improve economic profit estimates — especially, as in the latter case, for strategic investments like corporate acquisitions and R&D investments.

[10] While "Do-It-Yourself Company" is fictional, it is based in part on the financial statements of one of the largest U.S. home supply companies.

[11] For further insight, see Stewart, *The Quest for Value.*

Exhibit 3: Do-it-Yourself Company Income Statement ($ millions)

Net Sales	$3,800
COGS	2,700
Gross Profit	$1,100
SG&A	750
Pre-Opening Expenses	50
Operating Profit	$300
Interest Expense	35
Non-Operating Expense	20
Pre-tax Profit	$245
Income Taxes	75
Net Income	$170
Shares Outstanding	*100*
Earnings per share	$1.70

NOPAT Estimation

Exhibit 3 shows a basic income statement for Do-It-Yourself Company. A quick perusal of the income statement shows familiar items like net sales, cost of goods sold (COGS), selling, general and administrative expenses (SG&A) and *unadjusted* operating profit before taxes (EBIT).[12] Some obvious income statement accounts that need to be adjusted for the NOPAT calculation include pre-opening expenses,[13] interest expense, and non-operating expenses for which the two latter items reflect tax issues.

It is imperative to assess the after-tax operating profit of Do-It-Yourself Company as an un-levered firm. In this context, the tax figure shown in the income statement is biased due to several value-based considerations. Specifically, the tax figure is biased upward due to a rise in deferred taxes,[14] while cash taxes actually paid by Do-It-Yourself Company as an un-levered firm are biased downward due to (1) the tax subsidies received on debt and debt equivalents (capital and operating leases) and (2) the tax benefit received on *non*-operating expenses.

Let's begin the conventional economic profit accounting adjustments with operating leases. Suppose that Do-It-Yourself Company's leasing footnote shows that a $4 million rental payment is due each year for the next five years along with an overall total leasing commitment (unadjusted for present value effects) of $40 million thereafter. Assuming that Do-It-Yourself Company's pre-tax yield on cor-

---

[12] Depreciation while not listed separately is assumed contained within SG&A — as are annual restructuring charges that we introduce shortly.

[13] We assume that pre-opening expenses generate a limited future benefit — namely, two years. Note that additional accounts — beyond the standard reserve accounts that we covered before — will arise in any real world attempt to estimate NOPAT and invested capital.

[14] In our illustration, we assume that deferred taxes went up over the year's course.

porate debt is 7%, we estimate that the discounted value of the 5-year rental commitment is $16.40 million. On that figure, the implied interest expense on the capitalized operating leases is $1.13 million. The present value of the operating lease commitments and the implied interest cost are calculated as follows:

Do-It-Yourself Company: Capitalization of Operating Leases

Leasing footnote: Operating leasing payment of $4 million for 5 years.
Leasing payments beyond year 5 total $40 million.

Capitalization of Operating Leases ($ millions):
   5-year operating lease payments = $4
   Payments beyond year 5 = $40

Present value of 5-year operating lease commitments:

Year relative	Lease payment	Present Value
1	$4	$3.74
2	4	3.49
3	4	3.27
4	4	3.05
5	4	2.85
Total		$16.40

Pre-tax debt yield = 7%
Implied interest on operating lease = $0.07 \times \$16.40 = \$1.13$

Note:
[Present value of operating lease payments (*Perpetuity assumption*):
   Operating lease payment × (1/pre-tax debt yield) = $4/0.07 = $57.14]

Before proceeding, it is interesting to note that if the $4 million rental payment were to last for an indefinite time period (that is, if the lease payments were perpetual), then the capitalized value of the operating rental commitments would be $57.14 million ($4 million/0.07). This figure is $40.74 million higher than the present value figure that results with a 5-year operating leasing horizon!

At $4 million (0.07 × $57.14), the implied interest charge on the leasing perpetuity is noticeably higher than the $1.13 million figure that we calculated with a 5-year rental commitment. Hence, managers and investors must be aware of economic profit differences arising from varying assumptions about the maturity of operating leases.[15] For convenience, we'll use the capitalized value of the 5-year operating rental commitments (at $16.40 million) and the associated implied interest charges (at $1.13 million) in the value-based treatment of operating leases for Do-It-Yourself Company.

---

[15] Pamela Peterson also emphasizes this point in an insightful economic profit illustration for McDonald's Corporation. See Pamela Peterson, "Value-Based Measures of Performance," Chapter 4 in Frank J. Fabozzi and James L. Grant (Eds.), *Value-Based Metrics: Foundations and Practice* (New Hope PA: Frank J. Fabozzi Associates, 2000).

Suppose upon further inspection of the footnotes to Do-It-Yourself Company's financial statements along with independent company research, we find:

Do-It-Yourself Company: Footnotes and company research

Pre-tax related items:	Source
Increase in Deferred Taxes: $5	Balance sheet
Accumulated LIFO reserve and change: 90 and –15	Footnotes
Accumulated Goodwill Amortization and change: 150 and 50	Footnotes
2-Year Amortization of Pre-Opening expenditures	Research
After-tax item and other information	Source
Cumulative Restructuring Charges and after-tax change: 150 and 10	Research
Operating cash requirement: 2% of net sales	Research

With this information, we can make several value-based accounting adjustments to the pre-tax operating profit of Do-It-Yourself Company. These NOPAT adjustments include: (1) the implied interest expense on operating leases (calculated before), (2) the decrease in LIFO reserve due presumably to falling material prices, (3) the increase in accumulated goodwill amortization, and (4) the increase in net pre-opening expenditures due to company research that indicates that opening expenditures benefit the current year and the next one. Upon making these conventional economic profit accounting adjustments, we see that Do-It-Yourself Company's adjusted pre-tax operating profit rises from $300 million to $361.13 million.

Do-It-Yourself Company: Operating Profit Adjustments: (Bottom-Up Approach)

Item:	Amount	Source/Calculation
Operating Profit (EBIT)	$300.00	Income statement
Add:		
Implied interest on operating leases	1.13	$0.07 \times \$16.40$
Increase (decrease) in LIFO reserve	(15.00)	LIFO reserve change
Increase in accumulated goodwill amortization	50.00	Change in accumulated goodwill
Increase in net pre-opening expenditures	$25.00	Capitalization of ½ of Pre-Opening Costs
Adjusted Operating Profit	$361.13	

The next item for NOPAT consideration is the cash taxes paid by Do-It-Yourself Company as an un-levered firm. As mentioned before, we must adjust Do-It-Yourself Company's reported income taxes downward to account for the year-over-year increase in deferred income taxes. Also, if Do-It-Yourself Company were in fact an un-levered company, it would not receive the tax subsidy on the company's debt, nor would it receive the implied tax subsidy on the interest expense on operating leases.

Thus, we add back the debt-induced tax benefits to Do-It-Yourself Company's reported income tax. Also, we add back the tax benefit that Do-It-Yourself Company received on non-operating expenses shown in the income statement — since we are looking for a reliable operating profit figure for Do-It-Yourself Company as an *on-going* concern. Therefore, the adjusted cash operating taxes of Do-It-Yourself Company (before other after-tax items) were $89.65.

Do-It-Yourself Company: Adjusted Operating Taxes:

Reported Income Taxes	$75.00	Income statement
Subtract:		
Increase in deferred taxes	5.00	Balance sheet
Add:		
Tax subsidy from interest expense	12.25	$0.35 \times \$35.00$
Tax subsidy from implied interest	0.40	$0.35 \times \$1.13$
Tax benefit from non-operating expense	7.00	$0.35 \times \$20.00$
Cash Operating Taxes	$89.65	

Based on these findings, we see that Do-It-Yourself Company's after-tax operating profit (before any other after tax items) is $271.48. This figure results from subtracting the cash operating taxes, at $89.65, from the adjusted operating profit, at $361.13, that we estimated before. At $281.48, we now arrive at the firm's net operating profit after taxes (NOPAT) by adding back the after tax change in cumulative restructuring charges discovered from company research.

Do-It-Yourself Company: Net Operating Profit After Taxes (NOPAT)

After-tax Operating profit (*before* after-tax items)	$271.48	
Add:		
Restructuring charges (included in SG&A, net of tax)	$10.00	Research
NOPAT	$281.48	

Estimation of Invested Capital

One of the key benefits of economic profit measurement is that it links the income statement with the balance sheet. In a value-based context, we must not only look at how top line revenue leads to bottom line profit (NOPAT in our case), but we must also assess the firm's profitability relative to capital employed in the business. Also, we must recognize that for every income statement adjustment that we made for Do-It-Yourself Company there are capital-based balance sheet consequences. Exhibit 4 presents a standard balance sheet for Do-It-Yourself Company.

While the balance sheet is helpful in our goal of measuring Do-It-Yourself Company's operating capital — as it includes short-term operating asset and liabilities along with net property, plant, and equipment and recorded intangibles — it does not reflect all the required capital adjustments that go along with the income statement adjustments that we made before. Specifically, Do-It-Yourself Company's balance sheet does not reflect the invested capital effects arising from "off balance sheet" items — like LIFO reserve, accumulated goodwill amortization, present value of operating leases, and the build up of cumulative restructuring charges (arising from the assumed inclusion of *annual* restructuring expenditures in Selling, General, and Administration account on the income statement).

Exhibit 4: Do-it-Yourself Company Balance Sheet ($ millions)

Cash	$75
Accounts Receivable	105
Inventory	500
Other Current Assets	10
Total Current Assets	$690
Plant, Property and Equipment	$950
Accumulated Depreciation	(80)
Net Plant, Property and Equipment	$870
Intangible Assets	$40
Total Assets	$1,600
Accounts Payable	$200
Accrued Liabilities	120
Taxes Payable	20
Notes Payable	15
Total Current Liabilities	$355
Long-Term Debt	$530
Deferred Taxes	90
Paid-in-Capital	$225
Other	(25)
Retained Earnings	425
Stockholders' Equity	$625
Total Liabilities and Stockholders Equity	$1,600

In light of these economic profit omissions, we recast Do-It-Yourself Company's balance sheet to more closely approximate the firm's invested capital.[16]

Do-It-Yourself Company: Calculation of Invested Capital (Assets approach)

Net short-term operating assets	$350.00	Current assets less *non*-debt current liabilities
Add:		
Net Plant, Property and Equipment	$870.00	
Intangible Assets	$40.00	
Accumulated LIFO Reserve	$90.00	
Accumulated Goodwill Amortization	150.00	
Capitalized Pre-Opening Expenditures	$25.00	
Cumulative Restructuring Charges	$150.00	
Present value of operating leases	$16.40	
Invested (Book) Capital	$1691.40	

From this vantage point, we see that Do-It-Yourself Company's invested capital is $1691.40. This consists of the reported balance sheet items — including net short-term operating assets (current assets less *non*-interest bearing current

---

[16] As mentioned before, we use the "assets approach" to estimating invested capital in our illustrations.

liabilities) plus net plant, property, and equipment[17] and recorded intangibles — and the conventional "off balance sheet" capital adjustments — such as LIFO reserve, accumulated goodwill amortization, present value of operating leases and the like. At \$431.40 million, the above mentioned accounting adjustments make up 26% of Do-It-Yourself Company's book capital. This illustration suggests that the value-based accounting adjustments were worth the effort.[18]

ROIC DECOMPOSITION

We can now estimate the return on invested capital for Do-It-Yourself Company by combining its NOPAT and invested capital. In this context, we see that the home supply company's after-tax return on capital is 16.6%:

$$ROIC = NOPAT/Invested\ capital$$
$$= \$281.48/\$1691.40 = 0.166$$

While Do-It-Yourself Company's return on invested capital looks attractive, we would of course look at how this ratio and its components (NOPAT margin, net capital turnover) have changed over time and how its after-tax capital return compares with competitors within the home improvement industry. At any given point in time, we can also see how other economic profit-based company ratios contribute to the overall return on invested capital.

Exhibit 5 shows a decomposition of Do-It-Yourself Company's invested capital return in the context of its NOPAT margin — measured by the ratio of NOPAT to net sales — times the invested capital turnover ratio — measured by net sales over net invested capital. While this ROIC breakdown might look similar to a more traditional breakdown of return on assets and return on equity (ROE), managers and investors should be aware that economic profit-based ROIC is a noticeable improvement over traditional profit ratio measures since (1) ROE (like return on assets) does not account for the value-based accounting adjustments that we made and (2) ROE is distorted by debt-related financing decisions.[19]

---

[17] As noted previously, some analysts may choose to add-back accumulated depreciation or make other adjustments to estimate replacement value or original cost for plant, property, and equipment.

[18] Also, managers and investors might prefer to make a finer distinction between invested capital and operating capital. In general, operating capital excludes excess cash and marketable securities, other investments, and goodwill-related accounts. In our illustration, Do-It-Yourself Company's cash account is just 2% of net sales so we need only adjust book capital for the intangibles (presumed goodwill) and the accumulated goodwill amortization (contained in a footnote to financial statements). Therefore, Do-It-Yourself Company's invested capital is \$1691.40 while its operating capital is \$1501.40.

[19] According to the traditional Dupont formula, ROE can be calculated by multiplying return on assets — or net profit margin times asset turnover ratio — by the equity multiplier — or assets over equity. In this context, ROIC looks similar to ROA. However, in addition to the omitted economic profit accounting adjustments, the equity multiplier is a reflection of corporate leverage — since this ratio can be expressed as $1/(1 - DR)$, where DR is the total debt to assets ratio.

Exhibit 5: Do-It-Yourself Company: ROIC Decomposition

ROIC% = NOPAT/Capital = \$281.48/\$1691.40 = 0.166 × 100 = 16.6%

NOPAT Margin = NOPAT/Net sales = \$281.48/\$3800.00 = 0.074 × 100 = 7.4%

Capital turnover ratio = Net sales/Capital = \$3800.00/1691.40 = 2.25

ROIC% = NOPAT margin% × Capital turnover ratio = 7.4% × 2.25 = 16.6%

At 16.6%, we see that Do-It-Yourself Company's ROIC can be split up into a NOPAT margin, at 7.4%, times the net invested capital turnover ratio of 2.25. Other things the same, it should be clear that anything that management can do to increase the NOPAT margin — for example, cost savings on a given amount of revenue — and the capital turnover ratio — via improved capital efficiencies resulting from a lower net working capital to sales ratio and/or a lower plant, property, and equipment to sales ratio — will result in improved returns on invested capital.[20] These presumed *permanent* improvements should impact economic profit and stock price in a favorable way.

Real World Application

Jason Wolin and Steven Klopukh provide an interesting breakdown of return on invested capital for the Dayton Hudson Corporation.[21] Their insightful economic profit application is shown in Exhibit 6. Here, we see a cross-sectional comparison of the NOPAT margin and net invested capital turnover ratios for Dayton Hudson and its competitors — Costco, K-Mart, and Wal-Mart (shown as "Comps") — as well as a time-wise comparison of Dayton's 1-year invested capital return versus a 3-year average. Exhibit 6 also shows how income statement and balance sheet margins — such as gross profit margin and the net working capital margin (net working capital/sales) can be "rolled up" into a NOPAT margin and net invested capital turnover ratio.

From Exhibit 6, we note that Dayton Hudson's return on invested capital is noticeably higher than that of its close competitors. This upscale retailer has attractive capital returns because its NOPAT margin bests that of competitor

---

[20] Since the net invested capital turnover ratio is net sales over net invested capital, we can express this ratio as the *inverse* of the sum of (1) net working capital to sales ratio, (2) plant, property, and equipment to sales ratio, and (3) other assets to sales ratio. Looking at ROIC this way suggests that economic profit proponents are concerned with both top line revenue generation and bottom line economic profit (measured net of a firm's overall cost of capital).

[21] Jason Wolin and Steven Klopukh provide an insightful analysis of Dayton Hudson Corporation in an economic profit context. See Jason L. Wolin and Steven Klopukh, "Integrating EVA® into the Portfolio Management Process," Chapter 6 in *Value-Based Metrics: Foundations and Practice*.

firms. However, it seems that Dayton Hudson could generate even higher after-tax returns on invested capital if it could increase the invested capital turnover ratio. This in turn would require a capital-based examination of the firm's inventory policies and the economic profit consequences of the retailer's strategy of trying to best competitors by spending more money on new stores.[22]

Exhibit 6: Financial Decision Tree: ROIC Decomposition for Dayton Hudson Corp

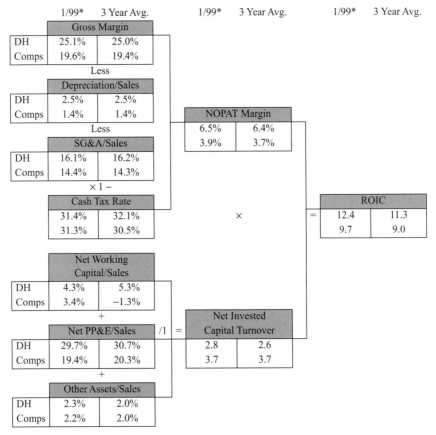

	1/99*	3 Year Avg.		1/99*	3 Year Avg.		1/99*	3 Year Avg.
Gross Margin								
DH	25.1%	25.0%						
Comps	19.6%	19.4%						
Less								
Depreciation/Sales								
DH	2.5%	2.5%		**NOPAT Margin**				
Comps	1.4%	1.4%		6.5%	6.4%			
Less				3.9%	3.7%			
SG&A/Sales								
DH	16.1%	16.2%						
Comps	14.4%	14.3%						
× 1 −								
Cash Tax Rate						**ROIC**		
31.4%	32.1%		×		=	12.4	11.3
31.3%	30.5%					9.7	9.0
Net Working Capital/Sales								
DH	4.3%	5.3%						
Comps	3.4%	−1.3%						
+								
Net PP&E/Sales		/1 =	**Net Invested Capital Turnover**					
DH	29.7%	30.7%		2.8	2.6			
Comps	19.4%	20.3%		3.7	3.7			
+								
Other Assets/Sales								
DH	2.3%	2.0%						
Comps	2.2%	2.0%						

* 12 months ended; Comps = Costco, K-Mart, and Wal-Mart
Source: Adapted from Exhibit 17 in Jason L. Wolin and Steven Klopukh, "Integrating EVA® into the Portfolio Management Process," in Frank J. Fabozzi and James L. Grant (eds.), *Value-Based Metrics: Foundations and Practice*, p.152.

[22] Dayton Hudson's operations are actually split between its Target division and department stores. Analysts and the Company have pointed to the higher capital turnover in the Target division being somewhat diluted by the lesser performing department stores. Several steps have been taken in an effort to improve this segment of the Company.

ROLE OF ECONOMIC DEPRECIATION

There are several other refinements that a manager or investor could make to arrive at a company's cash operating profit and invested capital. As touched on by the authors and others, these economic profit adjustments include a more advanced treatment of depreciation, acquisition goodwill, strategic investments, short-term operating assets, and environmental liabilities.[23] To expand on this, we'll show how the concept of economic depreciation — both positive *and* negative — can sharpen analyst estimates of NOPAT, invested capital, and the overall return on invested capital.

We'll first look at the inconsistency of using GAAP pronounced straight-line depreciation in the assessment of economic profit. We'll then show how positive economic depreciation resolves the straight-line depreciation bias in the return on invested capital. Following that, we'll discuss the role of negative economic depreciation (resulting from assets with appreciating cash flows) in providing improved capital return estimates for companies that purse growth opportunities via internal R&D investments and/or external corporate acquisitions.

ROIC Bias using Straight-Line Depreciation

For convenience, let's return to Do-It-Yourself Company. Suppose the popular home supply company has the opportunity to invest in a fleet of elevator lifting machines that will improve in-store distribution of products and save on labor costs. Further suppose that each machine costs $32,000 and generates a pretax (dollar) operating margin — or earnings before interest, taxes and depreciation (EBITD) — of $15,000 for four years. Exhibit 7 shows a yearly breakdown of Do-It-Yourself Company's unadjusted NOPAT and invested capital on a per machine basis.

With straight-line depreciation, the annual capital recovery is $8,000 per lifting machine. Also, with EBITD of $15,000 each year, we see that Do-It-Yourself Company's NOPAT — assuming a 35% tax rate — is constant at $4,550 per year. Likewise, the firm's yearly free cash flow estimates — NOPAT *less* net annual investment — are also constant at $12,550. As presented in Exhibit 7, these cash flow estimates do not give a manager or investor any reason to believe that the returns per lifting machine are improving or deteriorating with the passage of time.

Yet, Exhibit 7 shows that the after-tax return on invested capital figures are rising quite dramatically over time. At 56.88% for year 4, the return on invested capital (ROIC) is noticeably higher than the post-tax capital return of 14.22% for year 1 (we use beginning of year capital in these calculations). The

---

[23] Stephen O'Byrne provides a detailed numerical examination of several value-based accounting refinements including economic depreciation, acquisition goodwill, short-term operating assets, and environmental liabilities. See Stephen F. O'Byrne, "Does Value-Based Management Discourage Investment in Intangibles?" Chapter 5 in *Value-Based Metrics: Foundations and Practice*. Also, Al Ehrbar's insightful discussion of economic profit accounting issues can be found in his 1998 book. See Al Ehrbar, *EVA: The Real Key to Creating Wealth* (New York: John Wiley and Sons, 1998).

obvious culprit in the matter is the constant decline in invested capital caused by straight-line depreciation of $8,000 per year. That is, while NOPAT — as well as free cash flow estimates — for the lifting machine is constant each year, the denominator of the return on capital ratio continues to fall.

As we noted before with restructuring charges and write-offs of capital, managers and investors must be wary of projects that give the "illusion" of dramatically improving capital returns. That is not to say that capital budgeting opportunities cannot give great returns. However, in the case at hand, we'll see that the after-tax capital returns on the proposed lifting machines are not only constant each year but they are also equal to the (adjusted) after-tax internal rate of return of 20.10%. There are two key steps to show these financial results: (1) calculate the economic depreciation on the proposed capital investment, and (2) rework the NOPAT and invested capital figures to arrive at the correct after-tax return on invested capital.[24]

Estimation and Benefit of Economic Depreciation

Exhibit 8 shows how to estimate economic depreciation on Do-It-Yourself Company's proposed lifting machines. In a nutshell, economic depreciation is treated as the return of principal (or capital recovery) on an amortized loan such as a mortgage or automobile loan. With knowledge of the investment cost (present value at $32,000), the pre-tax operating margin (EBITD, at $15,000 for four years), we can calculate the pre-tax internal rate of return (IRR) on the lifting machine, at 30.92%. We can represent this present value relationship as:

$$\$32,000 = \$15,000 \times \text{Annuity factor (IRR,4 years)}$$
$$= \$15,000 \times [1/\text{IRR} \times (1 - 1/(1 + \text{IRR})^4)]$$

Exhibit 7: ROIC Bias Using Straight Line Depreciation

Year	0	1	2	3	4
EBITD		15000	15000	15000	15000
Depr.		8000	8000	8000	8000
EBIT		7000	7000	7000	7000
Taxes		2450	2450	2450	2450
NOPAT		4550	4550	4550	4550
Net Invest	32000	−8000	−8000	−8000	−8000
FCF*		12550	12550	12550	12550
IRR%	20.80%				
Capital	32000	24000	16000	8000	0
ROIC%**		14.22	18.96	28.44	56.88

* FCF = NOPAT − Net Investment
** ROIC = NOPAT/BOY Capital

[24] See Stephen F. O'Byrne, "Does Value-Based Management Discourage Investment in Intangibles?" Chapter 5 in *Value-Based Metrics: Foundations and Practice.*

Exhibit 8: Economic Depreciation on New Project

Year	0	1	2	3	4
Capital*	32000	26894	20210	11459	2
Level payment (project EBITD)		15000	15000	15000	15000
Pre-tax IRR%	30.92				
$ Interest return** (project EBIT)		9894	8316	6249	3543
Capital recovery (project depreciation)		5106	6684	8751	11457

* Year 4 capital difference from zero due to rounding
** $ Interest return = Pre-tax IRR × BOY Capital

Exhibit 9: Correction of ROIC Bias using Economic Depreciation

Year	0	1	2	3	4
EBITD		15000	15000	15000	15000
Depr.		5106	6684	8751	11457
EBIT		9894	8316	6249	3543
Taxes		3463	2911	2187	1240
NOPAT		6431	5405	4062	2303
Net Invest	32000	−5106	−6684	−8751	−11457
FCF		11537	12089	12813	13760
IRR%	20.10				
Capital*	32000	26894	20210	11459	2
ROIC%		20.10	20.10	20.10	20.10

*Year 4 capital difference from zero due to rounding
Note: After-tax IRR of 20.10% is also equal to (1-t)Pre-tax IRR:
(1 - 0.35) * 30.92% = 20.10%

In this expression, IRR is the pre-tax internal rate of return on one of Do-It-Yourself Company's proposed lifting machines. As noted before, each machine costs $32,000 and has an estimated 4-year pre-tax operating margin of $15,000. Also, with knowledge of the pre-tax IRR, at 30.92%, we can now calculate the yearly "interest" return and capital recovery (economic depreciation) on the proposed lifting machine. Exhibit 8 shows the yearly breakdown of "interest" and return of "principal," as well as the invested capital balance at the end of each year. In effect, we are merely splitting up the annual project EBITD of $15,000 into economic depreciation (capital recovery) and EBIT components.

We are now ready to calculate the revised NOPAT, invested capital, and after-tax return on capital figures for Do-It-Yourself Company's proposed lifting machine. With economic depreciation, we see in Exhibit 9 that the project NOPAT estimates are declining each year in the presence of companion declines in the amount of invested capital. Interesting enough though, the yearly decline in NOPAT and invested capital is such that the after-tax capital return is constant at

20.10%. Moreover, at this rate, the post-tax return on invested capital (ROIC) is now equal to the after-tax internal rate of return.

The importance of this illustration for managers and investors should be crystal clear. First, managers and investors should take a good look at invested capital returns to see if they are in fact increasing or decreasing. Incorrect capital budgeting decisions by managers and stock selection decisions by investors can result without a proper assessment of invested capital returns. Second, we know that investment opportunities should be evaluated in the context of an internal rate of return (after-tax return on invested capital using economic depreciation) measured relative to the cost of invested capital.

Viewed in terms of Do-It-Yourself Company's investment opportunity, the lifting machine is acceptable as long as the weighted average cost of capital is less than the firm's capital return (IRR) of 20.10%. While it is likely that the home supply company's after-tax "hurdle rate" is less than the IRR, we emphasize that if straight-line depreciation were used in economic profit assessment, the project would be rejected if the cost of capital were above 14.22% (ROIC for year 1 in Exhibit 7). In effect, the proposed lifting machines will create value for Do-It-Yourself Company's shareholders as long as the after-tax cost of capital is less than 20.10%. Otherwise, shareholder value will be destroyed at this company — or any real world company in like position — as manifest in a declining stock price.

Negative Depreciation (Acquisitions and R&D Investments)

While the concept of positive economic depreciation can be used to address an "old assets versus new assets problem,"[25] the concept of negative economic depreciation — appreciating cash flows and asset values — can be used to improve capital return and economic profit estimates for acquisitions and R&D investments. These strategic investments generally have sizable "back loaded" cash flows. To illustrate this economic profit refinement, we'll assume that Do-It-Yourself Company is contemplating the purchase of an internet-based ordering and supply company called "Why Wait Supply Company." For convenience, we'll use the free cash flow and enterprise valuation results from Chapter 6 in explaining the benefits of using negative economic depreciation over the "conventional" economic profit approach.[26]

---

[25] We explained how positive economic depreciation eliminates bias in invested capital returns that results from straight-line depreciation. However, it should be evident that if a manager or investor were looking at a rising stream of returns on existing assets, he/she might be misled into thinking that the "old assets" were quite attractive with little need for replacement. This faulty economic profit thinking could severely limit the firm's future growth opportunities.

[26] The major economic profit players have provided tremendous insight on the many accounting adjustments that can impact NOPAT and invested capital. Their (now) conventional economic profit adjustments include the treatment of LIFO reserves, goodwill, R&D, operating leases, deferred taxes and the like.

However, some of the economic profit players appear to have missed the measurement benefit of using negative economic depreciation over GAAP-pronounced straight-line depreciation — perhaps, because of the complexities that go with economic depreciation estimation.

Exhibit 10: Acquisition Forecast
(Portion of 10-Year Forecast)

Period	0	1	2	3	4	5
NOPAT		16.25	20.31	25.39	31.74	39.67
Operating Capital	90	96.25	104.06	113.83	126.04	141.3
Return on Operating Capital %		18.06	21.10	24.40	27.88	31.47
Acquisition Capital *	751.61	757.86	765.67	775.44	787.65	802.91
Return on Acquisition Capital %		2.16	2.68	3.32	4.09	5.04
Cost of Capital % **		9	9	9	9	9
Capital Charge		67.64	68.21	68.91	69.79	70.89
Acquisition EP (unadjusted)		−51.39	−47.90	−43.52	−38.05	−31.22

*Acquisition Capital = Operating Capital plus the amount paid in excess of the value of operating capital (goodwill or acquisition premium)
** Cost of capital assumption = 9% (applied to BOY Capital)

Exhibit 10 shows the first 5 (out of 10) years of capital return estimates for Why Wait Supply Company. In this exhibit, we see two measures of invested capital return: (1) the forecasted return on existing operating capital — namely, the ROIC's for Why Wait Supply Company in its status quo position — and (2) the conventional economic profit return on acquisition capital if Do-It-Yourself Company were to acquire the internet supply company. The favorable return estimates on operating capital are obtained by dividing the firm's NOPAT by the amount of operating capital. In sharp contrast, the meager return on acquisition capital figures shown in Exhibit 10 are based on the assumption that Do-It-Yourself Company acquires the internet ordering and supply company for its assessed discounted cash flow (DCF) value of $751.61 (recall Chapter 6).[27]

However, if Do-It-Yourself Company pays the present value of the 10 years of free cash flow estimates (shown in Chapter 6) for Why Wait Supply Company, then the proposed acquisition will neither create value nor destroy any value for its shareholders. In this context, the home improvement company's shareholders would be no better or no worse off if the acquisition capital were returned and placed in a similar risk (a similar beta) portfolio opportunity earning 9% per annum.[28] Equivalently, if Do-It-Yourself Company pays the DCF value of $751.61, then the net present value of the proposed acquisition must be zero. Moreover, from an economic profit perspective, the adjusted economic profit earned *each* year must also be zero since the adjusted return on acquisition capital will equal the cost of capital.

Another look at Exhibit 10 reveals the nature of the economic profit measurement problem at hand. Notice that the conventional economic profit acquisi-

---

[27] With a DCF value of $751.61 and existing capital of $90, it is interesting to note that acquisition goodwill makes up 88% of the assumed acquisition price. At that price, the bidding firm (Do-It-Yourself Company) is paying 46 times first year's NOPAT of $16.25. This is typical of an acquisition where the target firm (Why Wait Supply Company) derives most of its enterprise value from "back loaded" cash flows.

[28] Recall that we assumed a cost of capital of 9% in the calculation of enterprise value shown in Chapter 6.

tion returns are substantially less than the (assumed) cost of capital of 9%. Also, we see the logical inconsistency of simply measuring NOPAT over unadjusted acquisition capital. The economic profit on an otherwise zero net present value opportunity is negative in each and every year. The negative economic profit in the conventional economic profit approach to measuring acquisition capital is incorrect because there is no adjustment to NOPAT and invested capital for the appreciation in enterprise value due to a rising series of "back loaded" cash flows. This is a common occurrence for capital investments like corporate acquisitions and especially R&D investments. These strategic investments have low free cash flow and (NOPAT) earnings yield (if any) in the early years followed by substantial operating profits and invested capital returns thereafter.

Exhibit 11 shows how to adjust NOPAT and invested capital to obtain the correct cost of capital return on acquisition capital. Without getting into all the economic profit details here,[29] the *negative* economic depreciation each year — resulting from the yearly appreciation in enterprise value net of capital investments — gets added back to the DCF acquisition price of $751.61 that we calculated before. In turn, the net appreciation in enterprise value each year — negative economic depreciation net of annual capital investment — is then added back to NOPAT.

Exhibit 11: Acquisition EP using Economic Depreciation (Portion of 10-Year Forecast)

Period	0	1	2	3	4	5
Free Cash Flow		10	12.50	15.63	19.53	24.41
Less:						
Return on Enterprise Value		67.64	72.83	78.26	83.90	89.69
Equal:						
Decline in Enterprise Value		−57.64	−60.33	−62.63	−64.37	−65.28
Plus:						
Investment		6.25	7.81	9.77	12.21	15.26
Equal:						
Economic Depreciation		−51.39	−52.52	−52.86	−52.16	−50.02
Adjusted NOPAT		67.64	72.83	78.25	83.90	89.69
Adjusted Capital	751.61	809.25	869.59	932.22	996.59	1061.87
Adjusted ROIC %		9	9	9	9	9
Cost of Capital *		9	9	9	9	9
Adjusted Capital						
Charge		67.64	72.83	78.26	83.90	89.69
Adjusted Economic Profit **		0.00	0.00	−0.01	0.00	0.00

* Cost of capital assumption = 9% (applied to BOY Capital)
** Difference from zero due to rounding

[29] For further insight on the economic profit consequences of negative economic depreciation, see Stephen F. O'Byrne, "Does Value-Based Management Discourage Investment in Intangibles?" We discuss cost of capital estimation in Chapter 8.

For example, consider the NOPAT and acquisition capital adjustments for year 1. At –$57.64, the negative decline in enterprise value — or appreciation in enterprise value from year 0 to 1 — can be expressed in one of two ways: (1) the change in present value of free cash flow estimates (provided in Chapter 6) that occurs over years 0 and 1, or (2) the dollar-based cash yield for year 1 — free cash flow estimate of $10.00 for year 1 — *less* the total dollar return earned on enterprise value (at $67.64, which equals 9% of the acquisition purchase price of $751.61).

The decline in enterprise value can be expressed this way because the total dollar return is equal to the dollar-based free cash flow yield plus the overall change in market value — whereby positive economic depreciation represents a decline in enterprise value and negative economic depreciation represents an appreciation in enterprise value. Moreover, upon adding the new investment of $6.25 (at year 1) to the overall decline in enterprise value of $57.64, we obtain the correct economic depreciation figure for the acquisition.

As revealed in Exhibit 11, the negative economic depreciation for year 1 is –$51.39. Upon adding (the negative of) this figure to the unadjusted NOPAT of $16.25, we obtain the adjusted after tax operating profit of $67.64. Also, upon calculating the year 1 capital charge of $67.64 (9% of the acquisition purchase price of $751.61), we have the year 1 NOPAT and invested capital figures that provide a zero economic profit (NOPAT less capital charge) on the acquisition candidate. Repeating this rather complex — yet informative — procedure produces the desired economic profit results.

Our illustration of the concept of negative economic depreciation for strategic investments like acquisitions and R&D investments yields the following economic profit results: (1) adjusted NOPAT is equal to the yearly capital charge, (2) adjusted return on acquisition capital equals the cost of capital, and (3) the forecasted economic profit — adjusted NOPAT less adjusted capital charge — is equal to zero in every year. These cash flow and enterprise valuation findings are consistent with a value-neutral — or zero NPV — acquisition where a bidding firm pays the *full* DCF value of the forecasted free cash flow (and economic profit) on the target firm.

SUMMARY

There are many economic profit accounting adjustments that a manager or investor could make to measure a firm's return on invested capital. Indeed, some of the major economic profit players — including Goldman Sachs U.S. Research on the sell-side and consultants Stern Stewart & Co. — have observed some 160 accounting adjustments that can impact NOPAT and invested capital. In practice, however, most economic profit advocates — including ourselves as buy-side practitioners at Global Asset Management — seek to limit the number of accounting adjustments to a few of the more significant ones.

Some of the more important NOPAT adjustments that managers and investors should consider include: (1) increase in net capitalized research and development, (2) change in cumulative write-offs of special items such as restructuring expenses, (3) change in goodwill amortization, (4) change in LIFO reserve, and (5) implied interest expense on operating leases.

When making these NOPAT-related adjustments, we noted that cash operating taxes should be increased by the interest tax subsidies received on debt and implied corporate debt (operating leases), while cash operating taxes should be decreased (increased) by the rise (decline) in deferred tax liabilities from one year to the next. Also, cash operating taxes should be increased by the tax benefit received on non-recurring operating expenses and decreased by any taxes paid on non-recurring operating income. Of course, any value-based adjustments to NOPAT have invested capital consequences. Specifically, adjustments for operating leases, accumulated restructuring charges and capital write-offs, are some of the key capital adjustments that should be made. In addition, less widely practiced adjustments to approximate original cost or replacement value for plant and equipment as well as capitalized research and development can be used to enhance the accuracy of economic profit analysis.

We noted that there are even refinements that a manager or investor can make to the conventional approach to estimating return on invested capital. We illustrated the concept of positive economic depreciation to show how to adjust for the inherent bias in invested capital returns that result when using straight-line depreciation in the conventional economic profit approach. We noted that economic depreciation results in invested capital returns that are consistent with the internal rate of return on a company's capital investments. This is a desirable property of invested capital returns from a capital budgeting perspective.

We ended the chapter with a look at how negative economic depreciation can provide corporate managers and investors with accurate capital return estimates on strategic investments such as mergers and acquisitions and R&D investments. Whether or not managers or investors take the time to make such value-based refinements depends on a cost-benefit analysis. At the very least, managers and investors must be aware of the fact that even after making several conventional economic profit accounting adjustments to NOPAT and invested capital that bias may still be present in invested capital returns. Faulty investment decisions can result from such omissions.

As we move forward, it is important to keep a focus on the "big picture" aspect of economic profit measurement. Despite the complexities that are involved when estimating a company's economic profit in practice — dollar return on invested capital less dollar cost of capital — we are making a conscious effort to measure corporate financial success in a way that is directly linked to wealth creation. In addition to the numerous value-based problems that are associated with traditional accounting profit measures — such as "bottom line" net income and return on equity — accounting profit does not provide investors with a profit measure that "accounts" for the required return (debt *and* equity capital combined) on invested capital.

Even if accounting numbers could be used to correctly assess a firm's NOPAT and invested capital, the resulting dollar or percentage measures of "profit" would still omit the cost of capital driver — a key economic profit factor that we turn to in the next chapter. With a plethora of shareholder value limitations, accounting profit *per se* cannot measure a company's true economic profit or its fundamental ability to create wealth.

Managers and investors must realize that it is important to make the value-based accounting adjustments that we speak of in this chapter. However, managers and investors must also be cognizant of the key EP valuation factors — including achieving operating and capital efficiencies, understanding the risk-to-value impact of cost of capital change, understanding the impact of external influence on economic profit, and reconciling market implied expectations with internal (or warranted) projections of economic profit growth — that we introduced at the outset of this book.

Chapter 8

Economic Profit and the Cost of Capital

W hile consultants have spent a great deal of time on value-based accounting adjustments, they have spent far too little time on the role of cost of capital and invested capital growth in the wealth creation process.[1] These economic profit omissions are important because the cost of capital and the invested capital growth rate are two critical economic profit factors that drive share prices higher or lower.[2] Moreover, as managers and investors begin to recognize the primacy of cost of capital and invested growth, it will lead them to think beyond the currently assessed level of economic profit and to emphasize the importance of long-term economic profit planning in a corporate valuation context.

In this chapter, we examine the cost of capital and its variation impact on enterprise value. We begin with a review of the cost of capital. We then show how seemingly small changes in *wacc* can have a noticeable impact on enterprise value and stock price. Following that, we delve into robust theoretical and empirical issues that embroil the cost of invested capital.

From a theoretical perspective, we focus on competing theories of the capital structure — namely, Modigliani and Miller versus the traditional view — to demonstrate both the importance and complexity of the cost of capital issue. From an empirical perspective, we examine the benefits and limitations of conventional CAPM-based approaches to estimating the cost of invested capital. We also propose a factor model alternative that joins theoretical and empirical elements for estimating the cost of capital in practice.

On balance, we argue that the cost of invested capital is not only one of the most important EP factors that impact wealth creation, but it is also one of the most intriguing factors due to competing financial theories and empirical anomalies. As investment managers, the confusion surrounding the cost of capital provides opportunities to highlight inefficiencies in the equity market. Despite its complexity, the "buy side" message for economic profit practitioners regarding the cost of capital is crystal clear: Managers and investors must stop spending

---

[1] We emphasize in this chapter the wealth impact of a change in the cost of capital. We cover the strategic role of invested capital growth in Chapter 10.

[2] Indeed, accurately assessing the cost of capital and invested capital growth rate provides a framework for evaluating market implied expectations of economic profit growth. We cover managerial issues involving internal versus market implied growth rates in Chapter 11.

such an inordinate amount of time on accounting adjustments to estimate economic profit. Rather, they must redirect their efforts on making a realistic assessment of the cost of capital, and they must fully understand the wealth impact of a change in the cost of capital.

COST OF CAPITAL BASICS

One of the more significant ironies in modern day finance involves the cost of capital. On the surface, corporate managers and investment managers know that when companies invest in new projects, debtholders and stockholders require a risk adjusted return on their invested capital. Yet despite this obvious need by shareholders to be compensated for the financial and business risks undertaken by firms, corporate and investment players still worry about the "bottom line" impact on accounting earnings from capital investment decisions. This ambiguity and sometimes narrow focus on accounting earnings rather than economic profit is especially problematic because it causes companies to either avoid new investments that might enhance shareholder wealth, or it causes companies to make incorrect investment decisions based on an incomplete and short-term-oriented measure — namely, accounting earnings — of business success.

What is the Cost of Capital?

Central to economic profit measurement is the notion of a cost of capital. As aptly stated by classical economist Alfred Marshall over 100 years ago, a businessman's profit is measured by "What remains of his profits after deducting interest on his capital at the current rate."[3] While the concept of a cost of invested capital was recognized many years ago, the modern day view was formalized in a corporate valuation setting by Nobel Laureates Merton Miller and Franco Modigliani as a weighted average cost of debt and equity capital.

In more formal terms, we can express the firm's cost of invested capital (or *wacc*) as follows:

$$wacc = w_d \times r_d + w_e \times r_e$$

In this expression, *wacc* is a rate, and it can be interpreted as the cost of invested capital or the cost of financing capital. In turn, the (after-tax) cost of debt capital is denoted by r_d, while the cost of equity capital — as seen by the firm — is denoted by r_e. In practice, w_d is thought of as the "target" proportion of debt in the firm's capital structure, and w_e is (therefore) the target proportion of equity financing.

To see how this formula works, suppose a company's (after-tax) debt cost is 6% and its cost of equity is 12%. Further suppose that the firm's capital

---

[3] Alfred Marshall, *Principles of Economics*, Vol. 1 (New York: MacMillan & Co., 1890) p. 142.

structure consists of 33% debt and 67% equity. With these figures, the company's (after-tax) weighted average cost of capital is:

$$wacc = 1/3 \times 0.06 + 2/3 \times 0.12 = 0.10 \text{ or } 10\%$$

For convenience, let's also assume that the firm's existing assets of $100 million generate NOPAT perpetuity of $20 million.[4] Based on this assumption, the firm's NOPAT for any given year can be split into a capital charge of $10 million (10% of $100) plus an economic profit of $10 million.

As we will shortly see, a rise in the cost of invested capital will cause the capital charge to rise and the economic profit to fall. For a given NOPAT, a fall in the cost of invested capital will cause the capital charge to fall and the economic profit to rise. This example can be thought of as a modern day interpretation of Marshall's view that a firm is not truly profitable unless its profits cover the usual production and operating expenditures of an ongoing concern as well as the interest cost on invested capital at the current rate.

IMPACT OF A CHANGE IN THE COST OF CAPITAL

There are many economic and financial factors that can lead to a change in the firm's cost of invested capital. Without getting into the details here, suffice it to say that an unanticipated rise (decline) in the firm's debt-to-capital ratio (measured relative to target)[5] and/or heightened (lessened) business uncertainty about future cash flows might cause an increase (decrease) in a company's capital costs. At the macroeconomic or systematic level, an unanticipated rise (decline) in interest rates — due perhaps to an unanticipated rise in inflationary expectations — as well as unfavorable (favorable) commodity price developments — especially unforeseen changes in energy prices — can lead to unfavorable (favorable) change in a company's cost of invested capital. Moreover, monetary policy happenings at the economy-wide level can impact a company's capital costs in a favorable or unfavorable way.

However, regardless of the fundamental catalyst that causes the cost of capital to change, we emphasize that a change in *wacc* can have a meaningful impact on economic profit, enterprise value, and stock price. A rise in *wacc* will cause economic profit, enterprise value, and stock price to go down, while a fall in *wacc* will cause economic profit and valuation measures to go up. As we will shortly see, this happens even though the cost of invested capital changes by a seemingly small amount (measured in basis points). Thus, managers and investors

---

[4] We also assume no future economic profit growth opportunities in the cost of capital illustration that follows.

[5] As we will shortly see, the impact of capital structure on the cost of capital is a controversial issue in the theory of finance.

alike must be keenly aware of the fact that they can be the "best of the best" value-based accountants, yet miss altogether the sizable impact that changes in the cost of invested capital can have on economic profit and wealth creation.[6]

Impact of Change in *WACC* on Economic Profit

At a later point, we'll revisit company specific and other forces that may induce a change in the cost of capital. For now, let's examine the potential wealth impact of changes in the cost of invested capital. Based on a NOPAT stream of $20 million, initial capital of $100 million, and a cost of capital of 10%, Exhibit 1 shows what happens to the dollar capital charge and economic profit when the cost of capital changes. As before, when the cost of capital is 10%, the firm's capital charge is $10 million and the economic profit is $10 million.

If *wacc* rises by 200 basis points to 12%, then the firm's capital charge rises to $12 million and economic profit declines to $8 million. On the other hand, if the cost of capital falls to 8%, then the capital charge declines to $8 million and economic profit rises to $12 million. Taken together, Exhibit 2 presents a graphical depiction of the positive (and linear) relationship between the cost of invested capital and the dollar capital charge along with the concomitant inverse relationship between the *wacc* and a company's economic profit.

Exhibit 1: Economic Profit Impact of Cost of Capital Change (in $ millions)

wacc %	NOPAT Stream	Capital Charge	Economic Profit	% Change in EP
1	20	1	19	90
5	20	5	15	50
6	20	6	14	40
7	20	7	13	30
8	20	8	12	20
9	20	9	11	10
10	20	10	10	0
11	20	11	9	−10
12	20	12	8	−20
13	20	13	7	−30
14	20	14	6	−40
15	20	15	5	−50
20	20	20	0	−100

[6] Glassman and Hassett argue that the systematic decline in the equity risk premium over the 1990s has, and will have, the impact of lifting all equity securities, i.e., causing the cost of equity to structurally decline, thereby boosting price-to-earnings ratios and share prices. See James K. Glassman and Kevin A. Hassett, *Dow 36,000: The New Strategy for Profiting from the Coming Rise in the Stock Market* (New York: Crown Publishing Group, November 2000).

*Exhibit 2: Economic Profit Impact of Cost of Capital Change
(in $ millions)*

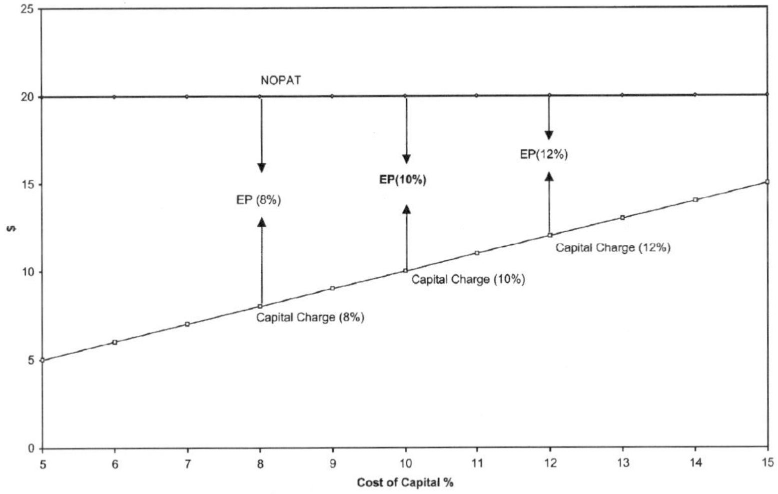

Impact of Change in *WACC* on Wealth Creation

We can also assess the impact of a change in the cost of capital on wealth creation — as measured by a change in *wacc* on net present value (NPV). In this context, Exhibit 3 shows the sensitivity of enterprise value and NPV to changes in the cost of capital. The exhibit is interesting in several respects. First, it shows that enterprise value and NPV are inversely related to changes in the cost of capital. When *wacc* rises from 10% to 11% the firm's wealth (NPV) falls by 9.09%. Conversely, if *wacc* were to fall by 100 basis points — from 10% to 9% — then the firm's NPV would rise by about 11%. Exhibit 3 shows even greater wealth effects if the cost of capital were to change by a larger amount. For example, when the cost of capital declines by 200 basis points then the firm's NPV would rise by some 25%.

Exhibit 3 also shows that the absolute percentage change in a company's wealth is dependent on whether the cost of capital rises or falls. As noted above, when the cost of capital declines from 10% to 8%, the firm's NPV rises by 25%. However, if *wacc* were to rise by 200 basis points — from 10% to 12% — then the firm's wealth would decline by about 17%. At the extremes, the exhibit shows that if the cost of capital were to fall from 10% to 6% — a 400 basis point decline — then NPV would rise by 67%, while the firm's wealth would decline by 29% for a comparative basis point rise in cost of invested capital. Although major changes in *wacc* on a scale of 400 to 500 basis points per year seem highly unlikely for the U.S. economy, such dispersions in capital costs have occurred in the international economy.[7]

---

[7] Indeed, capital costs can change quite dramatically in the emerging markets. One only needs to recall the excess volatility of capital markets when the Russian financial economy collapsed in August of 1998. This in turn led to a financial contagion in emerging market countries of Latin America and elsewhere.

Exhibit 3: Valuation Impact of Cost of Capital Change (in $ millions)

wacc %	Enterprise Value	Book Capital	NPV	% Change in Value
1	2000.00	100	1900.00	900.00
5	400.00	100	300.00	100.00
6	333.33	100	233.33	66.67
7	285.71	100	185.71	42.86
8	250.00	100	150.00	25.00
9	222.22	100	122.22	11.11
10	200.00	100	100.00	0.00
11	181.82	100	81.82	−9.09
12	166.67	100	66.67	−16.67
13	153.85	100	53.85	−23.08
14	142.86	100	42.86	−28.57
15	133.33	100	33.33	−33.33
20	100.00	100	0.00	−50.00

Before proceeding, it should be noted that the asymmetric wealth impact of a change in the cost of capital is manifest in normal present value relationships. This can be seen more clearly in Exhibit 4. The exhibit shows both the inverse relationship between enterprise value and the cost of invested capital as well as the "convexity" in the present value relationship between unanticipated changes in *wacc* and changes in wealth. In the unlikely event that cost of capital were only 1%, then the firm's enterprise value would be $2,000 million and its NPV would be $1,900 million. In contrast, if the *wacc* were unusually high at, say, 20%, then the firm's wealth would be entirely dissipated. At this extreme, the firm's enterprise value to invested capital ratio would be unity ($100/$100) — a rather unexciting wealth position for shareholders.

Moreover, over a *wacc* range of 1% to 20%, Exhibit 4 highlights the convex nature in the relationship between a company's enterprise value (and implicitly, its NPV) as a function of the cost of invested capital. The exhibit shows that when *wacc* changes from a low rate of 1% to a high rate of 20%, the firm's enterprise value "asymptotically" approaches its book capital. Over this same cost of capital spectrum, the firm's wealth (NPV) position displays a convex pattern toward zero.

TOWARDS A FIXED INCOME ANALOGY

The enterprise value and wealth effects shown in Exhibit 4 are also interesting from a fixed income perspective. Specifically, for those managers and investors who are familiar with present value techniques for fixed income securities, the behavior of the enterprise value (and implied NPV) function shown in the exhibit is similar to the duration and convexity properties of non-callable or option-free bonds.[8]

---

[8] For a rigorous explanation of duration and convexity properties of fixed income securities, see Frank J. Fabozzi, *Fixed Income Securities* (New Hope, PA: Frank J. Fabozzi Associates, 1997).

Exhibit 4: NPV Impact of Cost of Capital Change
(in $ millions)

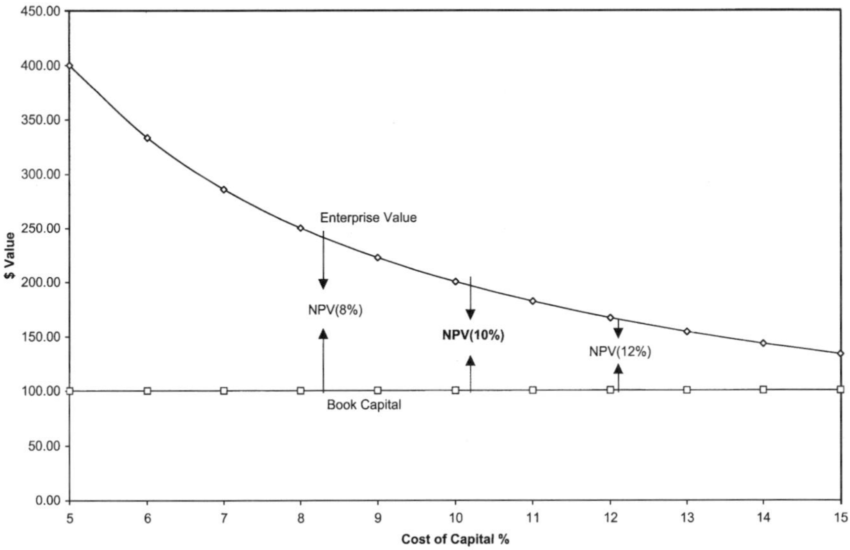

For example, as interest rates go up in the economy bond prices go down across the board. Conversely, we know that when interest rates go down, bond prices go up by an even greater percentage — due to the convexity of the bond's price/yield relationship — than the percentage price decline that occurs when interest rates go up. Like government and option-free corporate bonds, the firm's enterprise value and wealth show the same kind of interest rate sensitivity as that which is evident in the pricing of fixed income securities.

A Cautionary Word on the Fixed Income Analogy

While the pricing relationships between interest rates and bond prices and the cost of capital and enterprise value seem analogous, corporate managers and investors must be aware of differences that are important in the process of wealth creation. At this introductory point in our cost of capital discussion, it is worth emphasizing that we assumed that the firm's investment decision is fixed (pun intended) in the enterprise value calculation. Indeed, we made the simplistic assumption that there was no future investment opportunity and that the firm's existing capital stock generated NOPAT perpetuity of $20 million.

Other things the same, there is no compelling reason for the firm's enterprise value and NPV to change except from those changes that are driven by variations in *wacc*. Thus, in our illustration, the firm's enterprise value must rise or fall due to cost of capital changes just like the present value of the interest annuity and the present value of the par value on government and corporate bonds would rise or fall as interest rates change in the economy.

However, for theoretical reasons that we explain in the next section, corporate managers and investors must be careful not to confuse a change in bond yield with a change in the cost of capital. In principle, there are capital structure circumstances where offsetting bond *and* equity yield changes can leave the cost of capital unchanged.[9] In this context, it is helpful to recall that the cost of capital is a weighted average of the (after-tax) cost of debt and equity financing.

In order for the cost of capital to rise in the presence of, say, a rise in the required yield on bonds, we must presume that there is no offsetting reduction in the cost of equity capital. But having opened the box to a capital structure controversy in modern financial theory, we now take a look at the internal decision by corporate managers to finance a company with debt versus equity shares — and the concomitant impact (if any) of capital structure decisions on the weighted average cost of capital.

COST OF CAPITAL IN FINANCIAL THEORY

In 1958, Franco Modigliani and Merton Miller forcefully argued that capital structure decisions that merely vary the mix of debt and equity securities on a company's balance sheet have no impact on enterprise value (known as "MM Proposition I") and the cost of invested capital (known as "MM Proposition III"). Given the firm's investment decision, their capital structure argument implies that economic profit and NPV are invariant to the corporate leverage decision. Wealth is created in the MM world by investing in positive NPV (and therefore, discounted positive economic profit) opportunities. As a practical consequence, the substitution of debt for equity shares or the substitution of equity shares for debt by corporate managers is a dubious way to create economic profit and shareholder value.

Pivotal Role of the Cost of Equity

Without getting into all the Miller Modigliani details,[10] we can use "MM Proposition II" to shed light on the seemingly paradoxical view that the cost of invested capital is invariant to changes in the mix of debt and equity securities on the corporate balance sheet. Specifically, MM Proposition II states that the expected

---

[9] For example, the equity risk premium went up while interest rates were falling in the United States and most European markets during the market crisis of 1998.

[10] See Franco Modigliani and Merton H. Miller, "The Cost of Capital, Corporation Finance, and the Theory of Investment," *American Economic Review* (June 1958). The "MM Propositions" of corporate finance are also lucidly explained in Eugene F. Fama and Merton H. Miller, *The Theory of Finance* (Holt, Rinehart, and Winston, Inc., 1972).

return on a "levered" firm's (i.e., a company with corporate debt outstanding) stock is a function of the debt-to-equity ratio. We can express this relationship as:

$$r_e = wacc_u + (wacc_u - r_d)D/E$$

where r_e is the expected return on the levered firm's stock, $wacc_u$ is the expected return or cost of capital for an equivalent business risk "unlevered" firm, r_d is the cost of debt capital, and D/E is the ratio of debt to equity.

A graphical depiction of this expected return-leverage relationship is shown in Exhibit 5. With this formula, Modigliani and Miller argue that the expected return on levered stock is *linearly* related to the debt-to-equity ratio — one of several measures that can be used to capture financial risk. Indeed, MM Proposition II is a pivotal reason why the firm's enterprise value (MM Proposition I) and its cost of invested capital (MM Proposition III) are invariant to the corporate debt decision. We'll show this key MM development in the context of the cost of invested capital.

In more formal terms, we know that the cost of capital for the levered firm is a weighted average cost of debt and levered equity. We'll denote this as $wacc_l$. Upon substituting MM Proposition II into the general cost of capital formulation, we obtain:

$$
\begin{aligned}
wacc_l &= w_d \times r_d + w_e \times r_e \\
&= w_d \times r_d + w_e \times [wacc_u + (wacc_u - r_d)D/E] \\
&= wacc_u
\end{aligned}
$$

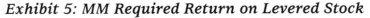

Exhibit 5: MM Required Return on Levered Stock

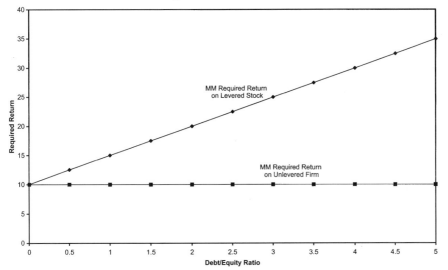

In this linkage between MM Propositions II and III, we see that the cost of capital for the levered firm, $wacc_l$, is equal to the cost of invested capital for the equivalent business risk unlevered firm — namely, $wacc_u$.[11] This is turn implies that unanticipated changes in the mix of debt and equity shares — as well as any internally induced debt and equity yield changes caused by variations in the debt-to-equity ratio — will have *no* meaningful impact on the weighted average cost of capital. Hence, corporate managers and investors alike must pay particular attention to real as opposed to illusory forces that impact a change in the cost of capital.

Invariance of Financing Decision on Wealth Creation

We can explain the economic profit and NPV consequences of the capital structure decision in the context of a perpetuity model on economic profit.[12] Specifically, with EP perpetuity, the firm's NPV can be expressed as the present value of its anticipated economic profit stream according to:

$$NPV = EP/wacc$$
$$= (NOPAT - wacc \times I)/wacc$$
$$= I(ROIC - wacc)/wacc$$

In this NPV expression, EP is the firm's estimated economic profit and — in the second expression — NOPAT is the net operating profit after tax. As before, ROIC is the after-tax return on invested capital, and *wacc* is the weighted average cost of debt and equity capital.

Since NOPAT is the firm's net operating profit after tax, but *before* financing costs — equivalently, NOPAT is the operating earnings of an "unlevered" company — and because "*I*" is the firm's fixed capital investment, we see that the wealth impact of the financing decision boils down to the impact of corporate debt policy on the weighted average cost of capital. However, for Modigliani-Miller reasons that we explained before,[13] the firm's cost of capital is *independent* of changes in the mix of debt and equity on the corporate balance sheet. Consequently, in the NPV formulation, it is implied that $wacc_l = wacc_u = wacc$.

In practical terms, the MM Propositions of corporate finance have a powerful message for corporate managers and investors. Specifically, if *wacc* is unaffected by internal changes in the mix of debt and equity, then the firm's assessed economic profit, NPV, and its enterprise value must also be independent of the corporate financing decision. In the MM world, the source of the firm's NPV —

---

[11] The invariance of cost of capital to changes in the corporate debt decision applies in a world of no taxes and a world with business taxes and *no* deductibility of debt interest expense. We'll examine the cost of capital issues that apply in a world with taxes and deductibility of debt interest expense at a later point.

[12] For further insight on EP-based wealth models, see Fabozzi and Grant, "Value-Based Metrics in Financial Theory," Chapter 2 in Frank J. Fabozzi and James L. Grant (Eds.), *Value-Based Metrics: Foundations and Practice* (New Hope PA: Frank J. Fabozzi Associates, 2000).

[13] See Franco Modigliani and Merton H. Miller, "The Cost of Capital, Corporation Finance, and the Theory of Investment." Again, to the extent that taxes apply, we assume (at this point) a world with corporate taxes and no deductibility of debt interest expense.

and therefore its annualized economic profit equivalent — is derived from the wealth enhancing investment decisions made by corporate managers — both now and in the future — that have an after-tax return on invested capital (ROIC) that on the average exceeds the cost of invested capital. Moreover, in a combined MM-EP view, the invariance of the economic profit spread (ROIC – $wacc$) to capital structure change is due to the invariance of the ROIC and $wacc$ (= $wacc_l$ = $wacc_u$) difference in the two-period NPV formulation.

Impact of Corporate Taxes with Deductibility of Debt Interest on $WACC$[14]

The capital structure irrelevance argument of Miller and Modigliani depends on the assumption of a well functioning or perfect capital market. In the real world, we know that market and informational imperfections exist such that the capital structure mix of debt and equity financing may impact both economic profit and the enterprise value of the firm. In this context, the cost of capital issue boils down to those factors that lead to capital market inefficiencies in the first instance and the significance of their impact on $wacc$.

Perhaps the most significant capital market imperfection — and the one most often cited in the theory and practice of corporate finance — is the issue of corporate taxes *with* deductibility of a company's debt interest expense. This tax imperfection leads to a debt tax subsidy that can impact the cost of capital. In a world with taxes *and* deductibility of debt interest expense, the firm's weighted average cost of capital can be expressed as follows:

$$wacc_l = wacc_u \, [1 - t_e \times D/C]$$

In this modified $wacc$ expression, t_e is the firm's "effective" debt tax subsidy rate and D/C is the "target" debt-to-capital ratio. As before, $wacc_l$ is the cost of capital for a levered company, while $wacc_u$ represents the cost of invested capital for an equivalent business risk unlevered firm.

Notice that if the firm's debt tax subsidy rate is equal to zero (that is, t_e equals zero) then the levered firm's $wacc$ is equal to the cost of capital for the unlevered firm. When this happens, a company's economic profit, NPV, and enterprise value are again invariant to the capital structure mix of debt and equity securities on the corporate balance sheet. However, if the firm's debt tax subsidy rate is positive (t_e greater than zero) — as emphasized in a more traditional view of capital structure theory[15] — then the levered firm's cost of capital is *lower* than the cost of capital for the unlevered firm. In this case, both the anticipated

---

[14] In this section, we draw on capital structure arguments covered in Fabozzi and Grant, "Value-Based Metrics in Financial Theory."

[15] We cover the traditional view on capital structure and the cost of capital in the next section. In this theory we'll see that economic profit and NPV are impacted by both investment *and* financing decisions — that is, leverage induced $wacc$ effects.

economic profit and the currently measured NPV of the levered firm are *higher* than that available to unlevered shareholders.

Based on this cost of capital formulation, we see that the pertinent capital structure issue boils down to the magnitude of the debt tax subsidy on the levered *wacc*. Having recognized that, it is important to note that Merton Miller argues[16] that even in a world with corporate taxes and progressive income taxes that the firm's effective debt tax subsidy (t_e in the levered cost of capital formulation) is close to zero. If Miller's debt tax argument is applicable in real world capital markets then the levered firm's cost of capital is again equal to the unlevered firm's cost of capital. In this instance, the firm's assessed economic profit and its current NPV are again independent of the particular method of corporate financing — including of course the "just right" mix of debt versus equity financing.

As with most corporate and investment practitioners, we do not question the existence of a debt tax subsidy on economic profit and enterprise value. However, we also recognize that the benefit of a debt-induced tax subsidy to the levered firm's shareholders may be overestimated — especially, as Merton Miller emphasizes, when one considers the offsetting tax effects of leveraged capital structures.[17] We especially believe that shareholders are better served when managers focus their investment decisions on real economic profit enhancement as opposed to misguided financing strategies that merely repackage the mix of debt and equity securities in order to lower the cost of levered capital. In this context, we emphasize the importance of wealth creation via positive NPV decisions, as opposed to capital structure changes that give investors the illusion of economic profit and wealth creation.[18]

TRADITIONAL VIEW OF LEVERAGE AND THE COST OF CAPITAL

While we emphasize the economic profit and wealth implications of the MM perspective on the cost of capital, we would be remiss for not shedding light on the wealth effects of the traditional approach to corporate debt policy. Whether rightly or wrongly so, the traditional perspective on cost of capital and capital structure — namely, that debt matters in the cost of capital equation — is the one that is employed most often in practice by senior corporate managers and investment managers. By covering these divergent viewpoints, managers and investors will — at the very least — have a better understanding of the cost of capital role in the creation of shareholder value.

---

[16] See Merton H. Miller, "Debt and Taxes," *Journal of Finance* (May 1977).

[17] See Miller, "Debt and Taxes."

[18] We are aware of — but do not cover in this chapter — the potentially positive NPV (and therefore economic profit) role that levered capital structures may have in disciplining corporate managers (agents) to act in the best interests of shareholders (owners) in a world with agency costs. For a practical discussion of the transaction costs role of corporate debt policy in creating ownership value, see Michael C. Jensen, "Eclipse of the Modern Corporation," *Harvard Business Review* (September-October 1989).

As with MM, the traditional approach can be examined in a world with no taxes *and* a world with taxes and deductibility of debt interest expense at the corporate level. We'll begin the traditional capital structure discussion in a no tax world — or similarly, a tax world with *no* deductibility of debt interest expense. In this context, we'll see that "debt matters" not just because of tax issues, but also because of an *inefficient* pricing response by investors to changes in equity risk as the level of debt changes on the balance sheet.

Inefficient Risk Pricing in the Traditional View

In the traditional view, it is argued that investors do not always have the information and/or the time needed to constantly monitor changes in the level of debt relative to equity. Consequently, there is a period where the required return on levered firm's stock does not fully account — in the MM sense — for the added financial risk that is associated with higher levels of debt.[19]

In more formal terms, the irrational response by shareholders to changing debt levels means that the required return on levered stock is (for a time) less than the efficient market response as manifest in MM Proposition II. Therefore, in the traditional view, the following risk pricing inequality applies for levered stock:

$$r_{e,T} < r_{e,\text{MM}}$$
$$r_{e,T} < [wacc_u + (wacc_u - r_d)D/E]$$

In this expression, $r_{e,T}$ is the expected return on the levered firm's stock in the traditional view, while $r_{e,\text{MM}}$ is the corresponding Modigliani-Miller required return on levered stock that we explained before.

The cost of capital implication of this risk pricing inequality is transparent. That is, if the required return on levered equity is not fully responsive to changes in the debt-to-equity ratio (or any other leverage ratio) then corporate managers can utilize debt financing to lower *wacc*. Unlike MM, this means that investment *and* financing decisions are no longer separable.

In the traditional view, corporate managers have two ways to increase economic profit and enterprise value — find real investment opportunities that enhance shareholder value and finance those positive investments up to the target level, with debt rather than equity. If the traditional view is applicable in real world capital markets, then shareholder value may rise in a compounding way to the announcement of investment opportunities that are financed with a sizable amount of debt.

Leverage Effects on ROE

In the above discussion, we focused on the mispricing of equity risk as the fundamental reason why debt policy can be used to enhance shareholder value. From

---

[19] The traditional view is a general one in corporate finance that predates the pioneering 1958 paper by Modigliani and Miller.

the traditional perspective, we could just as easily show that a larger proportion of debt in the firm's capital structure leads to *higher* profitability ratios — such as earning per share and return on equity.

We'll use the traditionally based Dupont formula to show the impact of leverage on the accounting return on equity. In this context, the return on equity (ROE) can be expressed in terms of the return on assets (ROA) and the inverse of one minus the corporate debt ratio according to:

$$ROE = ROA/(1 - D/A)$$

In this familiar expression, ROA is the accounting return on assets and D/A is the debt-to-asset measure of corporate leverage.

With a proportionately higher level of fixed obligations in the firm's capital structure, the Dupont formula shows that ROE goes up — since the denominator in the return on equity equation falls as D/A rises.[20] Conversely, as the debt/asset ratio declines relative to the firm's return on assets, its return on equity (ROE) goes down — as the denominator in the Dupont formula now goes up. In effect, when debt/asset ratio rises relative to ROA, a *smaller* amount of equity capital is generating the same amount of corporate profitability — thus the shareholder return on equity rises. A declining return on equity happens when a *larger* equity base is being used to earn the same amount of after-tax accounting profit.

Accounting Leverage: A Numerical Illustration

As a simple example of the link between the accounting ROE and leverage, assume that the firm's profit after tax is $10 million, and its assets are $100 million. Also assume that the firm is *initially* equity financed such that the debt/asset ratio is, for all practical purposes, zero. With 100% equity financing, the *unlevered* firm's accounting ROE is the same as its ROA, at 10%:

$$ROE = 0.1/(1.0 - 0.0)$$
$$= 0.1 \text{ or } 10\%$$

Let's now assume that the firm's corporate treasurer decides to engage in a financing strategy that effectively swaps the equity shares for more debt, such that D/A rises to say, 40%. With this *pure* capital structure change, the firm's return on equity rises from 10% to 16.7%:

$$ROE = 0.1/(1.0 - 0.4)$$
$$= 0.167 \text{ or } 16.7\%$$

As the firm moves to what it perceives to be its "target" capital structure, we see that the stockholders' ratio of profit-to-equity capital goes up. With this leverage change, it can also be shown that the firm's per-share earnings would rise as well.

---

[20] This assumes that ROA is fixed by a given investment decision.

Consequently, in the traditional view, it is argued that investors should be willing to pay *more* for the firm's enhanced profitability (as manifest in higher accounting ROE) and now seemingly dearer shares. This makes sense so long as the risk associated with the equity has not been negatively impacted in a material way.

ROE Volatility

Before proceeding, it may seem odd that investors should somehow feel better off just because the firm has a higher debt level. This of course is the general thrust of what MM were trying to say. Indeed, the flipside of the traditional Dupont formula is that it can be used to illustrate the underlying volatility of accounting return on equity at varying debt levels.

Exhibit 6 shows what happens to ROE when the return on assets varies from 10% to −10% in the presence of corporate debt levels ranging from 0% to 70%, respectively. Notice that as the firm's profitability expands or contracts — that is, ROA goes from 10% down to −10% — with a 10% debt load, we see that ROE fluctuates from 11.1% on the high side down to −11.1% on the downside.

In turn, Exhibit 6 shows that with a debt load of 40%, the ROE numbers swing from 16.7% down to −16.7%. As profitability expands or contracts with a 50% debt load, the shareholder's return on equity is even more volatile, with ROE figures ranging from 20% on the positive side and −20% on the negative side. On balance, the exhibit reveals that increasing leverage in "good times" conveys volatile benefits to the shareholders, while rising corporate debt loads in "bad times" is a source of heightened financial concern.

Moreover, according to MM Proposition II, the leverage-induced volatility in accounting return on equity should already be reflected in the required rate of return on levered stock. What is key here from an MM perspective is not so much the debt, but the business risk changes that can impact the required return on unlevered stock — in other words, the cost of capital as manifest in the equity risk premium for the unlevered firm, $wacc_u$. Hence, corporate managers and investment managers must be particularly cognizant of changes that result in heightened volatility in invested capital returns (ROIC) and sudden changes in the cost of invested capital.

Exhibit 6: ROE Impact of Corporate Debt Policy in Changing Profitability Scenarios

	Corporate Debt Ratio							
	0.0%	10%	20%	30%	40%	50%	60%	70%
	ROE %							
Expansion: ROA = 10%	10	11.1	12.5	14.3	16.7	20	25	33.3
Contraction: ROA = −10%	−10	−11.1	−12.5	−14.3	−16.7	−20	−25	−33.3

Exhibit 7: Impact of Capital Structure Change on Cost of Capital

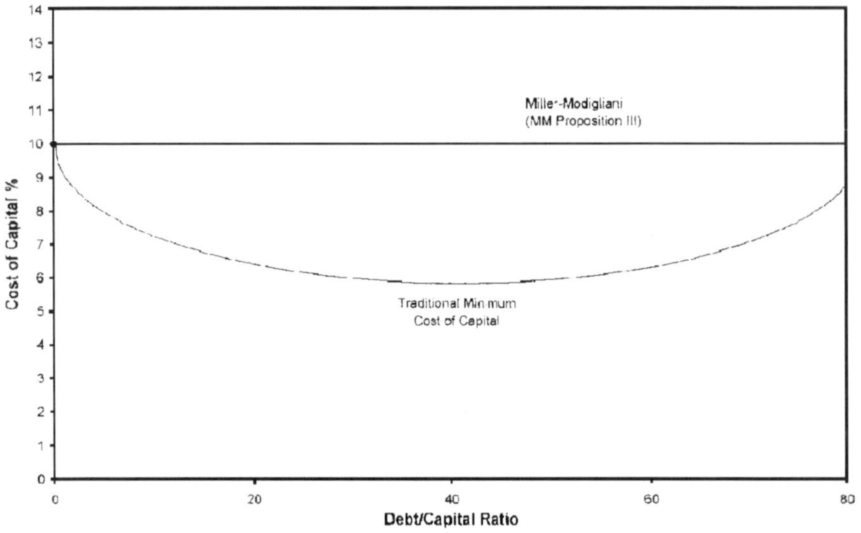

A COMBINED LOOK AT MM AND TRADITIONAL VIEWS

Based on the preceding foundation, let's now take a combined look at the MM and traditional positions on cost of capital and enterprise value. Exhibit 7 shows how corporate debt policy impacts the levered *wacc* in MM and traditional viewpoints, while Exhibit 8 shows the resulting impact of competing capital structure positions on enterprise value and shareholder value. We first discuss the traditional viewpoint with follow-up commentary on the graphical illustrations from the Modigliani and Miller perspective.

In the traditional view, we see that the cost of capital falls as the firm moves from being an unlevered firm to a levered firm. As we noted before, this happens because investors do not see the rising level of debt relative to equity and therefore do not require a higher level of return to compensate for the added financing risk.[21] As the presumably lower cost debt[22] is used to replace higher cost equity, we see in Exhibit 7 that the levered cost of capital, $wacc_l$, declines as the firm moves toward its "target" debt-to-capital ratio of, say, 40%.

---

[21] Of course, taxes *with* deductibility of debt interest expense provide further ammunition to the traditional argument that "debt matters."

[22] The traditional view largely looks at the direct cost (coupon rate or yield) of bond financing when estimating the cost of debt. It does *not* fully consider the indirect equity cost due to a higher level of debt financing and heightened financial risk for the shareholders.

Exhibit 8: Impact of Capital Structure Change on Enterprise Value

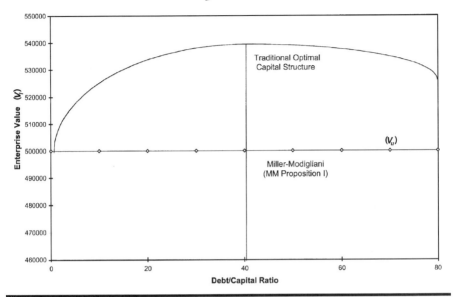

Beyond the target debt to capital ratio, the exhibit shows a sharp rise in the levered cost of capital. This happens in the traditional view because investors begin to discount the increased risk of distress or even bankruptcy. They then respond to heightened financial risk with a dramatic rise in the expected return on levered stock (not shown in the exhibit). This causes the levered firm's cost of capital to rise sharply with concomitant negative effects on enterprise value (we show this in Exhibit 8). Thus, in the traditional view, corporate managers have an incentive to finance their capital investment projects on the average with a target mix of debt relative to equity. Moreover, in the traditional view, debt policy impacts the cost of capital in a significant way — and, if correct, one that corporate managers and investors need to be apprised of.

In sharp contrast, Modigliani and Miller argue that the cost of capital is invariant to the corporate debt decision. This view is represented graphically by the horizon line in Exhibit 7, which starts at the unlevered firm's cost of capital and remains flat for varying degrees of corporate leverage. As noted before, the invariance of the unlevered *wacc* to changes in the debt-to-capital (or debt-to-equity) ratio is a manifestation of the efficient market response by ever-observant shareholders to changing levels of debt.

As manifest in MM Proposition II, the expected return on levered stock (recall Exhibit 5) is linearly related to the debt-to-equity ratio. Because of the efficient pricing of financial risk, the cost of capital remains invariant to the corporate debt decision. This leads to the rather profound cost of capital implication of the MM position on capital structure. Specifically, corporate managers would be much better off looking for real investment opportunities having positive discounted economic profit (i.e., positive NPV) — rather than spending valuable shareholder resources looking for seemingly efficient capital structures that simply give shareholders the illusion of economic profit and wealth creation.

Impact of Competing Positions on Enterprise Value

Exhibit 8 shows the capital structure implications of traditional and MM positions on enterprise value. In the exhibit, V_u represents the enterprise value of the *unlevered* firm — a firm having no long-term debt outstanding — while V_l denotes the *levered* firm's market value. In the traditional view, we see that when the debt-to-capital ratio raises from 0% to the target level of, say, 40%, the enterprise value of the firm and its outstanding shares go up. Over this debt range, the firm's market value goes up due to the presumably "good news" resulting from the falling cost of levered capital shown in Exhibit 7. The decline in levered *wacc* and the concomitant rise in economic profit (due to lower capital costs for a given NOPAT) causes investors to pay more for the levered firm's outstanding shares.[23]

On the other hand, if the debt-to-capital ratio exceeds the 40% target level, then economic profit and enterprise value *falls* as the heightened financial risk leads to an ever-rising cost of capital for the levered firm. At this point, the cost of levered capital rises due to sharp increases in the required return on equity capital. With a 50% debt load, corporate managers have pushed debt *beyond* the target level, and should therefore engage in substantial "de-levering" activities. Moreover, if the 40% debt level is in fact an optimal one, then economic profit and enterprise value decline with any sizable movement to the left *or* right of this target capital structure position. These traditionally based profit and valuation effects are of course a reflection of the possibility that the cost of capital is higher for any debt-to-capital ratio that is different from the presumed optimal level.

Again, in sharp contrast, MM argue that the firm's enterprise value is invariant to the corporate leverage decision. This is shown graphically in Exhibit 8 by the horizontal line emanating from the unlevered firm's enterprise value and continuing at that level over varying levels of the debt-to-capital ratio. Of course, the invariance of enterprise value to corporate debt policy is a reflection of the invariance of the levered cost of capital to the debt changes shown in Exhibit 7. Finally, the invariance of both enterprise value (MM Proposition I) and the cost of capital (MM Proposition III) are a reflection of the continuously responsive expected return on levered stock (MM Proposition II) to changes in the firm's

---

[23] In the Modigliani-Miller model, the higher EPS generated by corporate leverage is offset by a rise in the investor's required rate of return (in CAPM, for example, beta is linearly related to leverage) on the firm's outstanding stock. Consequently, in an efficient capital market, the company's stock price remains *unchanged* in the presence of the debt-induced rise in EPS and ROE. In the MM framework, corporate value is largely impacted by *real* economic profit opportunities as opposed to debt policies that give investors the "illusion" of value creation.

corporate debt decision. Given the firm's investment decision, the invariance of economic profit (NOPAT *less* dollar *wacc*) to changes in corporate leverage follows from the MM propositions.

COST OF CAPITAL ESTIMATES AND ESTIMATION ISSUES

Having been immersed in the theoretical controversy embroiling the cost of capital and its variation impact on economic profit, let's now take a look at (1) some empirical estimates of the cost of capital for wealth creators and wealth destroyers and (2) empirical challenges to estimating the cost of invested capital in practice. We'll first look at empirical estimates in the context of the return on invested capital (ROIC) and the cost of capital (*wacc*) for large U.S. wealth creators and wealth destroyers. We'll then cover some empirical challenges to the conventional CAPM approach to estimating the cost of capital. We conclude the chapter by providing corporate managers and investment managers with an economic profit-based factor model alternative to CAPM for estimating the cost of invested capital in practice.

ROIC and WACC Estimates for Wealth Creators

Exhibit 9 presents the after-tax return on invested capital (ROIC=NOPAT/ Invested Capital) and the cost of capital (*wacc*) for the top 10 U.S. wealth creators in the 1998 Stern Stewart Performance 1000 Universe. In the cost of capital estimates that follow, the capital asset pricing model (CAPM) is used to estimate the expected or required return on common stock.

Exhibit 9: Return on Invested Capital versus Cost of Capital: Top 10 U.S. Wealth Creators in 1998 Performance Universe

Name	MVA Rank	ROIC	*wacc*	RROC*
General Electric	1	17.34	13.76	3.58
Coca-Cola	2	36.33	12.13	24.20
Microsoft	3	52.94	14.20	38.74
Merck	4	23.15	14.51	8.64
Intel	5	42.71	15.14	27.57
Procter & Gamble	6	15.16	12.81	2.35
Exxon	7	9.44	9.91	−0.47
Pfizer	8	19.86	12.07	7.79
Philip Morris	9	20.15	11.93	8.22
Bristol-Myers Squibb	10	25.32	12.55	12.77

* RROC = ROIC − *wacc*

Exhibit 9 is interesting in several respects. First, and foremost, it shows that wealth creators have an after-tax return on invested capital that exceeds the cost of capital. Among the top 10 wealth creators, we see that 9 out of 10 companies had an ROIC that exceeded the *wacc*. For examples, the return on capital for powerful wealth creators like Coca-Cola, Microsoft, Intel, and Bristol-Myers Squibb were in excess of 25%, while their cost of capital estimate was less than 15%.

In addition, the economic profit spread (ROIC − *wacc*) for General Electric, Merck, and Philip Morris was attractive too, ranging from 3.6% for General Electric up to 8.6% for Merck. On the other hand, the exhibit shows that there can be exceptions to the positive economic profit rule. That is, the adverse economic profit spread for Exxon shows that some companies may have *currently* negative economic profit and still be considered a wealth creator if future or normalized economic profit is positive.[24]

Exhibit 9 is also important because it highlights a cost of capital point that is central to this chapter. Specifically, even though wealth creators like Coca-Cola, Microsoft, and Intel are largely equity financed, they have a *positive* cost of capital that exceeds 10%. Indeed, despite the fact that the stockholders' equity section of their balance sheets do not provide managers and investors with any indication of a required return on equity, the cost of capital figures shown in the exhibit reveal that equity financing is in no way a "free lunch" method of financing growth. In this context, the cost of invested capital for Coca-Cola and Microsoft — at 12% and 14%, respectively — are based on the CAPM required return for the equity shares of (mostly) unlevered companies using a *long-term* equity risk premium.[25] Recall that the economic profit data presented in Exhibit 9 is drawn from the Stern Stewart Performance Universe.

ROIC and WACC Estimates for Wealth Destroyers

In turn, Exhibit 10 presents the after-tax return on invested capital and cost of capital estimates for the bottom 10 firms (ranked by MVA or NPV) that were listed in the 1998 Performance Universe. These companies can be interpreted as large wealth destroying firms among the 1000 companies reported in the 1998 Performance Universe.

Exhibit 10 is also interesting in economic profit and cost of capital respects. First, it shows that wealth destroyers have an after-tax return on capital that is lower than the cost of invested capital. Among the bottom 10 U.S. firms listed in the 1998 Performance Universe, we see that all 10 companies had an ROIC that fell short of the *wacc*. At that time, the return on capital for wealth destroyers like USF&G, Digital Equipment, and Loews Corporation was less than 5%, while their cost of capital estimates was more than 10%.

---

[24] We introduced this EP possibility in Chapter 3 in the context of the EP-to-Capital versus NPV-to-Capital ratio.

[25] We address the potentially dynamic nature of the equity risk premium in an upcoming section to this chapter.

Exhibit 10: Return on Invested Capital versus Cost of Capital: Bottom 10 Companies in 1998 Performance Universe

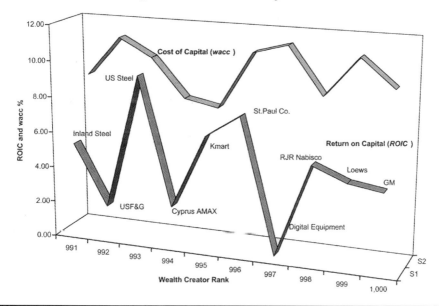

Second, the economic profit spreads (again, ROIC – *wacc*) for Cyprus AMAX, RJR Nabisco, and General Motors were problematic too, ranging from –3.3% for RJR Nabisco down to –5.6% for Cyprus AMAX. Moreover, it seems especially troublesome that a vital component of the U.S. economy such as General Motors would in recent times be ranked among the largest U.S. wealth destroyers.[26]

Exhibit 10 also reinforces in empirical terms a key cost of capital point that we made before. That is, the cost of capital is a weighted average of the after-tax cost of debt *and* equity financing. In economic profit terms, companies are considered to be wealth creators when — on the average — their invested capital returns exceed the cost of capital. On the other hand, companies are deemed to be wealth destroyers when ROIC falls short of the *wacc*. This can happen for wealth destroyers even though their after-tax capital return is more than sufficient to cover the after-tax cost of debt.

Due to their negative economic profit, companies such as Inland Steel, US Steel, and Kmart are deemed to be wealth destroyers even though ROIC may best their after-tax cost of debt. Moreover, RJR Nabisco has tried mightily over the past decade or so to finance their problematic asset mix (especially on the tobacco side) with seemingly cheaper cost debt financing. Hence, managers and investors must realize that it's not the debt per se, but rather the positive dis-

---

[26] Having said that, we note in Chapter 10 that General Motors was in the process of downsizing a negative economic profit spread business.

counted economic profit that dictates whether a firm is a wealth creator or a wealth destroyer. This EP interpretation is entirely consistent with the classic Modigliani-Miller position on capital structure.

ROLE OF CAPM

When estimating the required return on common stock, economic profit practitioners generally use the Capital Asset Pricing Model (CAPM).[27] As with any risk pricing model that purports to represent reality, there are benefits and limitations. On the benefit side, there are at least two compelling reasons to use the "single factor" capital asset pricing model when estimating the required return on common stock.

First, as we explained in Chapter 4, CAPM evolves from established investment theory. In this context, modern portfolio theory asserts that there exists a linear relationship between the expected return on an asset — represented by a share of common stock — and its level of "systematic (or beta) risk" in the marketplace. Second, and perhaps most important to the cost of capital discussion at hand, CAPM is supposed to capture the *linear* relationship between the expected return on levered stock and the debt-to-equity ratio. This in turn was central in our previous explanation of the MM approach to corporate debt policy. Indeed, both CAPM and MM theories are based on the premise that capital markets are efficient.

Benefits of Using CAPM

In more formal terms, the CAPM based expected return on common stock is linearly related to the level of systematic or beta risk according to:

$$r_e = r_f + (r_m - r_f)B_{e,m}$$

In this expression, r_e is the CAPM expected return on common stock, r_f is the risk-free rate of interest, $(r_m - r_f)$ is the expected market risk premium, and $B_{e,m}$ is the beta or systematic risk of stock in the marketplace. As predicted by CAPM, high beta stocks should have high expected returns, while low beta stocks should have comparably low expected returns. As shown, CAPM has a desirable cost of capital feature because risk is built into the formation of expected security returns.

Another cost of capital benefit of using CAPM to estimate expected return is that the model captures the *linear* relationship between expected security return and the debt-to-equity ratio that is central to the operational efficiency of MM Proposition II. In a pioneering study, Robert Hamada shows that the beta risk measure is linearly related to the debt-to-equity ratio.[28] As the corporate leverage

---

[27] For example, Stern Stewart and Goldman Sachs use CAPM-based approaches when estimating the cost of equity capital.

[28] See Robert S. Hamada, "Portfolio Analysis, Market Equilibrium and Corporation Finance," *Journal of Finance* (March 1969).

ratio goes up, the "levered beta" goes up in response to the higher level of financial risk. In turn, the higher beta leads to an increase in the expected rate of return on levered stock. This MPT-based interpretation of MM Proposition II can be used to reestablish the notion that the weighted average cost of capital and (therefore) economic profit and enterprise value are invariant to the corporate debt decision.

According to Hamada, the beta of the levered stock is linearly related to the debt-to-equity ratio according to:[29]

$$B_{e,m} = B_{u,m}(1 + D/E)$$

In this expression, $B_{e,m}$ is the beta of the levered stock, $B_{u,m}$ is the beta of the unlevered stock (or the beta of the unlevered firm), and D/E is the familiar debt-to-equity ratio that we spoke of before. With a CAPM substitution into the general weighted average cost of capital formula, it can be shown that the cost of capital for the levered firm is again equal to the cost of capital of the unlevered firm.

As Hamada contends, the levered $wacc$ is equal to the unlevered $wacc$ because the beta of the levered firm, $B_{l,m}$, is equal to the beta of the unlevered firm, $B_{u,m}$. Accordingly, the MM-CAPM cost of capital can be expressed as:

$$wacc_l = wacc_u$$
$$= r_f + (r_m - r_f)B_{u,m}$$

In this cost of capital expression, the beta of the levered firm is equal to the beta of the unlevered firm, $B_{u,m}$. Consequently, in the combined MM-CAPM view, corporate debt policy has no impact on the levered firm's cost of capital and, therefore, its economic profit and enterprise value.

CAPM Limitations

While CAPM is a robust formulation for the pricing of investment risk, several empirical studies have shown that beta alone does not fully account for the observed average returns in the marketplace. For example, in a long-term study using common stock returns over the 1941-1990 period, Eugene Fama and Kenneth French conclude that the celebrated CAPM relationship between average returns and beta risk is "weak," and "perhaps nonexistent."[30] Moreover, they also find that "two easily measured variables," including size (equity capitalization) and price-to-book value provide a "simple and powerful characterization of the cross-section of average stock returns for the 1963-1990 period."

While disagreement exists about why CAPM does not fully account for observed average returns, most empirical studies uncover several challenges to the

---

[29] Hamada's beta formula is similar in a world with corporate taxes and *no* deductibility of debt interest expense. As with MM, the tax issue boils down to the cost of capital consequence of deductibility of the debt interest expense. If Miller's 1977 argument is applicable, then Hamada's beta formula applies in a world without *and* with tax deductibility of debt interest expense.

[30] Eugene Fama and Kenneth French, "The Cross Section of Expected Stock Returns," *Journal of Finance* (June 1992).

single (beta) factor expected return model. These findings are of course problematic from a cost of capital — and therefore economic profit and NPV — perspective because the expected return on common stock is a critical component of the weighted average cost of capital. Indeed, CAPM anomalies are especially problematic for unlevered firms because the expected return on equity *is* the cost of capital.

Aside from the shortcomings of CAPM beta, the debate over what to use as an equity risk premium is a topic that should be discussed more given the sensitivity of enterprise value to changes in the cost of capital. Ibbotson Associates views the equity risk premium as the reward which investors require to accept the uncertain outcomes associated with equity securities.[31] The size of the risk premium will depend upon the extent of the risk and the investment horizon. Many consultants who utilize a CAPM framework tend to use the long-term (1926 to present) arithmetic (or geometric) mean return on large company stocks less the historical risk-free rate, resulting in a risk premium around 5% to 7%. Sell-side investment firms also tend to utilize a static equity risk premium, albeit a lower figure; generally 2% to 4% reflecting a shorter excess return period. The authors, as buy-side practitioners believe that a dynamic, *forward-looking* equity risk premium is most appropriate and have developed a proprietary model to calculate such.[32] Similarly, Jay Gould of StockVal, the security database and valuation modeling firm, developed a dynamic equity risk premium using an earnings discount model on a basket of companies with the highest degree of earnings certainty. No matter what system used, we believe that it is imperative to advance the theory on the equity risk premium so that there is greater accuracy of economic profit calculations and appropriate matching of time horizons.

CAPM Alternatives

There are of course alternative approaches to using CAPM when estimating the cost of equity capital. In this context, one of the authors[33] has developed a proprietary model akin to credit scoring that estimates a firm's required return on equity capital based on incorporation of a risk-free interest rate, base-dynamic market risk premium, plus an incremental premium determined from fundamental factors such as equity size (market capitalization), excess stock price volatility, leverage, *and* the growth and stability of a firm's economic profit over time. Holding other equity risk considerations the same, firms that have demonstrated stability (or consistency) in their company-specific economic profit growth are assigned a *lower* cost of capital than companies that otherwise have substantial firm-specific volatility in economic profit.

---

[31] See, for example, *Stocks, Bonds, Bills and Inflation — 2001 Yearbook* (Chicago: Ibbotson Associates, 2001).

[32] We provide an overview of this equity-risk pricing model in the next section.

[33] James A. Abate, cited in James A. Abate, Frank J. Fabozzi, and James L. Grant, "Equity Analysis using Value-Based Metrics," Exhibit 4 in T. Daniel Coggin and Frank J. Fabozzi (Eds.), *Applied Equity Valuation* (New Hope, PA: Frank J. Fabozzi Associates, 1999). The market premium in this proprietary EP factor model is based on the risk premium associated with the "least risky" equity in the marketplace.

Exhibit 11: Required Return versus Company Specific Risk Score

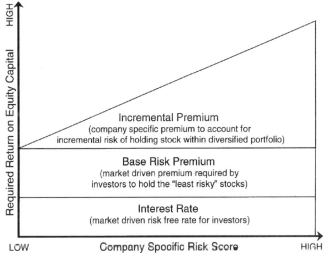

Source: James A. Abate, Frank J. Fabozzi, and James L. Grant, "Equity Analysis using Value-Based Metrics," Exhibit 4 in T. Daniel Coggin and Frank J. Fabozzi (Eds.), *Applied Equity Valuation* (New Hope, PA: Frank J. Fabozzi Associates, 1999).

Exhibit 11 provides a snapshot on how the required return on equity capital is estimated in this proprietary economic profit model. As shown, the model begins with a market driven interest rate and market based risk premium. To this, a company-specific risk premium is added to account for fundamental factors such as size and leverage, as well as the firm-specific risk premium implications from a scoring measure on the volatility of economic profit. The lower the company-specific EP volatility score, the lower the required return on equity capital. Conversely, the higher the company-specific EP risk score, the higher the assessed cost of equity capital. One obvious implication of the expected return model shown in Exhibit 11 is that a growth company with consistent economic profit growth will be assigned a lower cost of equity capital than a similarly positioned growth company (similar size, leverage, and industry considerations, for example) with substantial volatility (high company-specific risk score) in its economic profit profile.

There are of course other equity-risk pricing models that are used in lieu of the single (beta) factor CAPM. Fundamental factor models like BARRA have been used to build forecasts of equity returns based on beta, size, price to book ratio, earnings yield, and earnings momentum — among other "common factors" — that influence expected security returns.[34] Also, macro-factor models — such as Burmeister, Ibbotson, Roll, and Ross as well as Salomon RAM (Risk Attribute

---

[34] However, the obvious limitation of using established fundamental factor models to estimate the required return on equity capital is that the factors are often based on traditional accounting measures of profit and leverage.

Model) — have been used in practice to estimate the expected (or required) return on equity in the context of interest rate and economy-wide changes in corporate profits, among other macro-factors. In the next section, we'll introduce a fundamental EP factor model that can be used to provide insights into the estimation of expected returns *beyond* the single factor CAPM.

FACTOR MODEL APPROACH TO WACC ESTIMATION

In an attempt to capture systematic market (beta) and potential systematic *non*-market factors that influence expected security returns — and therefore the expected return on levered stock — factor models are now used in place of the single factor CAPM. In a nutshell, a factor model attributes expected return to a set of common factors that impact securities in the marketplace.

For example, an economic profit-based factor model with a systematic market factor (captured by beta[35]) and three systematic non-market factors can be represented as follows:

$$r_e = \text{CAPM} + b_1\text{Size} + b_2\text{NPV/Capital} + b_3\text{SDEP}$$

In this expression, r_e is the expected return on common stock. The standardized systematic *non*-market factors in the equation are represented by size (equity capitalization), NPV-to-Capital ratio, and the standard deviation of economic profit (SDEP). Also, the set of "b_i" coefficients represents the sensitivity of stock returns to the respective common factor.

We include size in the equity risk-pricing model for consistency with Fama-French. In *practice*, we recognize the empirical findings of Jensen, Johnson, and Mercer who suggest that equity size (especially, small cap stocks) may be endogenous to pervasive macroeconomic factors including interest rate developments and monetary policy.[36] Also, following Grant[37] and Yook and McCabe,[38] we include the NPV-to-Capital ratio in our economic profit factor model to capture the extra market risk associated with distressed or troubled firms.[39]

---

[35] Following Hamada, we assume in this EP-based factor model illustration that leverage is "fully reflected" in CAPM beta. For theoretical insight, see Robert S. Hamada, "Portfolio Analysis, Market Equilibrium, and Corporation Finance."

[36] Gerald Jensen, Robert Johnson, and Jeffrey Mercer, "The Inconsistency of Small-Firm and Value Stock Premiums," *Journal of Portfolio Management* (Winter 1998).

[37] James L. Grant, *Foundations of Economic Value Added* (New Hope, PA: Frank J. Fabozzi Associates, 1997).

[38] Ken C. Yook and George M. McCabe, "An Examination of MVA in the Cross-Section of Expected Stock Returns," *Journal of Portfolio Management* (Spring 2001).

[39] In our factor model, we employ the NPV-to-capital ratio rather than (Fama-French) price-to-book value ratio for two reasons: (1) the price/book ratio is plagued by accounting problems due to book value, and, most importantly, (2) NPV is a direct measure of wealth creation.

Exhibit 12: Standardization of Volatility of EP Factor in Unit Normal Distribution

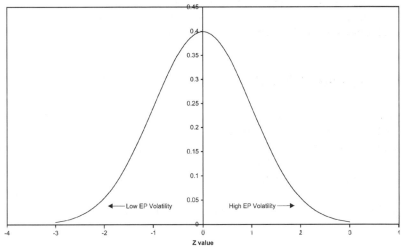

That is, the NPV-to-Capital ratio is a measure of a company's ability (or lack thereof) to invest in wealth creating projects. It is therefore a measure of company *strength* and resilience.[40] In this context, wealth creators have a high NPV-to-Capital ratio, while wealth destroyers have a low to negative NPV-to-Capital ratio — due to their fundamental inability to invest in projects that have an after-tax return on invested capital that exceeds the cost of capital.

Consequently, we argue that investors require a high expected return for investing in stocks of troubled firms — companies with relatively low to negative NPV-to-Capital ratio — while comparatively low expected return for investing in the stocks of stable and robust firms — namely, companies with strongly positive NPV. Moreover, we include the standard deviation of economic profit, SDEP, in the equity risk-pricing model to account for the market-adjusted volatility in a company's economic profit.

Factor Standardization Procedure

In a factor model, the factor values are standardized in a probability distribution called the "unit normal distribution." In a nutshell, this means that if the factor value for a stock were consistent with the average factor value for the representative stock in the marketplace, then the stock's standardized factor value would be zero. Atypical factor values can then be conveniently assigned in terms of standard deviation units from zero. Exhibit 12 shows how the standardization procedure works for the volatility of economic profit factor, SDEP.

[40] There are of course instances where the NPV-to-Capital ratio might reflect other economic profit factors such as cyclicality.

Exhibit 13: Standardized Factor Values

Factor:	Company A (Wealth Creator)	Company B (Wealth Destroyer)
Size (*equity cap*)	0.0	0.0
NPV/Capital ratio (*strength*)	2.0	−2.0
EP Volatility (*stability*)	−1.0	1.0

Exhibit 12 shows that if a company had an abnormally high volatility of economic profit, then its standardized factor value would be located to the right of zero in the unit normal distribution. Recall that a standardized factor value of zero is associated with the average firm in a market index. On the other hand, if a company had a relatively stable economic profit, then its standardized volatility of economic profit measure would be less than zero — a sign of economic profit stability in the marketplace. Moreover, this same kind of logic can be applied to other common factors including the size factor and the standardized NPV-to-Capital ratio.

As a practical illustration, Exhibit 13 shows the standardized factor values for the stocks of two companies. While the stocks of companies A and B have a market capitalization (that is, standardized size factors of zero) that is representative of stocks that would show up in a market "index" fund, these companies are fundamentally different in their ability to create wealth.[41] Indeed, Company A is a powerful wealth creator. This is because its standardized NPV-to-Capital ratio is *plus* two standard deviations from the average company in the marketplace.

Conversely, Company B with presumably negative NPV is a wealth destroyer. This is because its standardized NPV-to-Capital ratio is *minus* two standard deviations from the average company. Other things the same, investors should require a relatively low expected return to hold the stock of Company A, and a relatively high expected return to hold the stock of Company B.

Exhibit 13 also reveals that Company A is a stable company with relatively low volatility in its economic profit. In this context, Company A's standardized EP volatility factor is negative. Conversely, Company B has a high degree of economic profit uncertainty as manifest in its standardized EP volatility factor that is greater than zero. Taken together, the standardized NPV-to-Capital and EP volatility factors reinforce the notion that Company A is a powerful and consistent wealth creator, while Company B is a risky, troubled firm that in turn requires a high expected return on its stock.

Factor Model Illustration of Expected Return on Equity

Let's now "roll up" the individual factor contributions to estimate the required return on the stocks of Companies A and B. As mentioned before, each factor

---

[41] Consistent with our explanation in Chapter 4, this is an EP-based quantitative way of saying that indexing (and equity styles) *per se* is a naive approach to investing.

contribution is the product of the factor sensitivity (the relevant "b_i") and the standardized factor value. Assuming that NPV strength and EP stability are two common factors that are rewarded in real world financial markets, we'll assume that the NPV factor sensitivity is negative, while the factor sensitivity on EP volatility is positive. Drawing from our previous illustration, the factor values and assumed factor sensitivities are shown in Exhibit 14, along with the factor model assessment of required return for the stocks of companies A and B.

At 7.5%, Exhibit 14 shows that the required return on stock A is considerably lower than the expected or required return on stock B, at 12.5%. This in turn implies that the overall cost of capital for Company A is lower than the cost of capital for Company B. We contend that wealth-creating firms are rewarded for their implied wealth creation (*positive* standardized NPV-to-Capital ratio) and economic profit stability (*negative* standardized EP volatility) that in turn manifests itself in a comparatively low weighted average cost of capital. In turn, we believe that risky, troubled firms should be penalized with a high cost of capital for their fundamental inability to create wealth.

REFLECTION AND SUMMARY

We set out in this chapter to show why the cost of capital is central to the measurement of economic profit and wealth creation. Along this line, we demonstrated that a rise in *wacc* has an adverse effect on economic profit and a multiplied (or convex) negative effect on NPV and enterprise value. Conversely, a fall in *wacc* has a favorable effect on economic profit and a multiplied positive effect on NPV and enterprise value. Based on the powerful inverse relationship between the cost of capital and a firm's fundamental ability to create wealth, we argued that senior corporate managers and investment managers must be especially cognizant of the economic and financial factors that lead to a cost of capital change.

Exhibit 14: Factor Model Estimates of Required Return on Common Stock

Wealth Creator:
Required Return on Stock of Company A:
$r_{e,A} = 10\%^a + (-0.5\%) \times 0.0 + (-1.0\%) \times 2.0 + 0.5\% \times (-1.0) = 7.5\%$

Wealth Destroyer:
Required Return on Stock of Company B:
$r_{e,B} = 10\%^a + (-0.5\%) \times 0.0 + (-1.0\%) \times (-2.0) + 0.5\% \times (1.0) = 12.5\%$

[a] $CAPM = r_f + (r_m - r_f)B_{e,m} = 5\% + (5\%)1.0 = 10\%$

After looking at the sensitivity of enterprise value to a change in the cost of capital, we delved into the competing theories of capital structure — namely, Modigliani-Miller *versus* the traditional view — to examine company-specific reasons for a change in the cost of capital. We discussed that in an MM approach to economic profit analysis, the corporate debt decision has little if any impact on shareholder value. In the MM view shareholders are best served when corporate managers look for positive NPV investment opportunities. As a powerful corollary to this, shareholders are little served by managers looking for ways to enhance wealth by simply changing the mix of debt and equity capital on the corporate balance sheet or by other dubious forms of financial engineering.

The traditional theory of capital structure contrasts sharply with Modigliani and Miller. In the traditional view, wealth is created not only by investing in positive investment opportunities, but also by financing those investments with a "target" mix of debt and equity. In the traditional view, it is argued that managers can join investment decisions with corporate debt policy to impact discounted economic profit and (therefore) shareholder value. While the traditional view of capital structure has been embraced in practice — either directly or indirectly — by many corporate managers, its fundamental position on the wealth impact of corporate debt policy is based on the premise that the capital market is largely inefficient.

On balance, we ascribe to the Modigliani Miller position on the cost of capital. Indeed, we recognize that their capital structure view is entirely consistent with the NPV theory of the firm. In financial theory, it is argued[42] that corporate managers can base their investment decisions on positive NPV (equivalently, positive discounted economic profit) opportunities in their efforts to maximize shareholder utility for present and future consumption. Just like established NPV theory guides investment decisions, MM capital structure theory can be used to gain critical insight on the financing of those investment opportunities.

Thus, we believe that corporate managers should spend most of their time striving to find discounted positive economic profit opportunities for shareholders. From a cost of capital perspective, we believe that corporate managers and investment managers should worry about how economy-wide influences — such as interest rates, commodity price developments, and monetary policy — can increase or lessen business uncertainty for the representative firm. In this way, they will have a better understanding of the fundamental factors that impact the cost of invested capital and the wealth impact of cost of capital change. Lastly, the concept of using a dynamic equity risk premium that reflects both uncertainty of outcomes and the investment horizon is one that should be further advanced in academic and practitioner circles.

---

[42] See, especially, Fama and Miller, *The Theory of Finance*.

Chapter 9

External Influence on Economic Profit

A key issue that managers and investors must address is just how much of a company's economic profit is driven by company-specific decisions versus sector and/or market influences. Although questions of external influence have substantial theoretical and practical merit, they have received surprisingly little attention in the economic profit movement to date. Our goal in this chapter is to raise the consciousness of corporate managers and investors about the strategic role of external forces on economic profit and stock price.[1]

The apparent dearth of external economic profit research is troublesome because it makes little sense for companies to devise incentive compensation plans that are linked to economic profit improvement without a more general knowledge of whether a manager is actually responsible for economic profit change. Indeed, it makes little sense to reward (or punish) managers for that portion of economic profit improvement (deterioration) that is driven by sector and/or market influences having little to do with company specific actions taken by the firm's managers. Likewise, from an investment perspective, it makes little sense for security analysts and portfolio managers to adopt an economic profit-based research platform without a model that attempts to distinguish between company specific and external economic profit happenings.

This view that external forces can impact a firm's earnings and stock price is hardly a new one in the study of corporate finance and investment management. Yet, it is surprising how little the question of external market influence has been rigorously examined by corporate managers and investors in an economic profit context. This may be due to the fact that economic profit players were initially focused on the plethora of accounting adjustments (recall Chapter 7) that can be made to go from accounting profit to a more accurate assessment of a firm's net operating profit after tax (NOPAT). Whether or not this is in fact the case, we believe that it is time for corporate managers and investors alike to think more seriously about the central role of sector and market influences on economic profit and stock price.

---

[1] External forces on company earnings and stock price can of course come from many sources. This includes the impact of industry, sector and economy-wide influences on company earnings and stock price. At a later point, we'll explore the statistical relationship between sector returns and market returns as well as the correlation between industries returns and sector returns. Following that, we'll shed empirical light on the relationship between macro economic profit and the economic profit of some prominent wealth creators.

Along this line, we believe that knowledge of external influence on economic profit and stock price is especially important for corporations seeking to better understand what they can realistically ask their managers to achieve in the quest to deliver economic profit improvement and shareholder value. Likewise, we argue that an understanding of external market influence on economic profit is especially important for investment managers who utilize equity fundamental analysis to evaluate the active return and risk tradeoff of common stocks in an investment portfolio.

OVERVIEW OF EXTERNAL INFLUENCE ON STOCK RETURNS

We begin by emphasizing that the established literature on common stocks and the market portfolio is an integral part of a more general understanding of how systematic forces impact economic profit. Anyone who has studied finance — especially investment analysis — knows that the stock market as a whole can impact the performance of any company's stock. Indeed, Sharpe's single-index market model[2] developed during the early 1960s captures the "beta" sensitivity of company stock return to movements in the market as a whole. In addition, the well known beta factor is a cornerstone of Modern Portfolio Theory (via CAPM) in that it provides a risk foundation (albeit an incomplete one) for understanding the expected rate of return on stocks and portfolios.

In addition to the market pull on common stocks, studies by James Farrell, Jr. and Barr Rosenberg and Vinay Marathe during the mid 1970s point to the impact of systematic *non-market* factors on company stock performance.[3] For example, Farrell observed that stock returns tend to cluster into four distinct groups of common stocks. These homogeneous groupings include growth stocks, cyclical stocks, stable stocks, and oil stocks. In 1975, he noted that a low stock return correlation exists among the homogeneous groups, while a relatively high correlation exists for common stocks within each homogeneous grouping.

Farrell's — as well as Rosenberg and Marathe's — pioneering research on the stock market suggests that the performance of any particular stock — such as a growth or cyclical stock — is influenced by at least three effects. These common stock influences include (1) a pervasive market effect on all stocks, (2) a residual return effect due to systematic non-market influences on common stocks, and (3) the company specific return effect of real investment decisions made by the firm's

---

[2] See William F. Sharpe, "A Simplified Model for Portfolio Analysis," *Management Science* (January 1963).

[3] See James L. Farrell, Jr., "Homogeneous Stock Groupings: Implications for Portfolio Management," *Financial Analysts Journal* (May/June 1975), and Barr Rosenberg, "The Prediction of Investment Risk: Systematic and Residual Risk," Proceedings of the Seminar on the Analysis of Security Prices, University of Chicago, November 1975.

managers. Based on this three-way decomposition of stock return, it should be obvious that corporate managers and investors must isolate the systematic market and systematic non-market elements of stock performance when gauging the success or failure of managerial decision-making. Without this return attribution, it should be apparent that a naive look at unadjusted stock returns can — and in many instances, will — result in incorrect assessment of the ability of corporate managers to create or destroy wealth. This concept can have tremendous impact on compensation schemes where we have already started to see attempts at capturing company-specific attribution through "peer set-indexed" incentive stock options and the like.

Moving ahead to the 1980s and early 1990s, several studies document what is known as "anomalies" in the predicted CAPM relationship between average stock return and beta risk. During the early 1980s, empirical studies by Marc Reinganum and Rolf Banz point to anomalous size effects in common stock returns that cannot be explained by the single (beta) factor CAPM.[4] Also, during the early 1990s, research by Eugene Fama and Kenneth French point to abnormal returns associated with stocks that can be classified as small cap value stocks, while Rex Sinquefield (among others) reports that a "value style" of investing outperformed a growth style in the U.S. and international market.[5]

Recent studies have also shed light on the question of external influence on common stock returns. For example, Gerald Jensen, Robert Johnson, and Jeffrey Mercer[6] argue that the small cap premium and value premium on common stocks is not simply a function of time, but rather the result of expansionary or restrictive monetary policies followed by the U.S. Federal Reserve. Indeed, their research suggests that there are strong and consistent premiums when the "Fed" is following an expansionary monetary policy, while abnormal returns to small cap and value stocks seem to diminish when the Fed is pursuing a restrictive monetary policy. Moreover, Jensen, Johnson, and Mercer find that monetary policy has an especially pronounced effect on the return premium (measured relative to CAPM) earned on small cap stocks.

Also, a study by Kenneth Yook and George McCabe[7] finds that the value stock premium can be explained in part by the fact that companies with low NPV to capital ratios have comparatively high expected returns. The authors of the study offer several reasons for positive abnormal returns (again, measured relative to CAPM) on stocks of low NPV companies. These include (1) investor concern about

---

[4] See Marc Reinganum, "Misspecification of Capital Asset Pricing: Empirical Anomalies Based on Earnings Yield and Market Values," *Journal of Financial Economics* (March 1981), and Rolf Banz, "The Relationship Between Return and Market Value of Common Stocks," *Journal of Financial Economics* (March 1981).

[5] See Eugene F. Fama and Kenneth R. French, "The Cross Section of Expected Stock Returns," *Journal of Finance* (June 1992), and Rex A. Sinquefield, "Where Are the Gains from International Diversification?" *Financial Analysts Journal* (January/February 1996).

[6] Gerald R. Jensen, Robert R. Johnson, and Jeffrey M. Mercer, "The Inconsistency of Small-Firm and Value Stock Premiums," *Journal of Portfolio Management* (Winter 1998).

[7] Kenneth Yook and George McCabe, "MVA in the Cross Section Expected Stock Returns," *Journal of Portfolio Management* (Spring 2001).

credit or default risk, and (2) competitive forces (driven by restructurings and take-overs, etc.) that lead to positive change in earnings and stock price. Moreover, Eugene Fama and Kenneth French[8] support the idea that competitive forces in the economy lead to mean reversion in corporate earnings. They find that competitive pressures will lead to positive reversion in the profit outlook of firms with below average profits, while competitive forces will cause the abnormally high earnings of companies of fortune to revert downward to a long-term average over time.

Taken together, the presence of external influence on earnings and stock returns — and, by inference, the presence of external influence on economic profit — is apparent in these studies due to the fact that clusters or groups of companies with similar financial characteristics have correlated earnings and stock returns. As such, the practical implications of the stock market studies that have surfaced over the years is clear: corporate managers and investors must take account of the impact of systematic market and systematic non-market forces on corporate earnings and stock price before blindly ascribing company performance to individual managerial decisions.

THE CORRELATIVE STUCTURE OF SECURITY RETURNS

We begin our statistical journey on the impact of external influence on company performance by assessing (1) the correlative relationship between individual stocks and the market, (2) the correlative relationship between stocks and prominent sectors, and (3) the correlative relationship between stocks and industries (or sub-sectors) of broadly diversified sectors that comprise the market portfolio. Along the way, we'll see the strength of the statistical association between company and sector returns in areas like energy, financial services, health care, and technology. In the section that follows, we'll shed empirical light on the relationship between economy-wide economic profit and the economic profit of some powerful wealth creating firms. On balance, we'll see that industry, sector and economy-wide influences can impact common stock returns and economic profit in a meaningful way.

Exhibit 1 reports the market-based average correlation observed on the stocks that comprise the S&P 500, as well as the sector-based correlations of weekly stock returns within 11 broadly diversified sectors that comprise the market index. In each case the correlations are measured against equally weighted weekly price return indexes during the 5-years ending May 1999. At 0.43, we see that the stock market as a whole has a pronounced positive and statistically meaningful impact on price returns for the average company in the marketplace. This finding is important because it suggests that company returns — and by inference, economic profit — are influenced by a pervasive market effect that is generally outside the control of any particular firm's management.

---

[8] Eugene F. Fama and Kenneth R. French, "Forecasting Profitability and Earnings," *Journal of Business*, (April 2000).

Exhibit 1: Correlation Analysis: S&P 500-Sector Analysis

	Weekly Return Correlation**	Member Count
S&P 500 Companies* (companies with market)	0.431	500
Sector Name: (companies with sector)		
Energy	0.708	23
Financials	0.649	72
Transportation	0.602	11
Utilities	0.593	37
Communication Services	0.57	15
Basic Materials	0.562	54
Capital Goods	0.544	50
Technology	0.504	60
Health Care	0.50	30
Consumer Cyclicals	0.46	76
Consumer Staples	0.43	62
# companies examined in major sectors		490

* S&P 500 and sector indexes based on equally-weighted weekly price returns, five-years ended May 1999
** Correlation measures average of weekly stock return correlation of companies in respective market and sector indexes

Source: James Abate, white paper.

This view that external forces can impact company performance in a meaningful way is also reinforced by sector-related correlations shown in Exhibit 1. In this context, the exhibit shows that prominent sectors have a pervasive positive impact on the weekly price returns earned on companies within the 11 sectors used to characterize the S&P 500. For examples, the average correlation between the price return on 23 stocks that comprise the energy group with that sector index is 0.71, while the average correlation between the return on 72 stocks that comprise the financial sector with that sector benchmark is 0.65. These are sizable correlation values given that positive correlation ranges from a low of zero to a high value of unity.

Exhibit 1 shows that sector-based correlations can be quite variable. With average company and sector correlation values in a range of 0.6 to 0.7, we see that sectors can have a noticeable influence on the weekly price return earned on companies within the more "commodity-oriented" energy, financial, transportation, and utility sectors. While still quite positive, the sector influence on the representative firm in technology, health care, and consumer-oriented sectors is comparably lower — with sector-related price return correlation in a range of 0.4 to 0.5. These sector-based correlations are important because they quantify the commonplace notions that company performance is driven by sector performance, and that sector performance is in turn driven — to varying degrees — by market performance. We argue that it should not be such a surprise for corporate managers and investors to think that correlative sector and market effects are also present in economic profit given the linkage established throughout this book.

THE CORRELATIVE STRUCTURE OF INDUSTRIES

We can of course pursue an industry refinement to see a link between external forces and company performance. In this context, we'll look at the average weekly price return correlation of company stocks with industries (sub-sectors) for several of the sectors reported in Exhibit 1. Specifically, we'll look at the company-industry correlations within the sectors that are largely impacted by the general economy — including the energy and financial services sectors — as well as company-industry correlations within sectors reported in the exhibit having comparatively lower price return correlation in the marketplace. These latter sectors include the capital goods, health care and technology sectors.

Energy and Financial Stocks

Exhibit 2 shows the average price return correlation of company stocks with five industries in the energy sector. As before, we see that the weekly price return correlation of stocks with the energy sector index is 0.71. With respect to industry-based correlation, the exhibit shows that a high and consistent correlation exists between companies and industries that comprise the energy sector. For examples, stocks within the Drilling and Equipment industry have an average return correlation of 0.88 with that sub-sector, while the average stock within the Exploration and Production industry has a 0.81 correlation with that industry index.

Exhibit 2: Correlation Analysis: Energy Sector-Industry Analysis

	Weekly Return Correlation	Member Count
Energy Sector	0.708	23
(companies with sector)		
Industry Name		
(companies with sub-sector)		
Drilling & Equipment	0.878	5
Oils, International (Integrated)	0.827	5
Refining & Marketing	0.825	2
Exploration & Production	0.811	5
Oils, Domestic (Integrated)	0.786	6

Exhibit 3: Correlation Analysis:
Financial Sector-Industry Analysis

	Weekly Return Correlation	Member Count
Financial Sector *(companies with sector)*	0.649	72
Industry Name *(companies with sub-sector)*		
Investment Management	1	1
Savings & Loan	0.873	2
Insurance-Brokers	0.83	2
Money Center Banks	0.795	5
Investment Banking/Brokerage	0.776	4
Diversified Financial	0.751	9
Consumer Finance	0.739	4
Regional Banks	0.718	25
Insurance-Multi-Line	0.705	5
Insurance-Property/Casualty	0.648	6
Insurance-Life/Health	0.619	9

As with the energy sector, Exhibit 3 shows that a high degree of correlation exists among stocks of companies in the financial sector. This is manifest in the relatively high return correlation, at 0.65, between individual stocks and the financial sector more generally. However, with a breakdown of that sector into 11 industries, we see that the industry-based weekly price correlations in the financial sector are more variable than those observed in the energy sector with its five sub-sectors. For example, the return correlation of stocks within the Savings & Loan industry with that sub-sector is 0.87, while the corresponding correlation measure for company stocks with the Life/Health Insurance index is 0.62.

Again, the impact of external influence on stock returns is apparent — this time between companies and industries. Taken together, Exhibits 2 and 3 show that industry considerations have a pronounced impact on stocks of companies within the energy and financial sectors. Taken separately, however, we see that specific industries within these sectors can give additional insight on the relative consistency of external influence on company performance. Along this line, it seems that commodity price developments at the macro economic level can have a pervasive and consistent impact on the stocks of companies within and across industries that comprise the energy sector.

In a similar manner, it would appear that interest rate developments in the financial sector — another economy-wide factor that influences security returns — can impact the average stock within the sector, but — unlike the energy price effect — the intensity of the interest rate effect can vary by industries across the financial sector. Examples of this might include the interest rate sensitive money-center bank stocks where the underlying companies derive a significant portion of their revenue from the net interest margin, versus the more progressive oriented financial service "supermarkets" that have diversified their product lines and asset bases over the years toward relatively stable fee income sources of revenue and (economic) profit.

Technology and Health Care Stocks

As noted before, the correlation among health care and technology stocks with their respective sectors is positive, but comparatively lower than that observed on stocks in sectors that seem to be especially affected by the macro economy — including the energy, financial, transportation, and utility sectors. We'll now look at industry-related correlations within two sectors that comprise the somewhat less market sensitive sectors including health care and technology.

Exhibit 4 shows the weekly return correlation for companies within the health care sector and the industry-based return correlations for stocks within the sector. As shown, the price return correlation between the 30 stocks that comprise the health care sector and that sector index is 0.5. This is noticeably lower than the return correlation observed on company stocks in the energy and financial sectors — two sectors that seem particularly influenced by economy-wide factors such as commodity price developments and interest rate happenings. With seven reporting industries within the health care sector, it's interesting to see that the sub-sector correlations are quite variable.

On the highly positive side, the weekly return correlation of stocks within the HMO industry with that sub-sector index is 0.89. In contrast, the weekly return correlation of stocks within the Long Term & Managed Care and Medical Products industries is noticeably lower, at 0.66 and 0.52, respectively. This in turn implies that broad market effects to a degree influence companies within the health care sector, but with a price return intensity that depends on which industry the particular health care company resides. Intuitively, the level of governmental "control" seems to be a driver in the level of sub-sector performance homogeneity.

Exhibit 4: Correlation Analysis: Health Care Sector-Industry Analysis

	Weekly Return Correlation	Member Count
Health Care Sector (*companies with sector*)	0.5	30
Industry Name (*companies with sub-sector*)		
Special Services	1	1
Biotechnology	1	1
HMO	0.894	2
Drugs/Major Pharmaceuticals	0.669	6
Long Term & Managed Care	0.655	5
Diversified	0.634	7
Medical Products	0.52	8

Exhibit 5: Correlation Analysis:
Technology Sector-Industry Analysis

	Weekly Return Correlation	Member Count
Technology Sector (*companies with sector*)	0.504	60
Industry Name (*companies with sub-sector*)		
Electronics: Comp.Distr.	1	1
Electronics: Defense	1	1
Equipment Semi.	0.929	2
Electronics: Semi.	0.741	6
Computer Networking	0.734	4
Electronics: Instr.	0.665	3
Comm. Equipment	0.633	8
Computer Hardware	0.629	9
Photo/Imaging	0.554	4
Computer Software	0.516	12

Exhibit 5 presents the weekly return correlation of stocks in the technology sector with the tech sector index. Like the health care sector, the return correlation for the 60 stocks that comprise the technology sector is positive, at 0.5. However, this too is noticeably lower than the sector-based return correlation observed for the energy and financial sectors. With 10 reporting industries within the tech sector, it's again interesting to see that the return correlations on stocks are quite variable when measured against the respective sub-sector indexes.

For example, the price return correlation of stocks within the Semiconductor Equipment industry with that sub-sector index is 0.93, while the return correlation among the stocks that comprise the Computer Hardware and Computer Software industries are 0.63 and 0.52, respectively.

ECONOMY-WIDE INFLUENCE ON ECONOMIC PROFIT

Up to this point, this chapter has focused entirely on the correlative nature of security returns. Now, using the economic profit to NPV linkage established previously, we look at the components and behavior of economic profit at the macro level as well as its correlative impact on economic profit for some powerful U.S. wealth creators. As mentioned before, our overriding goal in presenting this research is to help corporate managers and investors better understand the nature of economic profit at the economy level and its pervasive influence on company performance.

Exhibit 6: Macro Economic Profit:
Top 500 Companies in Performance Universe: 1989-1998

	ROIC*	WACC	RROC*
1998	14.1	10.8	3.3
1997	14.04	11.41	2.63
1996	14.48	11.54	2.94
1995	16.14	12.04	4.1
1994	14.26	12.83	1.43
1993	13.48	12.08	1.4
1992	12.84	12.9	−0.06
1991	13.43	13.38	0.05
1990	12.83	13.24	−0.41
1989	14.19	13.39	0.8
Average	13.98	12.36	1.62
StDev	0.96	0.92	1.56

* ROIC = Equal-weighted ROIC of Top 500 Companies in 1999 Performance Universe
** RROC = ROIC − *wacc* = Economic Profit Spread

A LOOK AT MACRO ECONOMIC PROFIT

We'll begin our macro economic profit journey by focusing on the behavior of three economic profit related time series: namely, the U.S. return on invested capital (ROIC), the U.S. cost of capital (*wacc*), and the implied U.S. residual return on capital (RROC). We measure the first two variables over the 1989 to 1998 period — and then, by subtraction, obtain the third series.[9] In our index construction process, we use an equal weighting of the relevant ROIC and *wacc* percentages for the 500 largest MVA-ranked companies in the 1999 Performance Universe.[10] Exhibit 6 shows the percentage values for the return on invested capital, cost of capital, and residual return on capital in the U.S. for the 10-year study period. Exhibit 7 provides a graphical depiction of these macro economic profit series.

Exhibit 6 is interesting in several respects. The exhibit shows that over the ten years ending 1998, the U.S. return on invested capital was quite attractive. Specifically, the average return on invested capital during the 1989 to 1998 period was 13.98%. At the same time, the cost of capital averaged 12.36%. This in turn produced a positive U.S. residual return on capital of 1.62%. With an average residual return in excess of zero, and knowing that net capital spending[11] was

---

[9] It should be noted that the RROC is also equal to economic profit-to-invested capital ratio for any company and the macro economy. In this context, RROC is a not only the economic profit spread (ROIC less *wacc*), but also a size (measured by invested capital)-adjusted economic profit measure.

[10] We thank Al Ehrbar of Stern Stewart & Co. for providing the economic profit data used in this chapter. The 500 companies that we use to construct the economy-wide ROC and *wacc* series are ranked by market value added (MVA) at year 1999.

[11] We cover the critical economic profit role of net invested capital growth in Chapter 10.

positive during this period, we see that positive economic profit was created in the U.S. economy during the 10-year reporting period.

These favorable economic profit trends at the economy-wide level should be of no surprise to managers and investors who have followed the explosive growth in the U.S. stock market during the 1990s — especially for large capitalization U.S. companies like the 500 MVA ranked companies used in our economic profit survey. We can see that a large part of this stock market growth was derived from the decline in the cost of capital, attributed to a drop in interest rates and, arguably, a decline in the equity risk premium (though it is not reflected for purposes of calculating the cost of capital in Exhibit 7.)

Macro Economic Profit: 1989-1998

On a year-by-year basis, Exhibit 6 shows that the U.S. return on invested capital was somewhat volatile over the reporting period, while the U.S. cost of capital trended downward during the 10-years ending in 1998. During the 1989 to 1992 period, the return on capital fell from 14.19% in 1989 to 12.84% in 1992 due to the general slowdown in the economy. It then peaked at 16.14% in 1995 and leveled off at 14.1% in 1998. By itself, the time series behavior of the return on capital would imply (1) negative news for corporate managers and investors during the 1989 to 1992 period, (2) positive news in the post 1992 years through 1995, and then, (3) somewhat negative news as the U.S. return on capital settled in 1998 at the 14% level observed in 1989.

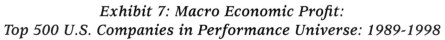

Exhibit 7: Macro Economic Profit:
Top 500 U.S. Companies in Performance Universe: 1989-1998

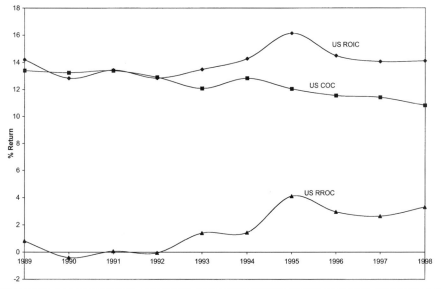

However, the behavior of the return on invested capital during the 10-year reporting period is just the beginning of a story on economic profit change and wealth creation. Exhibit 6 highlights the importance of looking at economy-wide developments in an economic profit lens — namely, capital returns less the cost of invested capital. Consider again the 1989 to 1992 period. While the U.S. return on invested capital was falling, we see that the cost of capital was also on the decline. The *net* result of these seemingly negative (ROIC falling) and positive happenings (*wacc* falling) is that economic profit growth was driven almost solely by the amount of net capital investment as the RROC was stable during the 1989 to 1992 period.

The economic profit picture in the U.S. economy during the post 1992 period is both interesting and instructive. Exhibits 6 and 7 show an especially attractive spread between the U.S. return on capital and the U.S. cost of capital. In this context, the U.S. residual return on capital went from zero in 1992 to a high of 4.1% in 1995 — a year of explosive growth in the U.S. stock market as not only the RROC expanded but net capital investment in the U.S. experienced strong growth as well.[12] These macro economic profit findings are supportive of positive stock market change in the post 1992 years. The economic profit depicted in Exhibit 7 also refute the broad assertion by some notable U.S. economists that investors on the average were inflicted by a measure of "irrational exuberance."

Another look at Exhibit 7 reinforces the notion that economy-wide economic profit (and wealth creation) is not determined solely by the level of capital investment, but is jointly dependent on invested capital returns and the cost of capital. For example, when the residual return on capital peaked at 4.1% in 1995, this favorable event occurred at a time when the return on capital had risen from 14.26% in 1994 to 16.14% in 1995, and when the corresponding cost of capital declined from 12.83% to 12.04%. Consequently, the residual return on capital peaked at a time when the return on invested capital peaked in the presence of a falling cost of capital. In turn, the cost of capital declined due to lower inflationary expectations, reduced business risk, and other factors.[13]

Notice also that in the post-1995 period, the residual return on capital stayed at a high rate of about 3% as the decline in the return on capital from its peak in 1995 was partially offset by additional declines in the economy-wide cost of capital. Indeed, we can draw from this evidence that the state of economic profit and wealth creation is not determined by a set of accounting adjustments that allow one to better estimate the economy-wide NOPAT, nor is the state of economic profit and wealth creation for a society driven solely by invested capital returns and net investment. Indeed, one must also know about the strategic role of the return on capital *and* the cost of capital in a society's quest to create wealth and improve its general standard of living.

---

[12] For example, the S&P 500 earned a total return of 37% in 1995.

[13] Since economic profit spread is defined as the difference between the ROIC and the *wacc*, it is noteworthy that the standard deviation of the two variables, at 0.96% and 0.92%, are roughly the same. This implies that "own volatility" in both economic profit spread variables can impact economic profit in a meaningful way.

MACRO ECONOMIC PROFIT INFLUENCE
ON COMPANY PERFORMANCE

With our macro economic profit foundation in place, let's now look at (1) the economic profit characteristics of some powerful U.S. wealth creators and — more to the point of this chapter — the correlative relationship between economic profit at the economy level and the economic profit of wealth creating firms. We'll begin our look at company economic profit performance in the context of the return on invested capital, the cost of capital, and the implied residual return on capital. We cover the economic profit fundamentals of the top five U.S. wealth creators that were listed in the 1999 Performance Universe for year-end 1998.[14] Following that, we'll look at market-related correlation in the economic profit of wealth creating firms.

THE RETURN ON INVESTED CAPITAL

Exhibit 8 reports the return on invested capital — one of two components that define the economic profit spread — for five U.S. wealth creators over the 1989 to 1998 period. The sample companies include Microsoft, General Electric, Intel, Wal-Mart Stores, and Coca-Cola. The ROIC exhibit is interesting in several respects. At a quick glance, we see that wealth-creating firms have attractive invested capital returns. In this context, the average return on capital for the five U.S. companies is in excess of 15%. Indeed, during the 10-year reporting period, the average return on invested capital for Microsoft, Intel, and Coca-Cola were especially attractive at 47.62%, 29.13%, and 30.84%, respectively.

Also, the invested capital returns for the five U.S. wealth creators are noticeably higher than the economy-wide average return on invested capital at 13.98%. Moreover, General Electric and Wal-Mart's average return on capital, at 15.39% and 16.79%, is attractive too when one realizes that these wealth creators were generating favorable capital returns on a large amount of invested capital. We also highlight the superior return on capital for these "largest-capitalization" stocks (and others not included here) as a principal reason why smaller stocks within the S&P 500, as a whole, underperformed during this period.

While the capital returns shown in Exhibit 8 are quite attractive, they are also quite volatile. For example, the standard deviation on the yearly capital return for Intel and Wal-Mart are 8.8% and 4.68%, respectively. Upon combining the average return on capital for Intel, at 29.13%, with its ROIC volatility estimate, we estimate that a 95% confidence interval on the computer chip maker's capital return for any given year ranges from a low of 11.53% to a high of

---

[14] As we noted before, companies are ranked by market value added (MVA) to invested capital in the Stern Stewart Performance 1000 Universe.

46.73%. In a similar manner, a 95% confidence interval for Wal-Mart's average invested capital return of 16.79% ranges from a low of 7.43% to a high of 26.15%. Thus, managers and investors should realize that fluctuations in ROIC adds to volatility in a company's economic profit spread (ROIC less *wacc*).[15] This view that Intel and Wal-Mart have high volatility per unit of average capital return is also supported by their relatively high coefficient of variation figures (standard deviation/average ROIC), at 0.3 and 0.28, reported in Exhibit 8. Also, in Chapter 3, we recognized a potential mispricing of Intel and how a higher cost of capital might reconcile such variance. In addition, we have previously discussed cost of capital determination based on economic profit and ROIC volatility.

Along the volatility theme, it's interesting to see that Intel's actual return on invested capital ranged from 16.32% to 42.71% during the 10-year reporting period. However, the "good news" for Intel shareholders is that invested capital returns were largely moving in the right direction — as Intel's ROIC of 16.32% occurred in 1989, while computer chip maker's invested capital return of 42.71% happened in 1997. In contrast, Exhibit 8 shows that Wal-Mart investors were not so fortunate on the ROIC volatility and trend. The discount retailer's return on invested capital declined from a high of 24.1% in 1989 to a low of 11.3% in 1996. Wal-Mart's return on invested capital then settled at 13.24% in 1998.

Exhibit 8: Return on Invested Capital for Top U.S. Wealth Creators in 1999 Performance Universe

Year	US*	Microsoft	GE	Intel	Wal-Mart	Coca-Cola
1998	14.1	56.16	19.29	35.44	13.24	31.22
1997	14.04	52.94	18.23	42.71	13.51	36.24
1996	14.48	47.12	17.66	36.39	11.3	35.97
1995	16.14	49.98	17.5	35.74	12.83	37.15
1994	14.26	47.55	14.48	28.29	13.72	35.4
1993	13.48	46.48	11.36	32.12	16	30.47
1992	12.84	43.18	13.25	25.36	18.81	29.13
1991	13.43	40.54	14.45	18.93	21.3	24.81
1990	12.83	44.51	14.22	19.96	23.1	24.86
1989	14.19	47.71	13.45	16.32	24.1	23.15
Average	13.98	47.62	15.39	29.13	16.79	30.84
SD	0.96	4.57	2.59	8.80	4.68	5.28
Var	0.91	20.88	6.73	77.41	21.88	27.84
CV	0.07	0.10	0.17	0.30	0.28	0.17
Correlation		0.491	0.537	0.469	−0.569	0.629

* US = Equal-weighted ROIC of Top 500 Companies in 1999 Performance Universe

[15] We cover the quantitative aspects of economic profit spread volatility in a later section. Suffice it to say at this point that the variance of the return on invested capital is an additive component (as is the volatility in the cost of capital) in the risk to economic profit calculation.

Exhibit 9: Return on Invested Capital: Top U.S. Companies in Performance Universe: 1989-1998

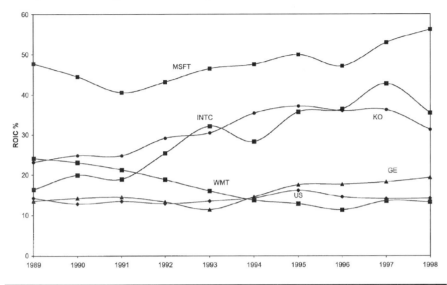

ROIC Correlation Measures

We'll now investigate the relationship between economy-wide return on capital and the invested capital returns for our sample of wealth creating companies. In this context, we expect to see a statistically meaningful relationship between economy-wide economic profit and the economic profit of wealth creating firms. We'll begin the empirical investigation with a graphical depiction of the yearly ROIC happenings over the 1989 to 1998 period for the five U.S. wealth creators. After that, we'll look at the correlative relationship between macro economic profit and the economic profit of our sample wealth creators. As before, the economy-wide ROIC series is based on the equally weighted return on invested capital for the first 500 MVA-ranked companies in the 1999 Performance 1000 Universe.

The graphical depiction of ROIC shown in Exhibit 9 is interesting in several respects. First, it's interesting to see that — with the noticeable exception of Wal-Mart — the return on invested capital series for the U.S. wealth creators are moving — to a variable degree — in the same direction. For example, during the 1989 to 1991 period, the return on invested capital for Intel, Coca-Cola, and General Electric were largely "flat," as was the economy-wide ROIC. During this 3-year timeframe, Microsoft's invested capital return declined somewhat, and then bottomed out at 40.54% in 1991 (which on an absolute level is still quite impressive and indicative of the enormous profitability in the software business). In 1992, we see the beginning of a sharp ascent in the invested capital returns for Microsoft, Intel, and Coca-Cola. In the post 1992 years — at least up to 1995 —

we see that the economy-wide ROIC began to rise as did the return on invested capital for General Electric.

Given that these wealth creators are from different industries, we would not expect to see the same co-movement between their respective capital returns and the economy-wide return on invested capital. However, we would expect to see a generally positive relationship between the ROIC series and the economy-wide ROIC. Along this line, Exhibit 9 confirms our expectations in that the return on invested capital for the individual wealth creators is related in a statistically meaningful way to the return on invested capital for the overall economy and not to each other. In this context, the exhibit shows that the correlation between capital returns — company ROIC and macro ROIC — are in fact related in a significant manner.

This view that economy-wide ROIC and company-based ROIC are correlated is manifest in the correlation values shown in Exhibit 8. For example, the correlation between return on capital for Microsoft and the economy-wide ROIC is positive and meaningful, at 0.49. Likewise, the correlation for General Electric's ROIC and market-based capital return is also positive and significant at 0.54. On the other hand, Wal-Mart's return on capital is negatively related to market ROIC during the 1989-1998 years. This negative relationship occurred in part because the economy-wide ROIC was rising during the post 1992 years while Wal-Mart's invested capital returns were largely falling during the 10-year reporting period. Exhibit 8 reports that the discount retailer's ROIC correlation with that of the economy was −0.57.

THE COST OF INVESTED CAPITAL

As we emphasized in Chapter 8, the cost of capital is a central element in the economic profit calculation. After all, economic profit is the simple difference between a company's net operating profit after tax (NOPAT) and the dollar cost of capital. Other things the same, a rise in the cost of capital causes economic profit (and stock price) to fall, while a decline in cost of capital causes economic profit (and stock price) to rise. However, as with the firm's NOPAT and return on invested capital, a company's capital costs can be impacted by external factors that induce changes in economic profit and stock price.

Indeed, as we will shortly explain, the systematic relationship between interest rate happenings at the economy level and the cost of capital for wealth creating firms seems stronger than the correlative relationship between the return on invested capital and the economy-wide ROIC. We'll also point out that interaction between the return on invested capital and the cost of capital provides additional insight for corporate managers and investors on the real factors that determine economic profit and wealth creation.

Exhibit 10: Cost of Capital for Top U.S. Wealth Creators in 1999 Performance Universe

Year	US*	Microsoft	GE	Intel	Wal-Mart	Coca-Cola
1998	10.8	12.64	12.64	12.64	9.82	11.24
1997	11.41	14.2	13.77	15.14	10.55	12.13
1996	11.54	11.8	12.74	13.61	9.91	9.72
1995	12.04	13.09	13.26	14.52	12	11.93
1994	12.83	14.68	13.35	15.7	12.54	13
1993	12.08	12.71	12.76	14.52	12.92	13.1
1992	12.9	14.28	13.67	15.38	14.13	13.23
1991	13.38	16.49	13.63	17.64	14.7	13.19
1990	13.24	16.93	13.62	17.43	15.16	13.31
1989	13.39	16.77	13.68	16.86	15.6	12.37
Average	12.36	14.36	13.31	15.34	12.73	12.32
St Dev.	0.92	1.85	0.44	1.63	2.15	1.14
Var	0.84	3.44	0.20	2.64	4.64	1.31
CV	0.07	0.13	0.03	0.11	0.17	0.09
Correlation		0.838	0.668	0.913	0.949	0.691

* US = Equal-weighted *wacc* of Top 500 Companies in 1999 Performance Universe

External Influence on Cost of Capital for Wealth Creators

Let's now look at the question of external influence on the cost of capital for some powerful U.S. wealth creators. In this context, let's look at cost of capital characteristics for the top five U.S. companies — again, Microsoft, General Electric, Intel, Wal-Mart Stores, and Coca-Cola. As with the ROIC findings that we explained before, the cost of capital findings are interesting in several respects.

Exhibit 10 shows that average cost of capital estimates for the five U.S. wealth creators range from a low of 12.32% for Coca-Cola[16] to a high of 15.34% for Intel. With the exception of Coca-Cola, the cost of capital estimates for the U.S. wealth creators are higher than the economy-wide cost of capital, of 12.36%. In terms of cost of capital variability, the exhibit shows that Wal-Mart's cost of capital was the most variable — at 2.15% or 215 basis points per year — while General Electric's cost of capital was the least variable — at 44 basis points per annum. This in turn implies that GE's cost of capital was the most predictable one among the U.S. wealth creators reported in the exhibit.

A closer look at Exhibit 10 shows that the cost of capital declined across the board for the five U.S. wealth creators reported during the 1989 to 1998

---

[16] Al Ehrbar quips that Coca-Cola uses a 12% cost of capital because it's 1% per month! For interesting case discussion of companies that use economic profit principles to enhance shareholder value, see Al Ehrbar, *EVA: The Real Key to Creating Wealth* (New York: John Wiley and Sons, 1998).

period. This is especially interesting when viewed in context of the economy-wide decline in the cost of capital during the 10-year reporting period. At year-end 1989, the U.S. cost of capital stood at 13.39%. It then declined by 259 basis points during the interim to settle at 10.8% at year-end 1998. In a similar manner, we see a consistent (as should be the case when using a single factor CAPM framework) decline in the cost of capital estimates for the five U.S. wealth creators. During the 10 years ending 1998, the cost of capital for Microsoft and Intel declined from 16.77% and 16.86%, respectively, to 12.64%. Over the same period, General Electric and Coca-Cola's cost of capital fell too — by over 100 basis points — presumably due (in part) to the economy-wide decrease in the U.S. cost of capital.

This view that external influence has a pervasive impact on the cost of capital for wealth creating firms is reinforced by the correlation estimates shown in Exhibit 10. Specifically, the exhibit shows that the correlation between changes in the economy-wide cost of capital and the cost of capital for our sample wealth creators ranges from 0.67 and 0.69 for General Electric and Coca-Cola, on up to economy-wide correlation values of 0.91 and 0.95 for Intel and Wal-Mart Stores, respectively. Indeed, with correlation values in excess of 0.6, the economy-wide correlations among the cost of capital estimates for the five wealth creators are higher than those observed for their return on invested capital.

At 0.84, the correlation between Microsoft's cost of capital and the economy-wide cost of capital is especially interesting because (1) the computer software maker has no long-term debt outstanding, and (2) its opportunity cost of capital — in the absence of any observable debt outstanding — has a correlative relationship with the economy just like the systematic cost of capital pull for all companies in the marketplace. Moreover, Intel and Coca-Cola are also interesting in this respect with a tiny amount of long-term debt outstanding. Exhibit 11 presents a graphical depiction of the economy-wide decline in the cost of capital during the 1989 to 1998 period, with an overlay of the volatile decline in the cost of capital estimates for the five U.S. wealth creators.

THE RESIDUAL RETURN ON CAPITAL

As expected, we have found that external influence has a pervasive impact on the two components that define the economic profit spread — the return on invested capital and the cost of capital. Let's now look at the time series behavior of the residual return on capital during the 1989 to 1998 period. As noted before, the residual return on capital — alternatively, the economic profit spread — is the difference between the return on capital and the cost of capital. We focus our attention on the U.S. residual return on capital and the economic profit spread for the top five U.S. wealth creators in the 1999 Performance Universe.

Exhibit 11: Cost of Capital: Top U.S. Companies in
Performance Universe: 1989-1998

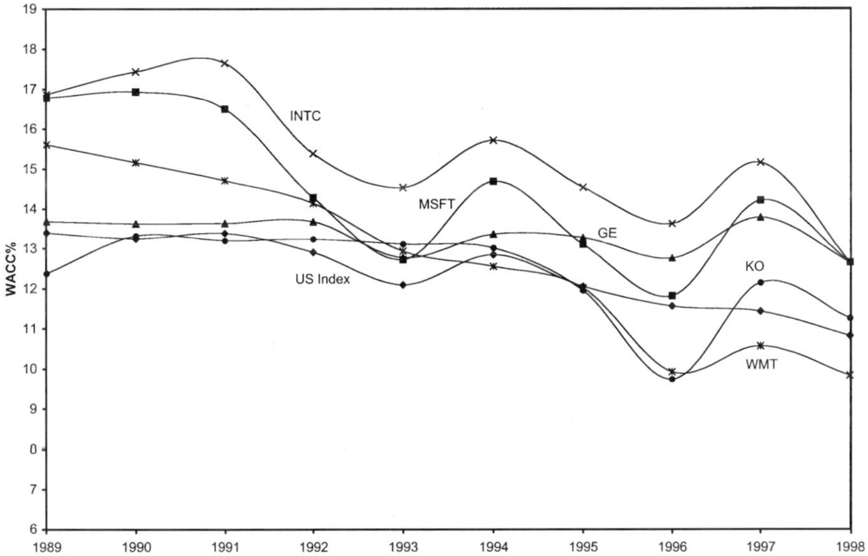

Exhibit 12 shows that the average residual return on capital for the five U.S. wealth creators is considerably higher than the economy-wide RROC during the 10-year reporting period. For examples, the RROC values for Microsoft, Intel, and Coca-Cola were especially attractive at 33.26%, 13.78%, and 18.52%, respectively. These economic profit figures are considerably higher than the economy-wide RROC, at 1.62%. Moreover, General Electric and Wal-Mart's average residual return on capital were attractive too, at 2.08% and 4.06%, when one realizes that their invested capital is generally higher than that observed for companies such as Microsoft and Coca-Cola. In this context, we emphasize that the economic profit spread times the amount of invested capital determines the dollar economic profit in any given year.[17]

The year-to-year behavior of the economic profit spread shown in Exhibit 12 is interesting too. As we noted before, the economy-wide residual return on capital was largely flat through 1992. It then turned positive in 1993 at 1.4%, peaked in 1995 at 4.1%, and then settled at 3.3% in 1998. By comparison, it's interesting to see that Microsoft's exceptional RROC declined slightly during the 1989 to 1991 period, and then began a relatively steady climb up to 43.52% by year-end 1998. Like Microsoft, Intel's residual return on capital "popped" in

---

[17] Along this line, it's interesting to note that while General Electric's RROC was sharply lower than that observed for Microsoft, Intel, and Coca-Cola, its dollar economic profit was both attractive and competitive. For example, at $4.37 billion for 1998, GE's economic profit was the highest among the top five U.S. wealth creators in our sample. In turn, General Electric's invested capital base at year-end 1997 was some 6 times the amount of capital employed at Microsoft and Coca-Cola.

1992 as the computer chip maker came out of an economic slump and began its powerful climb to a residual return on capital of 27.57% in 1997.

Exhibit 12 also shows that Coca-Cola experienced a noticeable rise in its residual return on capital during 1992. The beverage firm's RROC was around 11% during the 1989 to 1991 years, and then jumped to 15.9% in 1992. After that, Coke's residual return on capital rose above the 20% level and peaked in 1996 at 26.25%. General Electric's RROC was largely flat through 1993. After that, GE experienced a steady climb in its residual return on capital — rising from –1.4% in 1993 to 6.65% in 1998. By contrast, we see that Wal-Mart's residual capital return declined generally over the 10-year reporting period. The exhibit reports that the discount retailer's RROC declined from a high of 8.5% in 1989, to 0.83% in 1995, and then settled at 3.42% at year-end 1998. Exhibit 13 provides a graphical depiction of the time series behavior of the individual RROC series and that of the U.S. economy.

While we recognize that the residual return on capital series for each company is unique, we also recognize that the external influence — due to ROIC and COC happenings at the sector and economy level — can have a strong, yet varying, influence on the economic profit for any given firm. Exhibit 12 confirms our expectations in that a high correlation exists among the company-based residual return on capital series and the economy-wide RROC series. In this context, the market-based correlations in the residual return on capital series for Microsoft, General Electric, Intel, and Coca-Cola exceed 0.8. These correlation values range from 0.81 for General Electric up to Microsoft's RROC correlation with the market of 0.87. While Wal-Mart's market-based RROC was strongly negative over the 10-year reporting period, it too is interesting when examined in an economic profit context.

Exhibit 12: Residual Return on Capital for Top U.S. Wealth Creators in 1999 Performance Universe

Year	US*	Microsoft	GE	Intel	Wal-Mart	Coca-Cola
1998	3.3	43.52	6.65	22.8	3.42	19.98
1997	2.63	38.74	4.46	27.57	2.96	24.11
1996	2.94	35.32	4.92	22.78	1.39	26.25
1995	4.1	36.89	4.24	21.22	0.83	25.22
1994	1.43	32.87	1.13	12.59	1.18	22.4
1993	1.4	33.77	–1.4	17.6	3.08	17.37
1992	–0.06	28.9	–0.42	9.98	4.68	15.9
1991	0.05	24.05	0.82	1.29	6.6	11.62
1990	–0.41	27.58	0.6	2.53	7.94	11.55
1989	0.8	30.94	–0.23	–0.54	8.5	10.78
Average	1.62	33.26	2.08	13.78	4.06	18.52
St Dev.	1.56	5.72	2.74	10.14	2.79	5.94
Var	2.43	32.73	7.52	102.88	7.78	35.26
CV	0.96	0.17	1.32	0.74	0.69	0.32
Correlation		0.867	0.811	0.838	–0.753	0.842

* US = Equal-weighted RROC of Top 500 Companies in 1999 Performance Universe

Exhibit 13: Residual Return on Capital:
Top U.S. Companies in Performance Universe: 1989-1998

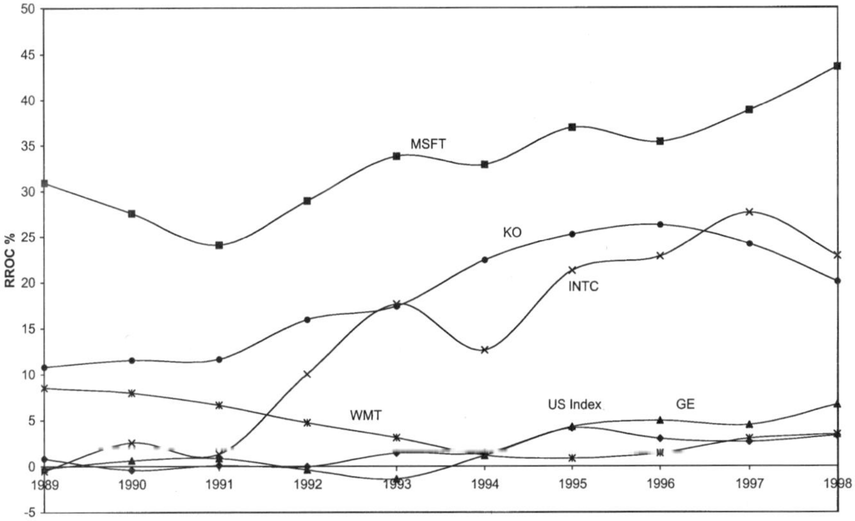

INTERACTION EFFECTS

In the previous section, we looked at the average residual return on invested capital and the time series behavior of the residual capital return. Let's now look at how the volatility (or variance) in the residual return on capital can be split up into three key risk elements. These economic profit-based risk elements include (1) the variance of the return on invested capital, (2) the variance of the cost of capital, and (3) the "interaction effect" that arises from the co-movement (measured by covariance or correlation) between the return on invested capital and the cost of capital.

In more formal terms, the variance of the residual return on capital, V(RROC), can be expressed as follows:

$$V(RROC) = V(ROIC) + V(wacc) - 2 \times C(ROIC, wacc)$$

In this variance expression, V(ROIC) is the variance of the return on invested capital, V(*wacc*) is the variance of the cost of capital, and C(ROIC,*wacc*) is the covariance between the return on invested capital and the cost of capital. In the V(RROC) expression, we view the term to the right of the "own economic profit variances" as the interaction effect — resulting from the contribution of the co-movement term, $-2 \times$ C(ROIC,*wacc*), to the variance of the residual return on capital.

Before proceeding to the data, let's first make sure that we understand how the return on invested capital and the cost of capital make a risk contribution to the variance of the residual return on capital. Note that the "own volatility" in the return on invested capital — as measured by V(ROIC) — adds to the risk that is inherent in residual capital returns. In a similar manner, the "own volatility" in the cost of capital, as measured by V(*wacc*), adds to the volatility of the residual return on capital. In turn, the risk contribution to V(RROC) due to the interaction effect is dependent on the sign of the covariance (or correlation[18]) between the return on invested capital and the cost of capital.

Since the return on invested capital can be thought of as an asset, or more precisely, the income flow generated by an asset, while the cost of capital can be thought of as a liability, or more precisely, the interest flow generated by a liability, we recognize that a negative correlation among assets and liabilities is risk increasing, while a positive relationship (again, measured by covariance or correlation) between assets and liabilities in a (corporate or investor) portfolio is risk decreasing.

Expressed in more practical terms, we can say that the risk of severe compression in economic profit for any given company and even the economy is higher when there exists a negative relationship between return on invested capital and the cost of capital. Conversely, the risk to company and economy-wide economic profit is lower when there exists a positive correlation between the return on invested capital and the cost of that capital. This finding for the correlation goes against the grain because managers and investors (especially) often form their expected return and risk estimates in terms of "assets only" investment portfolios — where negative as opposed to positive return correlation affords the best diversification or risk management benefits. However, one only needs to look at Wal-Mart as discussed previously. During this time period, Wal-Mart's ROIC declined but so did its *wacc* and, thus its RROC was favorably impacted from this positive correlation.

Moreover, while we all prefer a high return on invested capital and a low cost of capital, we need to also contemplate the risk to economic profit when the return on capital falls at a time when the cost of capital is high — do we need to be reminded of the volatile and poor stock market returns of the 1970s! Perhaps this economic profit risk consideration is why the Chairman of the U.S. Federal Reserve, Alan Greenspan, worries so much about inflation and its impact on the economy even though there has been a significant decline in governmental statistically measured inflation over the past decade.[19] On the other hand, a positive

---

[18] The covariance and the correlation of ROC and *wacc* are related in the following way: C(ROIC,*wacc*) = SD(ROIC) × SD(*wacc*) × p(ROIC, *wacc*), where SD(.) refers to ROC or *wacc* standard deviation, and p(ROIC,*wacc*) is the correlation between the return on invested capital and the cost of capital. Unlike the unbounded covariance, the correlation measure ranges from −1 to +1.

[19] Fed Chairman Greenspan is often cited (commended) in the financial press for espousing the virtues of sound monetary policy and, most notably, for attempting to engineer a "soft landing" in the U.S. economy in an effort to eliminate imbalances that lead to inflation and a significant rise in interest rates.

correlation between the return on invested capital (asset) and the cost of capital (liability), implies that ROIC is high when *wacc* is rising — that is, a time when a higher *wacc* may be more "affordable." Also, with positive correlation, a low ROIC will be associated with a comparatively low *wacc* — a cost of capital cushion that helps dampen the risk to economic profit from declining capital returns.

Decomposition of the Risk to Economic Profit

With this economic profit-risk background, let's now look at a decomposition analysis of the variance of the residual return on capital. As before, we'll focus on the economy-wide residual return on capital and the residual capital returns for the top five U.S. wealth creators in the 1999 Performance Universe. Consistent with the formula for the variance of the residual return on capital, we report (1) the variance of the return on invested capital, V(ROIC), (2) the variance of the cost of capital, V(*wacc*), and (3) the economic profit-risk impact of the "interaction effect" between the return on invested capital and the cost of capital $-2 \times$ C(ROIC,*wacc*).

The decomposition analysis on the residual capital return variance shown in Exhibit 14 is especially interesting for both the U.S. economy and wealth creators that we cover in this chapter. At the economy level, it's interesting to see that volatility in the return on invested capital, V(ROIC), accounts for just 38% of the overall volatility in the economy-wide residual return on capital. The unaccounted V(RROC) balance of 62% is explained (roughly) by a split between the variance of the cost of capital, V(*wacc*), and the interaction effect between the economy-wide return on capital and the cost of capital — that in turn is driven largely by C(ROIC,*wacc*).

Exhibit 14: Variance Decomposition: Residual Return on Capital

	US*	Microsoft	GE	Intel	Wal-Mart	Coca-Cola
V(RROC)	2.4334	32.7344	7.5175	102.8835	7.7822	35.2625
V(ROC)	0.9145	20.8754	6.7273	77.4128	21.8783	27.8388
V(*wacc*)	0.8419	3.4369	0.1952	2.6408	4.6401	1.3059
EXCov	−0.3046	−3.7900	−0.2678	−10.2734	8.4312	−2.7530
ADJCov	−0.3385	−4.2111	−0.2975	−11.4149	9.3680	−3.0589
Interact	0.6769	8.4221	0.5950	22.8299	−18.7361	6.1178
V(RROC)	2.4334	32.7344	7.5175	102.8835	7.7822	35.2625
Proportional contributions to V(RROC) from:						
V(ROC)	0.375824416	0.637720192	0.894880398	0.75243206	2.811305542	0.789474215
V(*wacc*)	0.345998422	0.104992289	0.025968479	0.025667909	0.596238073	0.037033251
Interact	0.278177162	0.25728752	0.079151123	0.221900031	−2.407543615	0.173492534
Sum	1	1	1	1	1	1

* US = Equal-weighted RROC Variance of Top 500 Companies in 1999 Performance Universe

A closer look at the economic profit findings in Exhibit 14 reveals that the negative covariance between the economy-wide return on invested capital and the cost of capital during the 10-year reporting period led to an additive risk contribution to the economy-wide V(RROC). As we noted before, a negative correlation among "assets" and "liabilities" in a portfolio leads to heightened risk to an investment portfolio. Again, we all cherish the robust economic growth and falling interest rates that occurred during the 1990s. But suppose — like the 1970s period of "stagflation" — the economic situation were reversed. In this context, we would see increased risk to economic profit due to the adverse combination of falling capital returns and rising interest rates. We emphasize that managers and investors must be ever cognizant about the myriad external influences — including the economy-wide ROIC and *wacc*, as well the "interaction effect" from these variables on economic profit.

The decomposition of residual capital return variance shown in Exhibit 14 also conveys some important economic profit risk knowledge for managers and investors. As shown, we see that knowledge of the behavior of the return on invested capital is important but not enough to explain what happens to a company's economic profit over time. For examples, the volatility in the invested capital returns — indeed, whether market induced, sector induced, or company induced — for Microsoft, Intel, and Coca-Cola accounts for about 64%, 75%, and 79%, respectively, of the volatility in their economic profit spreads. This in turn implies that volatility in the cost of capital and the interaction effect accounts for a range of 21% to 36% of the volatility in their residual capital returns. These cost of capital effects are especially interesting when one recognizes that Microsoft and Intel are largely debt free.

Finally, as we noted previously and as Exhibit 14 shows, the positive co-movement between Wal-Mart's return on invested capital and cost of capital led to a reduction in the volatility in its economic profit spread — due to the resulting negative interaction effect. To the unforeseen benefit of Wal-Mart's managers and investors, the economy-wide decline in the cost of capital (positive ROIC-*wacc* correlation for Wal-Mart) helped to cushion the volatile decline in the discount retailer's return on invested capital.

SUMMARY

We set out in this chapter to examine the impact of external influence on stock price and economic profit. As expected, we found that the systematic influence of the stock market as a whole has a pervasive positive impact on common stock returns. However, the degree of statistical association between common stock returns and market returns is dependent on the sector in which the company's stock resides. For example, financial and energy stocks seem to be strongly influenced by macro economic factors — such as interest rate and commodity price developments — while common stock returns within the consumer oriented, health care, and technology sectors are impacted positively, but to a lesser degree by general market influence.

We also noted that the correlation between industry and sector returns shows considerable variation. For example, a strongly positive association between industry and sector returns is apparent within the energy and transportation sectors, while a highly positive, yet variable, degree of industry association and sector return is apparent in the financial and health care sectors. Consistent with the general theme of this chapter, these stock return findings suggest that managers and investors must be aware of sector and market relationships, as well as industry relationships within sectors before ascribing company performance to corporate managers and investment performance to money managers.

From an economic profit perspective, we looked at the correlative relationship between the two factors that define the economic profit spread. Specifically, we looked at (1) the correlative relationship between the economy-wide return on capital and the return on capital for some powerful U.S. wealth creators, (2) the correlative relationship between the economy-wide cost of capital and the cost of capital for selected wealth creators, and (3) the correlative relationship between the economy-wide residual return on capital and the residual capital returns for selected wealth creators. Not surprisingly, we found that external influence has a pervasive impact on the return on invested capital, the cost of capital, and, in turn, the economic profit spread. We also noted that volatility in the economic profit spread is determined by volatility in the return on capital, volatility in the cost of capital, and the "interaction effect" between the return on invested capital and the cost of capital.

Before moving on, we believe that corporate managers and investors must be especially cognizant of the impact of external forces on economic profit and (therefore) stock price. We hope that the research presented in this chapter will cause managers and investors to take a closer look at the role of the economy, the role of sectors, and the role of industries — among other pervasive external forces — on economic profit and stock returns. For obvious reasons, this external look must occur before ascribing company performance to individual managers and before the outright purchase or sale of common stocks in an investment portfolio. In our view, this is the real "economic profit accounting" that will make the difference for senior corporate managers who strive to create wealth for shareholders, and, of course, for investors who seek to expand their portfolio return-risk tradeoff.

Chapter 10

Strategic Role of Invested Capital Growth

In our previous discussion of economic profit, we focused on the general financial characteristics of wealth creators and wealth destroyers.[1] In this context, we said that wealth creators have positive net present value because they have positive discounted economic profit. In turn, their economic profit spread is positive because the after-tax return on invested capital — both now and in the anticipated future — exceeds the weighted average cost of capital, *wacc*. However, absent from our discussion on economic profit and NPV at the company-specific level is a more robust statement about the strategic role of invested capital growth in the wealth creation process.

A fuller understanding of the preconditions of wealth creation requires a knowledge of whether a company's invested capital growth is positive — as in the case of internal expansion and/or external corporate acquisitions — or whether a company's invested capital growth is negative — associated with corporate downsizing and restructurings that were so vital to U.S. economic revival during the 1980s and early 1990s. In light of our capital growth omission, we seek in this chapter to broaden the economic profit horizon of managers and investors by providing a framework that distinguishes between "good company growth" and "misguided company growth."

The terms "growth-company" and "value-company" get bantered about in the corporate and investment world. This terminology is due in part to the growth and value equity styles that we criticized from an economic profit perspective in Chapters 4 and 5. In this chapter, we refer to growth companies in the popular jargon and real growth companies in an economic profit context. In the popular view, a growth company is often seen as a company that is rapidly expanding. In contrast, we take a real growth company (or "good company growth") to mean a company that is focused on maximizing economic profit and shareholder value. The difference between the two growth views lies in the fact that the economic profit approach links profit and invested capital, while the popular growth view seems entirely earnings focused, and thus is void of recognizing the strategic role of invested capital in the wealth creation process.

Likewise, we attempt to distinguish real value companies (or "good company value"). In the popular view, a value company is one whose stock price is

---

[1] See, for example, Chapter 3 where we explained that wealth creators have positive average economic profit, while wealth wasters have (discounted) negative economic profit. In this basic setting, we presumed that the invested capital growth rate is positive.

147

low relative to some accounting measure such as earnings per share or book value. We take a real value company to mean a firm that is efficiently restructuring — or de-investing out of — a negative economic profit situation in an effort to boost future economic profit and create shareholder wealth.

We begin the chapter with an emphasis on the general relationship between economic profit and capital growth. We then show the relationship between invested capital growth and net present value. We also explain the capital investment conditions that can lead to substantial wealth creation via internal/external expansion, and the capital shedding conditions that can lead to substantial wealth recapture via corporate revitalization activities. After explaining the role of invested capital growth in the wealth creation process, we provide some empirical evidence on the capital growth activities of companies that have created wealth — measured by substantially positive NPV — and the investment activities of companies that have, unfortunately, wasted wealth — via substantially negative NPV.

On balance, we find that wealth creators or real growth companies have attractive economic profit spreads (return on invested capital exceeds the cost of capital) in the presence of positive capital growth, while wealth wasters have negative economic profit spreads in the presence of higher than warranted capital investment activities that are financially imprudent. In terms of corporate revitalization, we emphasize that managers in so-called value companies must take advantage of the fact that downsizing a stale or troubled business having negative average economic profit spread is a precondition for the recapture of shareholder value. On the other hand, maintaining or — worse yet — continuing to expand a troubled company with discounted negative economic profit spread is a guarantee for further wealth destruction. Moreover, investors should take stock (pun intended) of the strategic role of invested capital in their assessment of real growth companies and real value (driven) companies. In other words, capital growth is wealth creating only if accompanied by a positive RROC or economic profit spread.

ECONOMIC PROFIT AND INVESTED CAPITAL GROWTH

We begin our focus on invested capital growth by demonstrating the relationship between changes in economic profit and the level of capital investment. In the model development, we take capital additions to mean those required beyond maintaining the NOPAT earnings stream from existing assets. To focus directly on the strategic role of invested capital growth, we express the change in economic profit for any given year as a function of the presumed constant residual return on capital[2] times the change in total (net) invested capital according to:

$$\Delta EP = \Delta C \times [ROIC - wacc]$$

[2] For simplicity, we take the RROC or economic profit spread to be constant in the model development so that we can focus directly on the strategic role of invested capital growth on economic profit and wealth creation.

In the above expression, we see that the change in economic profit for any given company is determined by (1) the sign and basis point magnitude of the residual return on capital (RROC) — where sign of the economic profit spread is dependent on whether the return on invested capital (ROIC) is higher or lower than the *wacc*, and (2) the sign and dollar magnitude of the change in invested capital (ΔC).

Of course, when ΔC is positive, the firm is making an internal/external (via acquisitions) growth decision, while when ΔC is negative, the firm is making an internal value decision by presumably restructuring business units and/or business processes. In either case — corporate expansion or corporate contraction — managers (and investors) must make a correct assessment of the expected economic profit spread — or expected residual capital return — when making strategic investment decisions.

NPV AND INVESTED CAPITAL GROWTH

Since we have previously shown that NPV and economic profit are linked via present value, it is a simple matter to show that changes in wealth are related to changes in invested capital. We'll use a simple economic profit perpetuity model to show this NPV result.[3] In order to emphasize the importance of capital growth, we'll (again) assume that the return on invested capital and the cost of capital are constant in the model development. The resulting constancy in the economic profit spread in turn implies that changes in economic profit and net present value are directly related to changes in the level of invested capital.[4]

With these simplifying assumptions, we express the change in NPV for any given company according to:

$$\Delta NPV = \Delta EP/wacc$$
$$= \Delta C \times [RROC]/wacc$$
$$= \Delta C \times [ROIC - wacc]/wacc$$

In this simple valuation development, we see that capital expansion or capital contraction can have a meaningful impact on wealth creation. Also, just like with changes in economic profit, changes in NPV are dependent on both the sign and magnitude of change in invested capital and the residual return on capital (RROC) — where RROC is the economic profit spread.

---

[3] We do not of course have to assume that economic profit is constant each year as in a perpetuity model. We could view economic profit as the annualized equivalent of the variable economic profit figures that produce the original NPV. Then, a similar interpretation of annualized economic profit change could be applied to induce a change in NPV.

[4] Our assumptions of a constant periodic return on invested capital and cost of capital in the presence of a changing capital investment level entails many subtleties which we pass over in this simple link between NPV, economic profit, and invested capital growth. For example, the reader may recall the complexity of the cost of capital and economic profit relationship that we covered in Chapter. 8. Indeed, embedded within this cost of capital complexity is the impact of a changing investment-financing decision on wealth creation.

Exhibit 1: Wealth Creation and Changes in Invested Capital

Capital Expansion ($\Delta C > 0$):		
RROC>0	ΔEP>0	ΔNPV>0
RROC=0	ΔEP=0	ΔNPV=0
RROC<0	ΔEP<0	ΔNPV<0

Capital Contraction ($\Delta C < 0$):		
RROC>0	ΔEP<0	ΔNPV<0
RROC=0	ΔEP=0	ΔNPV=0
RROC<0	ΔEP>0	ΔNPV>0

MANAGERIAL IMPLICATIONS

Exhibit 1 summarizes the general relationship between the sign of the economic profit spread (RROC) and predicted changes in economic profit and NPV for a given invested capital growth rate — that is, ΔC is assumed greater than zero, or ΔC is assumed less than zero. The economic profit-capital growth relationships are interesting in several managerial respects. First, and not-surprisingly, the exhibit shows that economic profit and NPV rise when the level of capital investment is expanded in a company having a positive expected economic profit spread (that is, $\Delta C > 0$ and RROC>0). This after all is the essence of real company growth as opposed to illusory company growth that merely expands the revenue and/or corporate asset base without regard to economic profit.

Exhibit 1 also shows that economic profit and wealth decline when a company expands in the presence of a negative residual return on invested capital ($\Delta C > 0$ and RROC<0). Imprudent capital expansion arises in a firm that is more focused on maximizing some financial or non-pecuniary variable, such as sales, assets, or even employees, that is inconsistent with the principles of economic profit and shareholder wealth maximization. Such misguided business expansion typically involves a size-maximizing manager replete with a corporate acquisitions agenda. Misguided investment decisions also arise with a manager, mostly in commodity-oriented industries, who expands a company at the peak of its competitive cycle.

Corporate Contraction

Exhibit 1 also presents two interesting facets of capital contraction. In this context, the exhibit implies that economic profit and shareholder value decline when a manager expands a stale or troubled company with a negative economic profit spread. The decline in economic profit is caused by the positive change in invested capital in the presence of a negative residual capital return (that is, $\Delta C > 0$ and RROC<0). Unfortunately, the manager who expands a troubled firm is moving in a direction of continued wealth destruction for the shareholders.

Exhibit 2: Excess Returns Relative to Capital Growth Rate
"Economically" Profitable Reinvestment

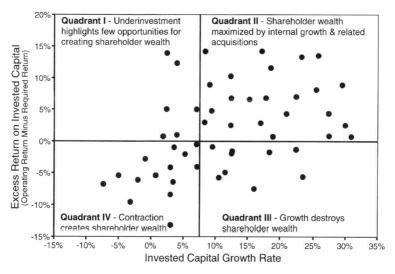

Obviously, equity investors should avoid a firm such as this. Moreover, debtholders would be well advised to demand an abnormally high-expected rate of return on the debt of companies such as this whose actions lead to excessive credit or even bankruptcy risk.[5] On the other hand, a corporate manager in a troubled company that is seriously concerned about wealth recapture must shed those business assets, units, or business processes that are plagued by the negative expected residual capital return. Corporate managers (and investors) must realize that turnaround value — or recaptured shareholder value — can be realized by contracting a stale business with a negative expected economic profit spread. In more formal terms, $\Delta C<0$ and RROC<0, leads to $\Delta EP>0$ and $\Delta NPV>0$.

A SCHEMATIC FOR DISCERNING "GOOD COMPANY GROWTH"

Exhibit 2 presents a matrix of excess returns or RROC and invested capital growth regions to more clearly identify the investment and economic profit com-

---

[5] On the question of risky-troubled companies, Grant argues that wealth destroyers are "plagued" by an abundance of adverse managerial noise — see James L. Grant, *Foundations of Economic Value Added* (New Hope, PA: Frank J. Fabozzi Associates, 1997). In turn, Yook and McCabe find empirical support for a view that low NPV-to-Capital ratio companies have abnormally positive expected returns — see Kenneth Yook and George McCabe, "MVA in the Cross Section Expected Stock Returns," *Journal of Portfolio Management* (Spring 2001).

binations that can lead to substantial wealth creation. Among the quadrants, we see a "good company growth" region (Quadrant II) and a "misguided company growth" region (Quadrant III). In addition, the exhibit shows a "good company value" region (Quadrant IV), and an "underinvestment" region (Quadrant I).[6]

In Quadrant II, we see that growth-oriented companies that continue to expand their capital base with a positive economic profit spread are poised for continued improvement in shareholder value. Investing in positive economic profit and (therefore) positive NPV projects — both now and in the anticipated future — is the essence of real company growth. On the other hand, Exhibit 2 shows that companies that are growing in the absence of positive NPV projects (Quadrant III) are heading in a direction that can lead to substantial compression in stock price and shareholder wealth.

The movement into Quadrant III is most unfortunate for shareholders in companies with managers who naively believe in overzealous capital growth objectives and possess an inordinate preoccupation with revenue and/or asset growth because this will ultimately destroy shareholder wealth.

Value Companies

Exhibit 2 also identifies two de-investment regions, Quadrants IV and I. There are several company types that might fall into these regions. For instance, we could be talking about a slow-to-negative growth company in the automotive, mining, steel, or railroad industries that are viewed — in popular jargon — as "Old Economy" companies. Typically, these Quadrant IV companies are in "restructuring mode" in an effort to drive capital efficiency higher. Also they are companies that have either negative economic profit or limited economic profit potential due to commoditization of their products.

We see that Quadrant I represents firms that are not growing a business despite a positive economic profit spread. Hence, Quadrant I is interpreted as a "underinvestment" region that is reflective of corporate managers who mistakenly downsize — as opposed to upsize — a positive economic profit spread business. In most cases, it is a signal to investors and competitors that a previously good business franchise has hit a growth plateau or maturity, and future expansion opportunities in the core business are limited. One only needs to look at many domestically-oriented food and beverage companies that have hit a slowdown in demand growth for their products. The problem for these "cash cows" usually arises when investors' perceptions shift as the companies move typically from Quadrant II into Quadrant I and the shift in economic profit growth becomes fully reflected in valuation.

In contrast, Quadrant IV can be viewed as a "good company value" region. With capital contraction, we see that companies in this region are downsizing or restructuring negative economic profit spread businesses — since the

---

[6] In effect, we define "growth" — whether good or misguided — in terms of companies that are still expanding their capital bases.

expected residual return on capital is less than zero. Based on the financial math of this region, we see that a negative change in invested capital times a negative economic profit spread (business) leads to a positive expected improvement in economic profit and shareholder wealth. This is what efficient corporate restructuring is really all about.

On balance, Exhibit 2 shows that Quadrants II and IV have the greatest potential for improvement in stock price and shareholder wealth creation. While companies and industries in these regions can be radically different — we would expect that forward-thinking growth-oriented companies would show up in Quadrant II, while forward-looking more cyclical, value-oriented companies would show up in Quadrant IV — we get to the same economic profit conclusion. That is, companies in Quadrant II are growing positive economic profit spread businesses that stand to create substantial shareholder wealth. Likewise, companies in Quadrant IV are restructuring stale or troubled businesses and should also see noticeable improvement in economic profit and shareholder wealth. Consequently, we view these wealth creating and positive economic profit regions as the "good company growth" and the "good company value" regions, respectively.

SOME EMPIRICAL EVIDENCE

In the following sections, we provide some empirical evidence on the capital growth and economic profit characteristics of wealth creating and wealth destroying firms. In this context, we compare the 1-year ahead economic profit spread with the prior 3-year capital growth rate for top- and bottom-ranked MVA groups of companies in the 1999 Performance Universe.[7] For convenience, we take top ranked MVA companies as the "wealth creator" sample, and bottom ranked MVA companies as the "wealth destroyer" sample.[8] We begin our company analysis with the top 10 and top 50 companies listed in the 1999 Performance Universe.

In our interpretation, the wealth creator samples are the "growth-oriented" companies that with proper management should fall into Quadrant II of the company growth and value matrix (Exhibit 2). Following our growth company investigation, we turn our attention to the economic profit spread versus the invested capital growth rate for the bottom 10 and bottom 50 MVA ranked companies in the 1999 Performance Universe, respectively. These samples of stale or troubled companies are the "value-oriented" companies that — with proper de-investment and efficient restructurings — should show up in Quadrant IV.

---

[7] We thank Al Erhbar of Stern Stewart & Co. for providing this economic profit data.

[8] For consistency with our growth- and value-company schematic, it would be more appropriate to sub-classify firms also by their investment activities — that is, capital expansion or capital contraction. This being said, we anticipated that the largest wealth creators would largely show positive changes in invested capital, while we were genuinely interested in learning more about the economic profit and capital investment features of wealth destroyers.

Exhibit 3: Economic Profit and Invested Capital: Top 10 Companies in 1999 Performance Universe

Company Name	1995-97 Capital Growth (%)	1998 Economic Profit Spread (%)
Microsoft	33.21	43.53
General Electric	7.76	7.37
Intel	9.58	22.52
Wal-Mart	5.12	3.42
Coca-Cola	8.70	19.97
Merck	7.83	18.14
Pfizer	17.93	6.91
Cisco Systems	82.25	25.11
Lucent Technologies	13.00	5.92
Bristol-Myers Squibb	4.43	15.54

Exhibit 4: Economic Profit Spread versus Capital Growth Rate: Top 10 U.S. Companies in 1999 Performance Universe

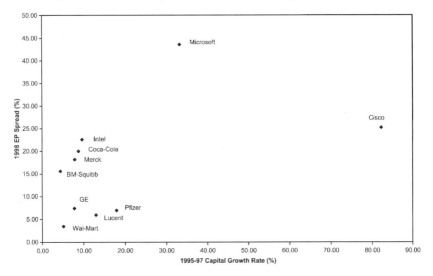

WEALTH CREATORS AND INVESTED CAPITAL GROWTH

We'll now look at the economic profit spread and invested capital growth rate for wealth-creating companies. In this context, Exhibits 3 and 4, table and graph respectively, show the 1998 economic profit spread versus the 3-year annualized capital growth rate for top 10 MVA-ranked companies in the 1999 Performance Universe. The growth in invested capital and economic profit characteristics for these powerful U.S. wealth creators are interesting in several respects.

The graphical display in Exhibit 4 shows that all 10 companies lie in Quadrant II of the returns relative to capital growth matrix (see Exhibit 2). This is evidenced by the fact that widely-recognized growth companies such as Merck, Coca-Cola, Intel, and Microsoft have the beneficial combination of a positive economic profit spread and a positive invested capital growth rate. This in turn is the essence of real company growth as manifest in the economic profit conditions shown in Quadrant II — namely, ΔC>0 and RROC>0 for good company growth or wealth creating firms.

Exhibit 3 reveals that the economic profit spread for a given capital growth rate can be quite variable. For example, if we fix the capital growth rate in a range of 5%-10%, we see that the residual return on capital starts at a relatively low positive economic profit spread of 3.42% for Wal-Mart, and then moves up to an attractive economic profit spread of 7.37% for General Electric. On the high positive side of economic profit spread for wealth creators — again for the specified capital growth rate — we see that the economic profit spread was 18.14% for Merck, 19.97% for Coca-Cola, on up to a 1998 residual return on invested capital of 22.52% for Intel.

At 43.53%, it is also noteworthy that Microsoft as a software company void of most tangible capital, as opposed to human and R&D capital, had the highest economic profit spread among the 10 U.S. wealth creators shown in the two exhibits. While this software giant's capital growth rate of 33.21% was higher than most of the other wealth creators, its growth in invested capital was considerably lower than the reported capital growth rate for Cisco Systems at 82.25%. Indeed, it seems that Microsoft and Intel got a better economic profit "bang" for their capital spending "bucks" when compared to Cisco Systems. While Cisco's 1998 RROC or economic profit spread is especially attractive at 25.11%, the internet-wiring giant had 82.25% capital growth rate over the prior 3-year reporting period. This figure exceeds the invested capital growth rates at 33.21% and 9.58%, respectively, for Microsoft and Intel by a wide margin.

It is also noteworthy that the average economic profit spread (not shown in Exhibit 3) for the top 10 U.S. wealth creators for 1998 was 16.84% with a cross-sectional spread volatility of 12.08%. These economic profit spread figures were preceded by a 3-year average capital growth rate of 18.98% and a capital growth volatility of 23.78%. On balance, we see that top-ranked, wealth-creating companies have attractive economic profit spreads in the presence of positive capital growth rates. This is the empirical essence of real company growth as these wealth creators strived to grow positive economic profit spread businesses. However, we also see that economic profit spreads and capital growth rates are quite volatile among top ranked wealth creators.

Invested Capital Growth for
Top 50 MVA Ranked Companies

While our above focus on the top 10 MVA ranked companies reveals that the "best of the best" growth companies have jointly positive economic profit spreads and invested capital growth rates, we would be remiss for leaving corporate managers and investors with the message that this beneficial economic profit combination will always be observed for these companies. As discussed previously, growth for their products may mature and, thus, limit future positive capital investment opportunities. Also, changes in the competitive landscape can drive down RROCs. In an attempt to demonstrate that not all widely-recognizable growth-oriented companies fall into Quadrant II of the capital growth matrix (Exhibit 2), we expand the company analysis to include the top 50 MVA ranked companies in the 1999 Performance Universe. As noted before, we employ top ranked MVA firms in our growth samples because of their revealed ability to create wealth.[9]

Exhibit 5 shows a graphical display of the 1998 economic profit spread (the dependent variable) versus the 3-year annualized capital growth rate (the independent variable) observed during the 1995 to 1997 period for the top 50 MVA ranked companies in the Performance Universe. Not surprisingly, the exhibit reinforces our previous observation (Exhibits 3 and 4) regarding the economic profit spread and capital growth characteristics of wealth-creating companies. However, the exhibit also reveals some troublesome economic profit and invested capital growth characteristics of other large companies that have previously created wealth.

Exhibit 5: Economic Profit Spread versus Capital Growth Rate: Top 50 U.S. Companies in 1999 Performance Universe

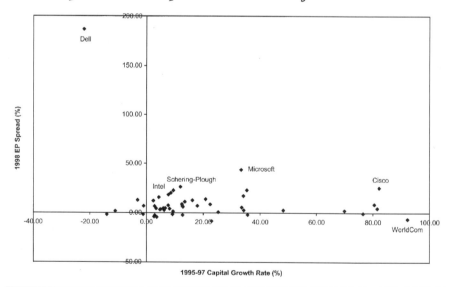

[9] We believe that a real growth company should be measured in terms of wealth creation as opposed to traditional financial measures such as growth in revenue, assets, and accounting earnings that have no direct link to invested capital.

Specifically, Exhibit 5 shows that most of the top 50 MVA-ranked companies were increasing their capital commitments in positive economic profit spread businesses. In this context, 70% (35 out of 50 companies) of the companies in the growth sample had jointly positive economic profit and invested capital growth. New among the sample list of real growth companies — in addition to powerful wealth creators like Merck, Coca-Cola, Intel, Microsoft, and Cisco Systems — were companies like Medtronic, Schering-Plough, and Abbott Laboratories in the health care sector, as well as EMC and Oracle in the technology sector. In the health care sector, Schering-Plough's 1998 economic profit spread of 26.13% was preceded by a 3-year annualized capital growth rate of 12.10%. Likewise, in the technology sector, Oracle's 1998 economic profit spread of 22.89% was joined with an invested capital growth rate of 35.26%. Indeed, these are the economic profit spread-capital growth combinations (recall Exhibit 2) that are manifest in real growth companies having a dedication to wealth creation.

Another Look at Fallen Growth

Exhibit 5 also gives us a look at some potentially wealth destroying companies despite their achievement of ranking in the top 50 MVA companies. Among the 11 companies (out of 50) that had a negative residual return on invested capital at year-end 1998, there were nine companies that experienced positive invested capital growth during the preceding three years. In our invested capital growth interpretation, these are wealth destroying companies that were expanding negative (expected) economic profit spread businesses.

Among these 9 companies that fell into Quadrant III of the invested capital growth matrix (Exhibit 2), we find Exxon and Mobil in the energy sector, Compaq Computer and Hewlett-Packard in the technology field, and WorldCom in the telecommunications sector. In terms of numerical values, the 1998 economic profit spreads for Exxon, Hewlett Packard, and WorldCom were −2.57%, −2.24%, and −6.54%, respectively. Their invested capital growth rates were 2.99%, 12.87%, and 92.19%, respectively. As we discussed previously in Chapter 3, the presence of negative economic profit spread with positive NPV indicates that the market is anticipating a positive spread in the future. Failure to achieve a positive economic profit spread would in principle result in a dramatic reduction in the NPVs for these companies.

Exhibit 5 is interesting in two additional respects. Among the 11 companies that had a negative economic profit spread during 1998, there were two companies that had negative invested capital growth rates. At −1.59% and −1.87%, the 1998 residual capital returns for IBM and AT&T were negative. However, these negative economic profit spreads are paired in the exhibit with negative invested capital rates of −1.07% and −13.91%, respectively. As we noted before, this is a sign of "good company value" as the technology and telecommunication giants were shedding assets having negative economic profit spreads. This positive restructuring activity places IBM and AT&T (again, at that time) in the good company value region — labeled Quadrant IV — in the capital growth matrix (Exhibit 2).

We would be remiss if we did not recognize the unusual economic profit position of Dell Computer. Exhibit 5 shows that the computer maker had a hugely positive economic profit spread, at 186.68%, in the presence of a negative invested capital growth rate, at –22.15%. While as investors, we would be two of the last to say anything negative about Dell's future growth potential — given the computer maker's phenomenal achievement in creating wealth — we must admit that in the context of invested capital growth, it makes little sense to downsize a successful growth company that has a tremendous economic profit spread. To us, Dell is a growth company anomaly, as it fell into Quadrant I of the capital growth matrix at year-end 1998.[10] However, a closer analysis of Dell reveals the firm's success lies in its ability to effectively maintain its components inventory on the balance sheet of its suppliers and limit its finished goods inventory through its build-to-order sales process. In essence, Dell manages to limit its own capital through the use of sophisticated supply-chain software and systems and thus analysis of Dell's return on capital is really a focus on the profit margin component and risk assessment.

We also note that the average economic profit spread for the 50 MVA ranked companies during 1998 was both attractive and volatile. The average residual return on capital for the 50 U.S. companies was 10.75% in the presence of a cross sectional spread volatility of 27.18%. In turn, the preceding average 3-year capital growth rate for the top 50 U.S. wealth creators was about 20% in the presence of cross sectional capital growth volatility of 26%.

WEALTH DESTROYERS AND INVESTED CAPITAL GROWTH

We have now arrived at one of the more intriguing areas of our economic profit and capital growth investigation. Specifically, previous research has documented that wealth destroyers have negative economic profit because their return on invested capital falls short of the weighted average cost of capital. Previous research also emphasizes that troubled companies are "plagued" by an abundance of adverse managerial noise — such that it can be very difficult for a troubled company to dig its way out of a wealth destroyer position. [11] However, the "good news" for wealth destroyers is that the capital growth matrix (Exhibit 2) indicates that a negative economic profit spread is a necessary but not a sufficient condition for continued wealth destruction. That is, we also need to know what a troubled company's management is doing with regard to the level of invested capital.

Specifically, we know that wealth will be destroyed if management is expanding a negative economic profit spread business and is unable to turn around the spread in the future. However, wealth can be created if managers are downsizing or restructuring a negative economic profit spread business. As we pointed out

---

[10] It is also problematic to see that Disney grew a zero spread business (1998 RROC = –0.6%) at a capital growth rate of 76.52% over the preceding three years.

[11] See Grant — *Foundations of Economic Value Added.*

before, the magnitude and sign of the invested capital growth rate — whether it is positive or negative — play a strategic role in the assessment of real — versus that which is illusory — company value. Exhibits 6 and 7, table and graph respectively, present some interesting findings regarding the economic profit and invested capital growth characteristics of wealth destroying companies. In this context, the exhibits show the 1998 economic profit spread versus the prior 3-year invested capital growth rate for the bottom 10 MVA ranked companies in the Performance Universe.[12]

Exhibit 6: Economic Profit and Invested Capital: Bottom 10 Companies in 1999 Performance Universe

Company Name	1995-97 Capital Growth (%)	1998 Economic Profit Spread (%)
UAL Corp.	17.77	3.13
CSX	17.00	−2.55
Cyprus AMAX	2.35	−7.32
US Steel Group	6.80	−1.02
St. Paul Companies	−2.97	−10.29
Union Pacific	19.73	−4.84
Loews Corporation	0.66	−7.81
Nabisco	1.67	−4.09
CNA Financial	−0.48	−10.51
General Motors	−10.53	−7.37

Exhibit 7: Economic Profit Spread versus Capital Growth Rate: Bottom 10 U.S. Companies in 1999 Performance Universe

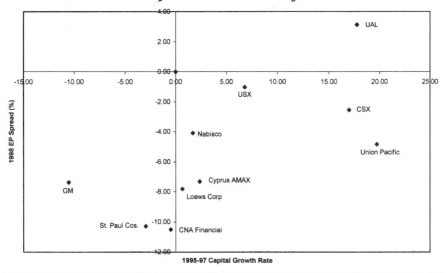

---

[12] We actually used the bottom 11 companies in the Performance Universe due to insufficient data for Park Place Entertainment.

In these exhibits, we see that nine of the bottom 10 MVA ranked companies in the 1999 Performance Universe had a negative economic profit spread at
year-end 1998. Among the wealth wasters, we see that six of these companies
were expanding negative economic profit spread businesses. In terms of numerical values, Exhibit 6 shows that CSX and Union Pacific had negative economic
profit spreads of –2.55% and –4.84% that were preceded by 3-year (1995-1997)
invested capital growth rates of 17% and 19.73%, respectively. Also, Nabisco and
Cyprus AMAX Minerals had residual capital returns of –4.09% and –7.32% with
preceding 3-year annualized capital growth of 1.67% and 2.35%, respectively.
While Nabisco and Cyprus AMAX capital growth rates were lower than those
observed for CSX and Union Pacific, they too were expanding negative economic
profit spread businesses during the reporting period.

In terms of economic profit and wealth creation, it is interesting to see
that General Motors and St. Paul Companies fell in Quadrant IV of the capital
growth matrix (recall Exhibit 2). In effect, these companies were downsizing negative economic profit spread businesses. This restructuring activity should prove
positive for General Motors, as its MVA rank was dead last in the 1999 Performance Universe. Moreover, as a fallen "pillar of capitalism," GM's jointly negative residual capital return of –7.37% and negative invested capital growth rate of
–10.53% suggest that the automotive giant was (and some would argue finally)
taking concrete managerial steps to improve shareholder wealth in an economic
profit context.

Among the 10 wealth destroyers shown in Exhibit 6, it is also interesting
to see that UAL Corporation (United Air Lines) had a positive residual return on
capital of 3.13% in the presence of a positive invested capital growth rate of
17.77%. In effect, UAL was expanding a positive economic profit spread business, which of course is characteristic of "good company growth."

However, referring back to Chapter 9 on "External Influences," a key
analysis step for UAL is to broaden the research to cover the highly competitive,
somewhat commodity-like airline industry as a whole. Specifically, it is prudent
to examine whether UAL's positive economic profit spread is consistent with its
industry peers. Most importantly, one needs to assess whether this strong capital
investment by UAL and perhaps others has the potential to create excess capacity
thereby driving the economic profit spread down or even to a negative level. On
balance, the empirical findings shown in Exhibit 7 suggest that wealth destroyers
are justly labeled so because of misguided expansion of negative economic profit
spread businesses. We will further examine this wealth destroyer observation in
the next section with a larger set of troubled companies.

Invested Capital Growth for
Bottom 50 MVA Ranked Companies

Exhibit 8 expands the focus on stale or troubled companies — certainly, from a
net present value perspective — to include the bottom 50 MVA ranked companies

in the 1999 Performance Universe. Among the 50 (out of 1,000) companies at the bottommost of the survey, there were 46 companies with a negative economic profit spread, two companies with insufficient data, and two companies having a positive economic profit spread at year-end 1998. With mostly negative economic profit spreads — at 92% of bottom 50 companies in the Performance Universe — this finding is consistent with earlier research that shows that troubled companies have a fundamental inability to earn a return on invested capital that exceeds the weighted average cost of capital.

There could of course be a ray of hope for these wealth destroyers if they were currently downsizing negative economic profit spread businesses. However, Exhibit 8 is not too encouraging on the wealth creation opportunity as 31 of the 50 reported companies (or 62%) were expanding negative economic profit spread businesses. For some troublesome examples, we see that companies like Cummins Engine, IKON Office Solutions, and SAFECO Corporation had sharply negative economic profit spreads, −5.86%, −7.11%, and −6.98%, in the presence of 3-year prior invested capital growth rates of 10.83%, 23.08%, and 21.22%, respectively. Indeed, Genesis Health Ventures, Integrated Health Services, and Pioneer Natural Resources were expanding negative economic profit spread businesses, −3.03%, −0.77%, and −20.84%, at invested capital growth rates of 52.96%, 84.55%, and 89.52%, respectively.

Exhibit 8: Economic Profit Spread versus Capital Growth Rate: Bottom 50 U.S. Companies in Performance Universe

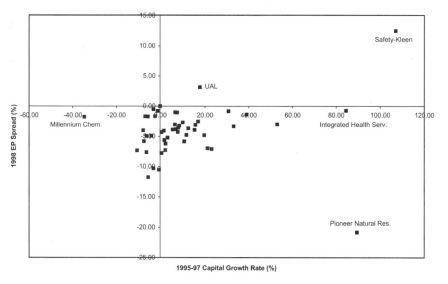

Another Look at Wealth Recapture

In terms of wealth recapture, Exhibit 8 shows that not all of the bottom 50 companies in the 1999 Performance Universe fell into Quadrant III of the company growth and value matrix (Exhibit 2). In this context, there were 15 companies that were downsizing or restructuring negative economic profit spread businesses. These companies lie in the "good company value" region, Quadrant IV. We noted previously that General Motors was taking positive steps to restructure its negative economic profit spread business. Exhibit 8 also shows that companies such as Asarco, Beverly Enterprises, National Steel, and Occidental Petroleum were recently taking steps to restructure underperforming businesses with negative residual returns on capital. For instance, the economic profit spreads for Asarco and National Steel were −11.78% and −4.98%, respectively, in the presence of invested capital growth rates of −5.37% and −6.17%, respectively. Moreover, Millennium Chemicals was sharply downsizing a negative economic profit spread business at a capital growth rate of −34.68%

Exhibit 8 also shows that there were two bottom-ranked MVA companies that actually had positive economic profit spread and invested capital growth. As we noted with UAL, one could argue that the two companies were lowly ranked on the MVA scale because investors were highly pessimistic about their future economic profit potential — even though the year-ahead economic profit spreads and invested capital growth rates for the two companies, UAL and Safety-Kleen, plotted favorably on the capital growth matrix.

SYNTHESIS OF INVESTED CAPITAL GROWTH FINDINGS

We'll now "roll up" the invested capital growth findings for wealth creators and wealth destroyers. In this context, Exhibit 9 displays the 1998 economic profit spread versus the prior 3-year annualized growth rate in invested capital for the top 50 and bottom 50 companies listed in the Performance Universe.[13] The combined focus on this group of uppermost and bottommost ranked companies allow us to make some important observations about the economic profit and investment characteristics of wealth creators and wealth destroyers. These summary observations should in turn be helpful to managers and investors who are interested in the real growth and real value characteristics of companies in the marketplace.

With two exceptions,[14] Exhibit 9 shows that Quadrant II of the company capital growth matrix (Exhibit 2) is occupied mostly by top 50 MVA ranked companies in the 1999 Performance Universe. This suggests that real growth companies are largely doing what they should be doing — namely, expanding positive economic profit spread businesses to create shareholder wealth.

---

[13] For scaling reasons, we omitted Dell Computer in the combined exhibit. We previously covered the Dell anomaly — a technology company with sizable economic profit spread and negative capital growth rate during the reporting period.

[14] The company exceptions were UAL Corporation and Safety-Kleen.

Exhibit 9: Economic Profit Spread versus Capital Growth Rate: 100 Companies in 1999 Performance Universe

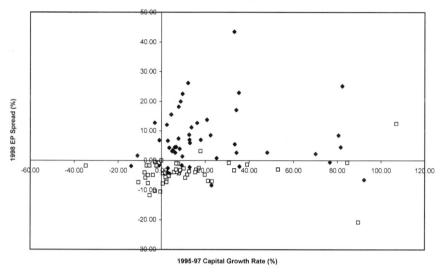

A look at Quadrant III of the capital growth matrix reveals mostly companies that were expanding negative economic profit spread businesses. Just as importantly, we see a preponderance of popularly labeled "value" companies that were expanding negative economic profit spread businesses. These findings are obviously problematic for shareholders in companies that are naively classified as value companies. From an economic profit and therefore shareholder wealth perspective, it makes no sense to expand a negative economic profit spread business even though the accounting profit from such businesses still looks attractive.[15]

With most of the bottom 50 companies appearing in Quadrant III of the capital growth matrix, we are left with the unfortunate conclusion that underperforming companies get into trouble in the first place because they either (1) have little understanding of what shareholder wealth creation is really all about, or worse yet, (2) they choose to ignore the principles of wealth creation and proceed on a plan of expansion without regard to the negative ramifications. Wealth creation means investing in jointly positive economic profit and NPV businesses, while wealth recapture happens when managers recognize that contraction creates shareholder wealth in the face of a currently negative economic profit spread.

To reiterate this key point, there are some companies that understand that wealth creation means downsizing or restructuring a negative economic profit spread business at certain times. As we noted before, about 15% of the bottom 50

---

[15] At the portfolio level, this especially reinforces our criticism in Chapters 4 and 5 of equity management styles — whether "growth" or "value" oriented — from an economic profit perspective.

MVA ranked companies at year-end 1998 had the beneficial combination of a negative economic profit spread and a negative invested capital growth rate. Using a math analogy, we can say that a "negative" times a "negative" produces a "positive" impact on economic profit and wealth creation. This beneficial economic profit combination is one of the managerial keys to producing a turnaround that unlocks the real value in previously underperforming companies.

REFLECTION

We believe that real company growth and the creation of shareholder wealth means expanding positive economic profit spread businesses. In contrast, we believe that capital expansion in firms that maximize something other than economic profit leads to shareholder wealth destruction.

Instead of the investment style labels used so frequently, we emphasize that real company value means downsizing or restructuring underperforming businesses with a negative economic profit spread — since the beneficial combination of the negative residual capital return and negative capital growth has the potential for significant economic profit turnaround and (therefore) wealth creation. On the other hand, continuing to expand an underperforming business with negative expected economic profit characteristics — as manifest in a return on capital that falls short of the anticipated cost of capital — destroys shareholder wealth.

We looked at a sample of companies that are at the topmost and bottommost rank of creating shareholder wealth. On balance, we found that wealth creating companies focus on what they should be focusing on — namely, the expansion of positive economic profit spread businesses. However, we also pointed out that the cross-sectional scatter of economic profit spreads and invested capital growth rates for sample wealth creators were quite volatile.

Unfortunately, we confirmed that the predominance of lowly-ranked companies — from an economic profit perspective — were inappropriately expanding businesses in need of contraction and revitalization. We argued that companies that continue to expand stale or troubled businesses have little regard for what wealth creation is really all about. Worse yet, this unfortunate managerial characteristic appears to be mostly found in companies widely recognized as "value style" investments. This can result in sometimes overly anxious investors awaiting a turnaround but overlooking management's poor regard for shareholder wealth creating changes.

Finally, while many companies have a public commitment to creating long-term shareholder value, they seem to have little understanding of what it means to implement a "good company growth" or a "good company value" strategy in practice. Driving a value creation message throughout the entire organization — from top management to staff employees — is of course a necessary condition for wealth creation, but it is not a sufficient condition for actual wealth creation. Indeed, managers (and investors) must realize that shareholder value is created when companies invest in positive net present value opportunities, while shareholder value is wasted when companies invest in negative NPV opportunities. In essence, real company growth is manifest in wealth creation via capital expansion, while real company value is manifest in wealth creation through capital contraction.

Chapter 11

Reconciling Market Implied Growth Expectations

In our *focus on value* journey thus far, we explained several economic profit factors that managers must assess in their quest to transform an otherwise average company into a great company. In this context, we said that corporate managers must strive to achieve a solid return on the existing capital employed within the business. We said that managers must understand the risk (to value) impact of cost of capital change, and they must invest positively for economic profit growth. Moreover, we said that managers and investors must make a distinction between the portion of economic profit that is due to company specific actions by managers and that which is driven by industry, sector, and market influences.

But suppose that managers follow our economic profit advice in their quest to transform into a great company. By following the prescribed economic profit success formula does this mean that managers will, in fact, have a great company with a great stock? Unfortunately, the answer to this question is not quite so simple. That is, the answer depends on whether, and by what magnitude, market implied expectations of economic profit growth are already reflected in the firm's current stock price. At this point, it is worth reiterating the *five* economic profit considerations that we introduced at the outset of this book — namely:

- generating favorable returns on existing assets
- examining risk in a cost of capital context
- investing positively for economic profit growth
- understanding the magnitude of external influences (industry, sector, and macroeconomic factors) on company performance
- reconciling market implied with internal (or warranted) expectations of economic profit growth

As we explain in this chapter, it is this *fifth* economic profit factor — reconciling market-implied expectations of economic profit growth — that speaks to the issue of whether or not a manager has created a great company that will also be a great stock for investors. By way of introduction, we point out that if internal growth expectations are already embedded in the current stock price, then a company's stock price will fully reflect the positive economic profit steps that a firm is taking with respect to the first *four* economic profit factors that we listed above. In an ideal world where internal and market implied expectations of economic profit generation are joined, managers can *focus on value* in the context of their company-specific decisions that are designed to enhance shareholder wealth.

However, when internal expectations of economic profit growth differ from that which is reflected in enterprise value, then managers must be cognizant of such divergent growth expectations and must take immediate action to reconcile the difference. For example, when market implied expectations of economic profit growth are lower than that which the firm can actually deliver on its current and anticipated growth assets, then managers should, for their company's benefit, take immediate steps to inform the capital market at large that enterprise value and stock price are much too low in light of the firm's economically profitable opportunities for reinvestment of invested capital. We emphasize that for enterprise value and stock price to go up, managers must provide the capital market with "new real growth information" — as opposed to short-term oriented or accounting-based "illusory" information — about its opportunities to generate economic profit both now and in the foreseeable future.

Consider also what happens to enterprise value if market implied expectations of economic profit growth are higher than that which the firm can realistically achieve on its current and anticipated growth assets. In this context, corporate managers and investors need only recall the decline of many of the great consumer-oriented food and household product companies in the early 1990s or, more recently, the free fall in technology stocks that happened during 2000 and early 2001 when companies were unable to meet Wall Street's high growth expectations. Clearly, the focus on earnings shortfalls was easy in a "reporting" sense. That being said, the true culprit was over-investment of capital into businesses with declining rates of return on capital.

As another introductory example that highlights the importance of reconciling economic profit growth expectations, consider the stock of a troubled company where management is restructuring a stale business to generate a positive economic profit turnaround. In this situation, the internal expectation of economic profit growth is now presumably higher than market implied growth expectations. While one would naturally expect the stock of such a company with a newly found focus on value to rise quite smartly in the marketplace — due to the company's positive economic profit steps and anticipation of the benefits — the stock may languish for a time if no one really believes that the heretofore distressed company is the one that will emerge from the abyss of wealth destruction.[1]

In this chapter, we argue that if corporate managers really want to have a great company with a great stock then they need to convince the capital market that market implied expectation of economic profit growth is much lower than that which the firm can actually deliver on its existing and future growth assets

---

[1] As noted before, Grant argues that wealth destroyers are plagued by an abundance of adverse managerial "noise." Without a consistent message of positive economic profit change, this makes it difficult for such tainted firms to turn their depressed stock prices around. See James L. Grant, *Foundations of Economic Value Added* (New Hope, PA: Frank J. Fabozzi Associates, 1997).

for a sustainable period of time. In this context, we argue that managers must surprise the capital market positively about the firm's underlying economic profit stream, and, therefore, its achievable net present value (NPV). When this happens, market implied expectation of economic profit growth should rise to match internal company expectations. This in turn leads to a fundamental improvement in enterprise value, NPV, and stock price. In reality, a "contrarian" approach towards investing in companies striving to achieve (or return to) a great company status, yields the maximum surprise quotient to investors.

In the next section, we'll use a simple constant growth economic profit model to explain how growth in economic profit impacts a company's NPV and its enterprise value. This foundation is helpful because it shows what happens to enterprise value when internal expectations of economic profit growth are synchronous with market-implied growth expectations. We then use this framework to explain why divergent economic profit growth expectations can cause a stock to be undervalued or overvalued in the capital market — indeed, even though managers may be diligently following the first four (of five) economic profit factors that we explained in previous chapters. Along the way, we focus on a real value-based form of company analysis that is grounded in economic profit principles. Finally, we conclude the chapter (and the book) with an emphasis on what forward-looking managers must do in their quest to truly have a great company with a great stock. We also explain how active-minded investors can potentially earn abnormal rates of return on the debt and equity securities of companies by using a disciplined economic profit approach.

MARKET IMPLIED GROWTH

In our earlier discussion on economic profit valuation, we were concerned with how a future economic profit stream can be converted into enterprise value, NPV and, of course, stock price. When expressed in terms of market value added to invested capital, we said that a company derives its NPV from the present value of expected economic profit generated by existing and anticipated future growth assets. While numerous economic profit valuation models exist — with single to multiple growth stages[2] — we'll use a constant growth economic profit model to explain the NPV importance of reconciling market implied and internal expectations of economic profit growth.

Another Look at Constant Growth Economic Profit Model

In the constant growth economic profit model, the firm's NPV can be expressed as:

$$NPV = EP_1/(wacc - g)$$
$$= EP_0(1 + g)/(wacc - g)$$

---

[2] Recall our economic profit valuation explanations in Chapter 6.

In the first expression, NPV is the firm's net present value, EP_1 denotes expected economic profit (at period 1), *wacc* is the familiar weighted average cost of capital, and g is the constant expected economic profit growth rate. In the second expression, we see that next period's economic profit can be estimated with knowledge of the current economic profit, EP_0, and the long-term (or sustainable) economic profit growth rate, g.[3]

Notice at this point in the model development, we made no distinction as to whether the NPV parameter estimates — namely, EP_1 (or current economic profit, EP_0, *times* one *plus* the growth rate), *wacc*, or g — are market assessed inputs in the market value added equation, *or* whether these parameters are based on internal estimates of economic profit made by corporate managers. For this — or any other — valuation procedure to have practical merit, we must specify the variables involved in the NPV estimation process, and whether or not there is a divergence of opinion about the relevant economic profit parameters. By knowing this information, we can gain substantial pricing insight on how a real growth-oriented company can reap the benefits of being a great company and a great stock, and how a currently troubled company can elicit meaningful positive change in its low expectations stock price.

Company versus Market Implied Growth

For convenience, we'll focus on two primary constituencies that make a regular assessment of the firm's market value added. In particular, we discuss (1) the capital market at large, which in turn allows us to reflect on a market consensus about economic profit parameters, and (2) a company's senior managers, which allows us to reflect on internal economic profit parameters. Along the way, we'll use the letter "m" to denote market-assessed estimates of economic profit parameters, and the letter "c" to denote company or internal expectations of economic profit parameters.

Since our emphasis in this concluding chapter concerns the pricing implications of a divergence of opinion about sustainable economic profit growth rates, we'll assume that market and company estimates of *current* economic profit, EP_0, and the cost of invested capital, *wacc*, are the same. At the same time, we'll assume that disagreement exists among economic profit players about the long-term economic profit growth rate, g. With these simplifying assumptions, we can direct our enterprise valuation attention to a divergence of opinion between the market implied economic profit growth rate, g_m, and the company-specific growth rate, g_c — where g_c is based on what a firm's managers can *realistically* earn on current and anticipated future growth assets.

---

[3] We note that current economic profit, EP_0, reflects all the value-based accounting adjustments that we discussed in Chapter 7. When looked at in valuation terms, we see that economic profit measurement is much more than a set of accounting adjustments. We emphasize the real economic profit factors (enumerated several times before) that lead to substantial wealth creation.

Exhibit 1: Impact of Economic Profit Growth on Company Valuation (in $ millions)

EP(0)	wacc	g	NPV*	Capital	Enterprise Value
100	0.1	0.01	1,122	1,000	2,122
100	0.1	0.02	1,275	1,000	2,275
100	0.1	0.03	1,471	1,000	2,471
100	0.1	0.04	1,733	1,000	2,733
100	0.1	0.05	2,100	1,000	3,100
100	0.1	0.06	2,650	1,000	3,650
100	0.1	0.07	3,567	1,000	4,567
100	0.1	0.08	5,400	1,000	6,400
100	0.1	0.09	10,900	1,000	11,900

* NPV = EP(0) $\times$ (1 + g)/(wacc - g)

VALUATION OF ECONOMIC PROFIT GROWTH

Before examining the financial consequences of a divergence of opinion between company and market-assessed economic profit growth rates, we'll first show the sensitivity of NPV and enterprise value to changes in the economic profit growth rate along the same lines as our *wacc* sensitivity analysis in Chapter 8. This economic profit growth focus is helpful because it provides an understanding on how shareholder wealth changes when market implied and company expectations of economic profit growth are joined. Following that, we'll shed light on corporate and investor implications of a divergence of opinion between internal and market implied growth rates in economic profit.

Exhibit 1 shows the theoretical impact of changes in the economic profit growth rate on NPV and enterprise value. In this illustration, we assume that (1) current economic profit is $100 million, (2) the cost of capital is 10%, and (3) the economic profit growth rate ranges from a low of 1% to a high of 9%. As with any discounted cash flow model, the long-term growth rate (in economic profit) must fall short of the cost of invested capital.[4]

Exhibit 1 shows that if the economic profit growth rate is only 1%, then the firm's net present value is $1,122 million. At 5% growth, the firm's NPV rises to $2,100 million, while with 9% growth in economic profit the firm's NPV soars to $10,900 million. Based on these findings, it should be clear that numerically small changes in economic profit growth have the potential to add tremendous value to a firm's invested capital. Moreover, in a hypothetical efficient capital mar-

---

[4] For simplicity, we use a constant growth economic profit model to explain the consequences of a divergence between company and market implied economic profit growth rates. We could of course use a multiple stage economic profit model to argue the same financial implications. While the mathematics of a multi-stage economic profit model is more complex, the last stage within, say, a two- or three-stage growth model must be one where the economic profit growth rate falls short of the *wacc*.

ket[5] — where market implied and internal expectations of economic profit growth are always joined — such growth changes lead to direct and immediate improvement in the market value of the firm and its outstanding debt and equity securities.

Exhibit 2 presents a graphical depiction of the NPV and enterprise valuation findings listed in Exhibit 1. The graphical depiction provides a look at how economic profit growth impacts shareholder value in a *non*-linear way.[6] In this context, we see that as market implied growth, g (= $g_c = g_m$), ranges from 1% to 9%, the firm's NPV and enterprise value rise at an increasing (or non-linear) function of the economic profit growth rate. From a practical perspective, this means that anything management can do to demonstrate an increase in the economic profit growth rate will have an immediate impact on shareholder value.

As emphasized in Chapter 10, such managerial growth actions can take at least two forms. For growth-oriented companies, this means increasing the level of capital spending in positive economic profit spread businesses. For value-oriented businesses, this means restructuring stale or possibly distressed companies for substantial economic profit improvement. Either way, the constant growth economic profit model — as well as multi-phase economic profit growth models — suggests that investing for positive economic profit change is a key ingredient in the managerial quest to have a great company with a great stock.

Exhibit 2: Valuation of Economic Profit Growth

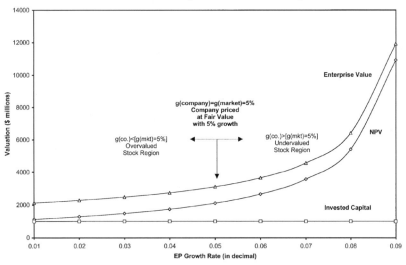

---

[5] The concept of an efficient capital market — as lucidly explained in Eugene Fama's classic 1970 *Journal of Finance* article — states that current security prices "fully reflect" all available and relevant information for the pricing of securities. In this chapter (and previous ones) we apply the efficient market — as well as the inefficient market — concept in an economic profit context.

[6] We explained in Chapter 8 how variations in the cost of capital also impact enterprise value and NPV in a *non*-linear way.

DIVERGENT OPINION ON ECONOMIC PROFIT GROWTH

As noted before, the NPV and enterprise value functions shown in Exhibit 2 presume that the capital market is efficient in the sense that company and market implied expectations of economic profit growth are "fully reflected" in stock price. This efficient pricing condition is operative when the internal growth rate of economic profit is equal to the market implied growth rate, such that $g_c = g_m = g$. Suppose however that — due to possible asymmetric information about future growth opportunities — there exists an imbalance in growth expectations such that the internal assessment of economic profit growth is higher than market implied growth in economic profit. This imbalance will in turn provide the opportunity for the company to surprise the capital market *positively* about its fundamental ability to invest for positive economic profit change. This growth imbalance will also provide astute investors with an opportunity to earn active returns on their investment portfolios by following an economic profit approach to equity securities analysis.

For instance, suppose that the capital market was anticipating that the firm could grow its economic profit at a rate of 5%   consistent with the company's long-term history. Further suppose that management has "inside" company information regarding its productive-investment opportunities to grow economic profit at, say, 7% per annum due to an enhanced distribution plan that will increase revenue and operating asset efficiency. We now see in Exhibit 2 that with 5% economic profit growth, the market has incorrectly assessed the firm's NPV at $2,100 million and its enterprise value at $3,100 million. (In this case, enterprise value is equal to the initial invested capital of $1,000 million plus market-assessed NPV.)

Consequently, with the potential for 7% actual growth in economic profit, the firm has the opportunity to disclose to the capital market its fundamental ability to invest positively for economic profit change. With 7% growth in economic profit, the firm's discounted economic profit stream (namely, its NPV) is worth $3,567 million, and its enterprise value is $4,567 million. This NPV change represents a whopping 70% increase in the present value of the firm's anticipated economic profit stream. Moreover, Exhibit 2 shows that NPV and enterprise value rise steeply when the capital market realizes that market implied expectation of economic profit growth is much lower than that which the company can actually achieve with its current and anticipated growth assets.

Conversely, Exhibit 2 shows what happens to NPV and enterprise value when internal expectation of economic profit growth is lower than market implied growth. If, for example, the company's internal growth rate was 3% — compared with market implied economic profit growth of 5% — then NPV and enterprise value are headed for a significant downward revision. With 3% internal growth, the firm's NPV drops to $1,471 million from market assessed NPV of $2,100 million. This represents a 30% decline in the discounted value of the firm's economic profit stream. Likewise, enterprise value falls to $2,471 million when the capital market realizes that actual company growth falls short of that which is embedded in the firm's current valuation. In many cases, problems such as this arise when investors naively extrapolate past results into the future. As we discussed extensively in Chapter 10, companies that fall into Quadrant I, despite high residual returns on capital, begin to stop growing their invested capital bases. Clearly, with no capital growth, growth in economic profit is unsustainable.

With the potential for a 70% rise in shareholder value upon the announcement of a 200 basis point rise in the economic profit growth rate, corporate managers are well advised to pay particular attention to real investment activities (via internal company growth and/or external corporate acquisitions) that have the potential to materially change the company's economic profit growth rate. Of course, with the potential for a 30% decline in shareholder value upon market recognition of a 200 basis point decline in the economic profit growth rate, managers are also well advised to take the necessary actions (corporate restructurings and the like) to prevent a free fall in the firm's stock price.

Judicious Recognition of Falling Economic Profit Growth

Before proceeding, we emphasize that if internal growth in economic profit still falls short of market implied growth after the firm's managers have considered *all* conceivable investment opportunities, then a company's managers must immediately inform the capital market that market implied economic profit growth is much higher than that which the firm can realistically achieve on its current and anticipated future growth assets.[7] While no rational manager likes to see — let alone, precipitate — a substantial decline in enterprise value and stock price, we believe that the ensuing uncertainty that will arise in the absence of a forthright announcement about the economic profit shortfall will result in a much larger decline in enterprise value and stock price than that which would naturally occur with complete disclosure. Of course, astute investors who follow an economic profit approach would be well advised to anticipate and move out of the shares of companies before internal expectations of economic profit growth fall below market implied expectations.

Indeed, as we have emphasized in previous chapters, heightened uncertainty about the economic profit outlook can lead to a rise in the cost of capital — due to the increased financial and business risks — that in turn exacerbates the decline in the company's NPV, enterprise value, and stock price. For instance, if *wacc* was to rise from 10% to, say, 12% in the presence of a *volatility-induced* 200 basis point decline in the economic profit growth rate (from 5% down to 3%), then the firm's NPV would decline to $1,144 million (from $2,100 million, when initially priced at 5% market implied economic profit growth) and its enterprise value would fall to $2,144 million (from $3,100 million). One only needs to witness the dramatic stock declines in companies such as Xerox and Lucent Technologies in early 2001 as examples of business deterioration coupled with financial stress.

---

[7] Consider, for example, the misguided economic profit growth expectations that were built into technology stocks before the free fall in prices during late 2000 and early 2001.

The resulting 46% decline in NPV — caused by the *doubly* negative combination of falling growth in the presence of a rising discount rate (commonly referred to as "stagflation" at the macroeconomic level) — is noticeably higher than the 30% decline in NPV that would otherwise occur with a judicious announcement by management that its internal growth rate falls short of that which is embedded in enterprise value and current stock price. Indeed, the mere recognition by corporate managers that internal and market implied economic profit growth rates could diverge in a meaningful way is an important consideration in any company's quest to create — rather than destroy — substantial shareholder wealth.

ROLE OF THEORETICAL COMPANY ANALYSIS

We can recast our NPV and enterprise valuation findings into a format that is more noticeable by investment analysts. To begin, we have mentioned several times before that analysts often look at accounting profit measures such as ROA and ROE, as well as relative valuation measures such as the price-to-earnings and price-to-book ratios when evaluating corporate financial success (or distress and failure). For reasons that we have enunciated before, these traditional financial measures do not accurately measure the firm's net creation of wealth (namely, the firm's NPV), and they most certainly do not measure real economic profit (or "true" profit) because of inadequate "accounting" for the dollar cost of equity capital.[8]

Relative Economic Profit and Wealth Measures

Let's now look at the NPV and enterprise valuation findings in a framework that can be called "theoretical company analysis."[9] In this context, Exhibit 3 reports the NPV-to-Capital and (accompanying) Economic Profit-to-Capital ratios for varying assumptions about the firm's sustainable economic profit growth rate. Notice that if the firm's long-term economic profit growth rate is only 1%, then the

---

[8] We are aware of some empirical research which suggests that economic profit measures do not provide security analysts with insight on companies (and their stocks) beyond that obtainable from traditional metrics like ROA and ROE. Without getting into the details here, we believe that much of this comparative economic profit research is too short-term focused, emphasizing only the current period's economic profit or the change therein.

   As buy side investors, we find some economic profit studies to be too limited in scope because they do not "account" for potentially exploitable differences between internal (or warranted) expectations of economic profit growth and that which is already reflected in stock price. Moreover, as investors with a penchant for blending financial theory and practice, we take comfort in knowing that — unlike GAAP-based accounting measures of profitability — the discounted stream of economic profit is inextricably linked to wealth creation.

[9] The microeconomic theory of the firm and the theory of finance are well known branches of the general field of economics. We seek to introduce a blended form of theoretical company analysis that joins economic profit principles that arise in the economics of the firm (such as NPV analysis) and the theory of finance (such as capital structure). In this effort, we seek a closer link between how real world companies are evaluated with financial data and how companies should be evaluated based on economic profit valuation principles.

firm's NPV is worth 1.12 times its invested capital. Also, with an economic profit growth rate of 5%, the firm's NPV-to-Capital ratio climbs to 2.1, while with 9% growth in economic profit, the firm's NPV soars to 10.9 times its invested capital.

In turn, Exhibit 4 depicts the *non*-linear relationship between the firm's expected Economic Profit-to-Capital (y-variable) and NPV-to-Capital (x-variable) ratios as the economic profit growth rate ranges from a low of 1% up to a high of 9%. Notice that the growth-induced Economic Profit-to-Capital and NPV-to-Capital relationship is a concave one. Viewed in more practical terms, Exhibit 4 shows the relationship between expected economic profit for the coming period and the firm's NPV (both measured relative to invested capital) when (1) the economic profit growth rate goes up, and (2) when internal expectations of economic profit growth are joined with market implied growth — namely, $g_c = g_m = g$. For convenience, we'll refer to the theoretical pricing relationship that is manifest in Exhibit 4 as the "Fair Value Curve." As before, it should be evident from this graphical depiction that economic profit growth has a pervasive and powerful impact on the firm's net creation of wealth.

Company Analysis with Divergent Opinions on Economic Profit Growth

Suppose again that due to information asymmetries regarding economic profit growth, the firm's internal (and presumably, correct) assessment of its growth opportunities is higher than that which is reflected in its NPV, enterprise value, and therefore stock price. This fortuitous situation is represented in Exhibit 5 by the economic profit growth condition, $g_c > [g_m = 5\%]$. In this context, Exhibit 5 shows that with, say, 7% economic profit growth the firm's NPV-to-Capital ratio should rise from a market-assessed wealth relative of 2.1 on up to 3.57 (see solid arrow pointing to the right[10]).

Exhibit 3: NPV and Economic Profit-to-Capital Ratios for Constant Growth Economic Profit Model

g	NPV*/C	EP(1)/C
0.01	1.1222	0.1010
0.02	1.2750	0.1020
0.03	1.4714	0.1030
0.04	1.7333	0.1040
0.05	2.1000	0.1050
0.06	2.6500	0.1060
0.07	3.5667	0.1070
0.08	5.4000	0.1080
0.09	10.9000	0.1090

* $NPV = EP(0) \times (1 + g)/(wacc - g)$

---

[10] Recall that we used the Economic Profit-to-Capital versus NPV-to-Capital graphing format in Chapter 3 to provide an economic profit explanation as to why Intel's stock was potentially undervalued at year-end 1997.

Exhibit 4: Theoretical Economic Profit-to-Capital versus NPV-to-Capital Ratio

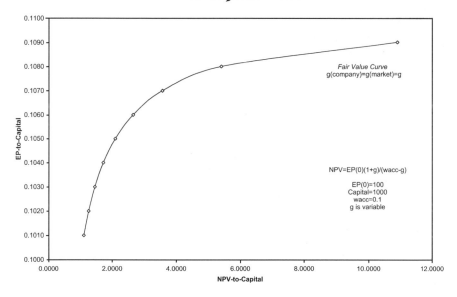

Exhibit 5: Theoretical Company Analysis: Economic Profit-to-Capital versus NPV-to-Capital Ratio

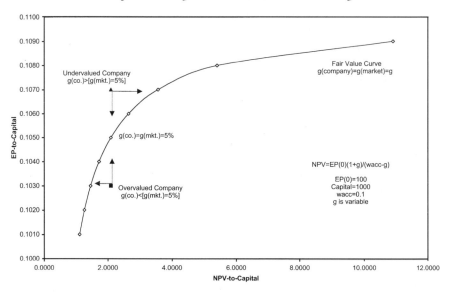

When this happens, the firm's NPV rises from \$2,100 million up to \$3,567 million — representing, as before, a 70% gain in shareholder value. Clearly, when internal expectations of economic profit growth exceed the growth rate that is embedded in market-implied NPV, then the firm has a wealth incentive (indeed, an obligation to the shareholders) to expeditiously announce the fortuitous growth opportunities to the capital market. In this example where $g_c > g_m$, we see that reconciling differences between company and market-implied economic profit growth allows the firm's managers to surprise the capital market positively in their quest to have a great company with a great stock.

Notice too that in the absence of new and consistent information about the company's economic profit growth rate, the capital market at large expects to see compression in the firm's future economic profit. This is because market implied growth in economic profit is still 5%, rather than 7%. This economic profit situation is represented by the downward pointing dashed arrow in Exhibit 5 showing the potential economic profit compression if the Economic Profit-to-Capital ratio of 0.107 were to decline back to 0.105 — which in turn is consistent with the market assessed 5% long-term growth in economic profit. Consequently, in the absence of a sustainable (or consistent) economic profit growth change, the market-assessed NPV-to-Capital ratio remains at 2.1 and shareholder wealth remains unchanged.

Growth Implications for Overvalued Companies

In contrast, suppose that a company's economic profit growth rate falls short of that which is embedded in current valuation. This unfortunate condition is represented in Exhibit 5 by the economic profit growth condition, $g_c < [g_m = 5\%]$. In this instance, the firm's NPV, enterprise value, and stock price are overvalued in the capital market when measured relative to market-assessed parameters based on an economic profit growth rate of 5%. Should the growth rate actually decline from 5% to 3%, the firm's NPV-to-Capital ratio should decline from 2.1 down to 1.4714. This change is represented in Exhibit 5 by the solid arrow pointing leftward. Expressed in percentage terms, this represents a 30% decline in the firm's net creation of wealth.

Notice too that with a 5% economic profit growth rate, the capital market would be expecting a revision if economic profit were to fall short of that consistent with an Economic Profit-to-Capital ratio of 0.105 for a given NPV-to-Capital ratio of 2.1. This Economic Profit-to-Capital revision from 0.103 up to 0.105 is reflected in the upward pointing dashed arrow shown in Exhibit 5. As we emphasized before, when internal expectations of economic profit fall short of market implied expectations, then the firm must forthrightly make known the negative news to prevent a volatile decline in its stock price. In the absence of an honest announcement about the detrimental change in economic profit growth, the capital market at large may overreact to the falling growth and demand a substantially higher equity risk premium. Thus, managers (and investors) must beware the *doubly* negative risk-to-value of a falling growth rate when paired with a concomitant rise in the cost of invested capital.

Exhibit 6: Theoretical NPV-to-Capital versus
Economic Profit-to-Capital Ratio

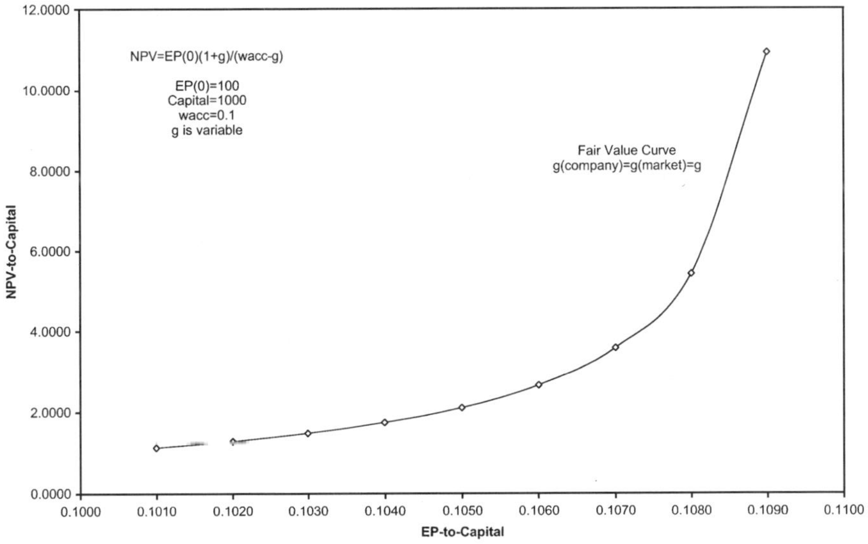

ANOTHER LOOK AT THEORETICAL COMPANY ANALYSIS

Another interesting way of looking at companies in an economic profit context is obtained by reversing the order of the variables shown in Exhibit 5.[11] In this context, Exhibit 6 shows the theoretical relationship between the NPV-to-Capital ratio (this time, y-variable) and the Economic Profit-to-Capital ratio (x-variable) for varying rates of economic profit growth. The exhibit shows the relationship between capital adjusted NPV and economic profit as the long-term economic profit growth rate ranges from a low of 1% up to a high of 9%.

Not surprisingly, Exhibit 6 shows that the NPV-to-Capital ratio is a *non-linear* and increasing function of the Economic Profit-to-Capital ratio. As before, we can interpret points along the curve as "fair value" combinations of NPV and economic profit relatives that arise when internal expectations of economic profit growth are precisely equal to market implied growth rates. In this ideal world, the firm's productive-investment decisions toward increasing the economic profit growth rate are continuously and fully reflected in shareholder value measures — such as NPV, enterprise value, and stock price.

---

[11] We note that both approaches to visualizing companies in an economic profit context — namely, the Economic Profit-to-Capital versus the NPV-to-Capital and the NPV-to-Capital versus the Economic Profit-to-Capital — are contained in earlier (and separate) writings of the authors.

Exhibit 7: Theoretical Company Analysis: NPV-to-Capital versus Economic Profit-to-Capital Ratio

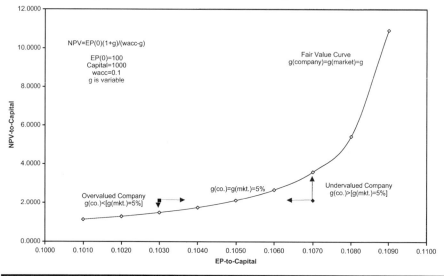

Information Asymmetry

Suppose again that information asymmetry exists between internal expectations of economic profit growth and market implied expectations. In this context, Exhibit 7 shows that points that lie below the Fair Value Curve — this time, in NPV-to-Capital versus Economic Profit-to-Capital space — represent wealth and economic profit combinations that reflect undervalued companies. This can be attributed to internal expectations of economic profit growth that exceed market implied expectations — such that $g_c > g_m$. Conversely, the exhibit shows NPV and economic profit combinations that lie above the Fair Value Curve represent companies that may be overvalued in the capital market. This happens because internal expectations of economic profit growth fall short of market implied expectations — such that $g_c < g_m$.

For example, consider the "Undervalued Company" shown in Exhibit 7. At that NPV-to-Capital and Economic Profit-to-Capital combination, the internal growth rate in economic profit, at 7%, exceeds the market-implied expectation of economic profit growth, at 5%. If the firm can demonstrate that the sustainable growth rate of economic profit is really 7%, then the firm's NPV-to-Capital ratio is headed for a substantial revision, from 2.1 up to 3.57. When this happens, the firm's NPV rises from $2,100 million to $3,567 million, for a wealth gain of 70%.[12] Notice that with 5% embedded economic profit growth, the capital market is anticipating that the Economic Profit-to-Capital ratio will decline from 0.107 to 0.105 such that the NPV-to-Capital ratio remains at 2.1.

---

[12] This of course is the same NPV result that we obtained before when analyzing the Economic Profit-to-Capital (y variable) versus NPV-to-Capital (x variable) graphical relationship.

Now consider the "Overvalued Company" position shown in Exhibit 7. In this case, we see that internal expectation of economic profit growth, at only 3%, falls short of market-implied expectations, again at 5%. This time, the firm's NPV-to-Capital ratio is poised for a decline from 2.1 down to 1.47. When this happens, the firm's NPV falls from $2,100 million down to $1,471 million, for a wealth decline of 30% in the absence of any further negative information (such as a volatility induced rise in the cost of invested capital). Notice too that with 5% market-implied growth, the capital market incorrectly perceives (due to information asymmetry) that the Economic Profit-to-Capital ratio will rise from 0.103 to 0.105.

INVESTOR IMPLICATIONS

Up to this point, we have largely focused on the managerial implications that arise from a divergence of opinion between internal (or company) and market implied expectations of economic profit growth. We said that when economic profit growth divergence exists, then managers must make it known to the capital market that the firm either has or lacks productive-investment opportunities that exceed those that are embedded in its enterprise value and stock price. Reconciling the market-assessed growth rate with what a company can actually deliver is one of the managerial keys to having a great company with a great stock. Of course, reconciling market implied economic profit growth with internal growth expectations that fall short of embedded expectations is one of the managerial keys to avoid having a permanently distressed company with a disappointing stock.

From the investor's perspective, a divergence between internal and market implied expectations of economic profit growth presents some fascinating opportunities for active-minded investors who employ an economic profit approach to equity securities analysis. One only needs to look back to Exhibit 5 (or, equivalently, Exhibit 7) to contemplate how active investors could potentially earn a risk-adjusted return on common stocks from their "bottom up" economic profit analysis.

Using quantitative and qualitative economic profit tools, active investors can discover companies where the internal expectation of economic profit growth is different from the market implied growth rate. They can then buy stocks of companies where internal economic profit growth expectations are higher than market implied growth rates (namely, $g_c > g_m$) with the expectation of potentially substantial stock price appreciation. On the other hand, active investors can sell the stocks of companies where internal economic profit growth expectations fall short of market implied growth ($g_c < g_m$) with the expectation of avoiding a substantial capital loss. Indeed, the creative investor can utilize an economic profit approach to potentially earn risk-adjusted returns in a "long short" or market neutral approach to active investing.

Exhibit 8: Excess Returns Relative to Valuation

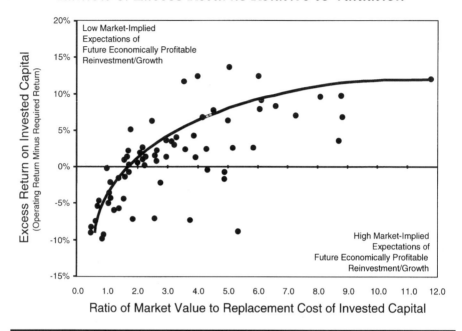

Ratio of Market Value to Replacement Cost of Invested Capital

A REAL WORLD LOOK AT INVESTMENT STRATEGY

Before concluding this chapter (and this book), we illustrate how an economic profit approach to company analysis has real world practical merit. To help fill any remaining void, Exhibit 8 shows the "Excess Return on Invested Capital" versus the "Market Value of Invested Capital to Replacement Cost of Invested Capital"[13] for a universe of companies.[14]

In this graphical display, the excess return on invested capital is simply the after-tax return on invested capital (ROIC, including the relevant accounting adjustments that we spoke of in Chapter 7) *less* the weighted average cost of capital (*wacc*, that we explained in large detail in Chapter 8). Also, we report the market value of invested capital (or enterprise value) measured relative to replacement cost of invested capital for consistency with the conventional analyst way of evaluating companies in a profitability versus "price-to book" context. There is *no* slippage of economic profit focus here because the market value of invested capital-to-

---

[13] Note that the "excess return on invested capital" is equivalent to the Economic Profit-to-Capital ratio that we utilize in this chapter, and it is also equivalent to the "economic profit spread" that we discussed before. Also, the use of market value-to-replacement cost of invested capital is really just a scaling on our previous usage of the NPV-to-Capital ratio.

[14] These are companies that we track in an economic profit context at Global Asset Management.

replacement cost of invested capital ratio is *directly* related to the NPV-to-invested capital ratio that we used in the previous theoretical company illustrations.[15]

Exhibit 8 shows a scatter plot of companies measured relative to a curve of "best fit" through the data points. Consistent with our earlier explanation of a Fair Value Curve in Exhibit 5, those points in the exhibit that lie above the curve are potentially undervalued companies (low market implied expectations of future economic profit growth), while those data points that fall below the curve represent potentially overvalued companies (high market implied expectations of economic profit growth).

For companies that lie above the curve, the capital market at large is expecting compression in future economic profit downward (see Exhibit 8). However, for any given market value-to-replacement cost of invested capital ratio, actual internal expectations of economically profitable reinvestment for combinations above the curve imply a noticeably higher valuation for any company's stock. Astute investors can therefore expect to earn potentially attractive risk-adjusted returns on stocks that plot above the curve because of the fortuitously positive (and presumably consistent) economic profit positions of these companies.

Conversely, for companies that plot below the curve, the market expects a high degree of future economic profit growth and, thus, failure to meet or exceed such high expectations would negatively impact such firms' NPV. Investors need to be especially cognizant of the downside valuation risk in this situation. Taken together, we see that the stocks of companies that plot above the curve in Exhibit 8 are potential buy opportunities, while stocks that plot below the curve are potential sell (or short sell) candidates. Moreover, the "longs" and "shorts" can be combined into an economic profit based approach to long-short investing.

From this starting point (see Exhibit 8), analysts should weave together all five economic profit considerations. The company research framework is a disciplined way to isolate the key economic profit variables that impact firm value. A rigorous analysis of invested capital growth, the correlation or leverage that capital growth has to future revenue, cash flow and eventually economic profit, and how that reconciles to the market's expectations of future economic profit growth is key to identifying investment opportunities.

SOME CLOSING THOUGHTS

Taking the theory of efficient markets literally, the correct expectation of economic profit growth is always "fully reflected" in stock prices. In such a world,

---

[15] As we have explained before, the enterprise value-to-invested capital ratio can always be written as:

$$V/C = 1 + NPV/C$$

In this expression, V is enterprise value (or market value of invested capital) and C is a measure of invested capital. Hence, V/C is greater than one when NPV is positive, while V/C is less than unity when NPV is negative. The market value of invested capital-to-replacement cost of invested capital is also a measure of "Tobin's Q."

internal expectations of economic profit growth are precisely equal to market implied growth rates. In the real world of practitioners, corporate managers can *focus on value* by emphasizing the first four (of five) value drivers that we explained in this book: namely, (1) generating a solid return on existing capital, (2) examining risk (to value) in a cost of capital context, (3) investing positively for economic profit growth, and (4) understanding the magnitude of external factors (industry, sector, and macroeconomic forces) on corporate performance and shareholder wealth.

Given that inefficiencies most certainly do exist in real world capital markets, managers (and investors) must be especially cognizant of the *fifth* economic profit-value driver that we explained in this chapter — specifically, the importance of reconciling internal (or warranted) expectations of company economic profit growth with market implied growth. By this, we mean that if internal expectations of economic profit growth exceed that which is reflected in stock price, then managers should disclose this information to the capital market as quickly as possible to ensure that shareholders receive maximum value on their security holdings. Likewise, when internal expectations of economic profit growth fall short of market implied expectations, then corporate managers need to — in the absence of any profitable investment opportunities — make this adverse information known to the capital market to avoid a doubly volatile decline in shareholder value arising from lowered economic profit growth expectations and a rising cost of capital.

From an investment perspective, we said that the economic profit approach to company analysis explained in this book can be used to discover mispriced securities in the capital market. By buying the stocks of companies having internal economic profit growth opportunities that exceed the market implied growth rate that is imbedded in stock price, investors can hope to generate an active reward (that is, positive "alpha") on investment securities. This includes both the bonds of companies with impending risk profile upgrades and the stocks of companies with expectations of economic profit growth "surprise capability" driven by improved invested capital growth prospects and/or better operating leverage from their capital growth.

We also pointed out that investors should sell (or short sell) those securities with an internal economic profit growth rate that falls short of that which is reflected in current stock price. As a case in point, the relative underperformance in consumer stocks in the early 1990s and the more appropriately labeled free fall in technology stocks (especially internet and biotech) that happened during 2000 and early 2001 are testaments to the economic profit view that market implied expectations can differ quite significantly from internal (or warranted) expectations of what companies can realistically achieve on their existing and future growth assets. Going forward, this solidly supports our introductory and now concluding message to corporate managers and investors — namely, *focus on value*.

Index